AF618126

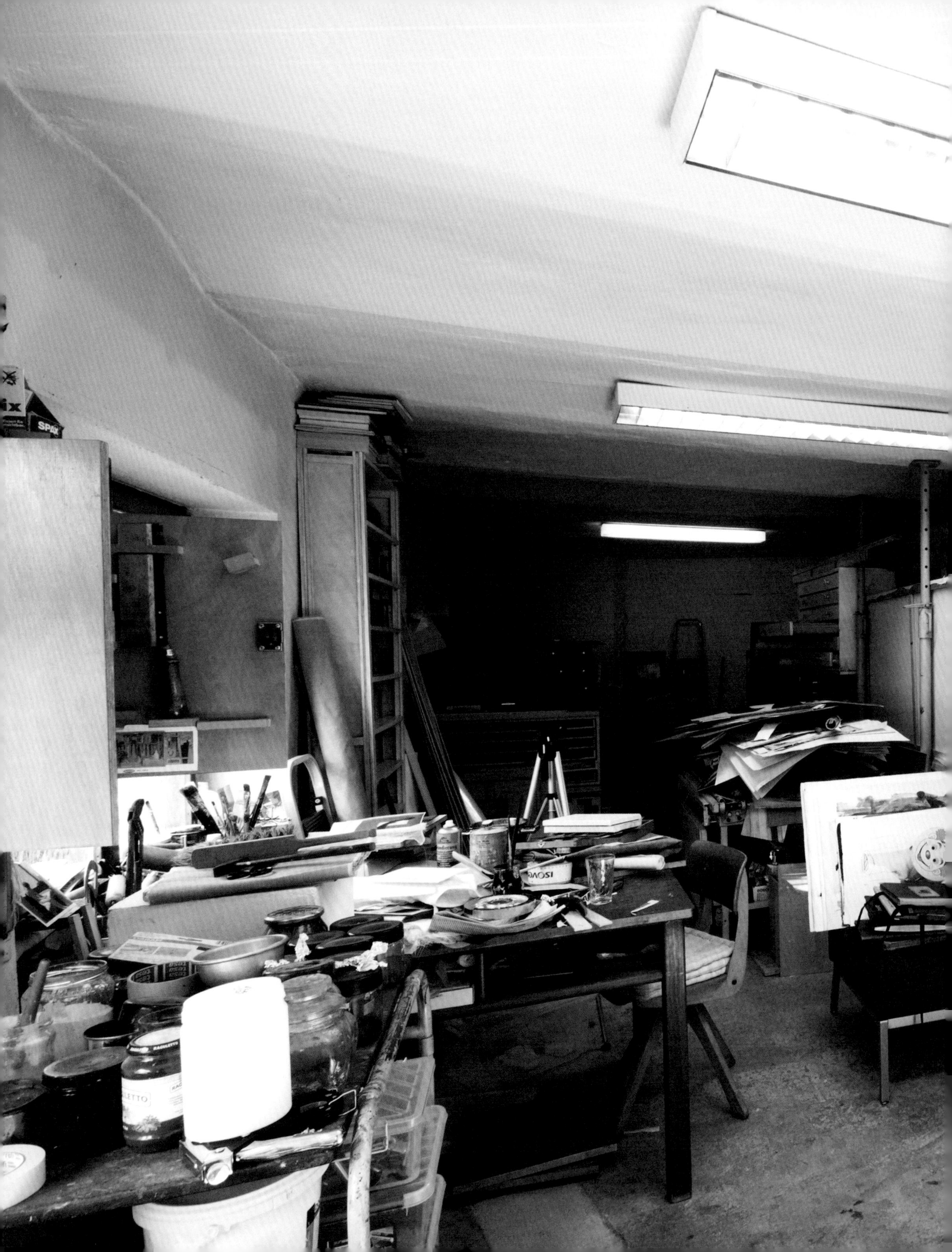
SPAX

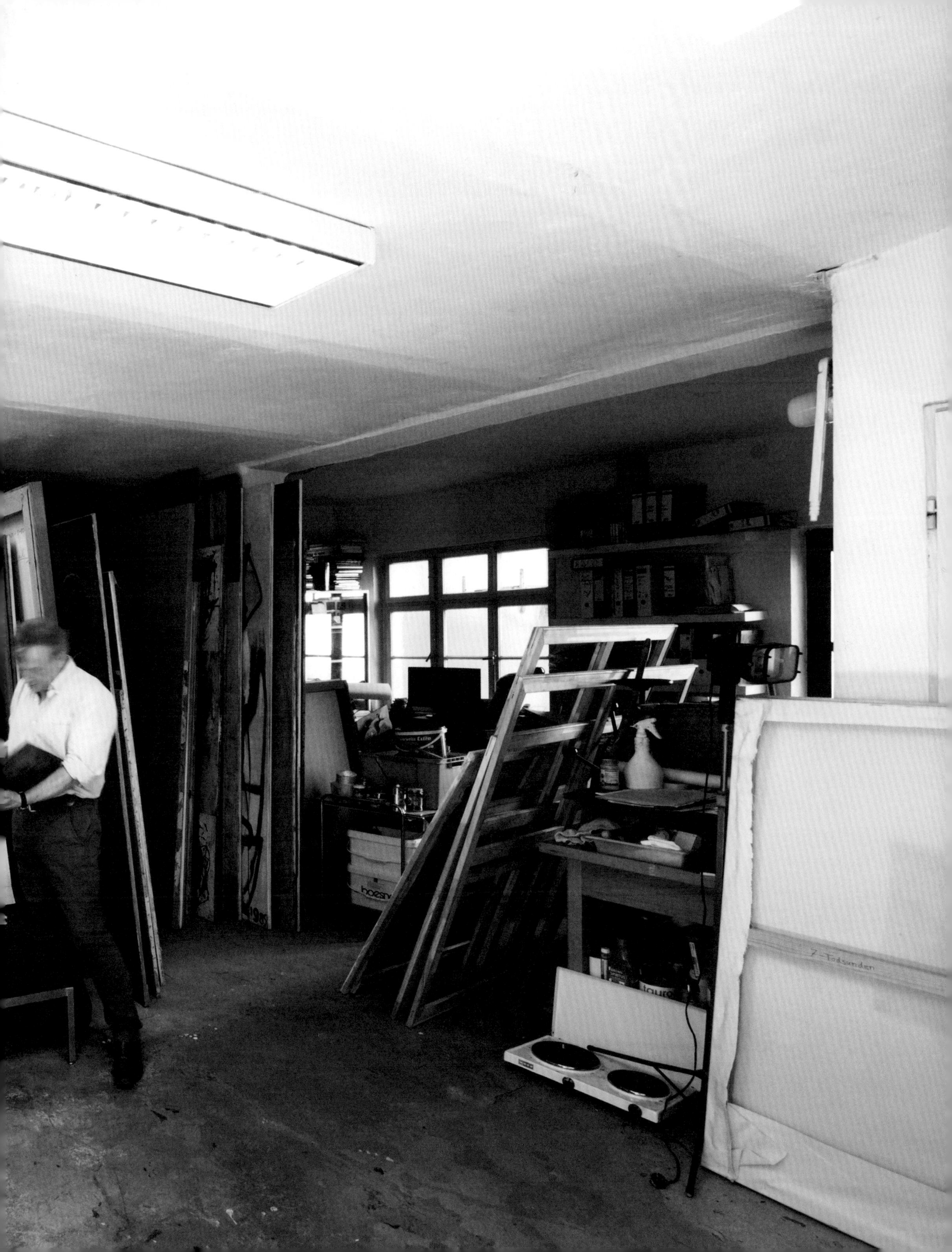
7-Todsunden

DAS PALIMPSEST UND DIE MALEREI VON RAINER DISSEL

Dr. Danièle Perrier * unter Mitwirkung von Dr. Julia-Constance Dissel

Vingt fois sur le métier remettez votre ouvrage
Polissez-le sans cesse et le repolissez;
Ajoutez quelquefois, et souvent effacez.
Nicolas Boileau, L'art poétique

Zwanzig mal nimm dir dein Werkstück vor
feile an ihm und feile wieder;
füge etwas hinzu und vor allem reduziere!
Nicolas Boileau, L'art poétique

Rainer Dissel ist Maler im wahrsten Sinne des Wortes. Seit dem Studium, das er in den 1980er-Jahren an der renommierten Akademie der bildenden Künste (Städel-Schule) in Frankfurt absovierte, fühlt er sich von der abstrakten Malerei angezogen, einer Malerei, die auf sich selbst verweist. So steht sein Werk ganz im Zeichen der Auslotung malerischer Ausdrucksformen. Doch Malerei ist nicht nur Form, sondern immer auch Ausdruck und Aussage, um diese zu transportieren, greift der Künstler nicht nur auf die Leinwand als Malgrundlage zurück, sondern er bedient sich historischer Kassen- und Kunstbücher oder von Blinden angefertigter Bodenputztücher und integriert Fundobjekte aus dem persönlichen Alltagsleben sowie textuelle Versatzstücke, die mit der Malerei eine bedeutungstragende Allianz eingehen.

In den Arbeiten der 1980er- und frühen 1990er-Jahre bevorzugte Rainer Dissel sehr große Leinwände, ein Trend, der in den USA, wo sich Dissel nach dem Studium lange Zeit aufhielt, mit dem Abstrakten Expressionismus begann und der bis weit in die 1980er-Jahre andauerte. Der Bildaufbau erfolgt jedoch im klassischen Sinn: Die Leinwand wird grundiert, erhält eine Imprimitur und wird dann mit diversen dünnen Malschichten lasiert. Am Ende ensteht so eine additive Farbmischung mit teils diaphaner Wirkung. Dissel bevorzugt selbstgefertigte Eitemperafarbe und Öl-Harz-lasuren als Malmittel, eine altmeisterliche Technik, die nicht nur für Farbbeständigkeit, sondern vor allem auch für ihre Farbintensität und Tiefenwirkung ausgewiesen ist. Diese Technik verleiht der Bildoberfläche der Arbeiten Dissels eine Art Leichtigkeit, als würden diese atmen. Am Beispiel von NOCTURNAL EMISSION (Abb. 1) wird das besonders ersichtlich: Der graue Farbgrund wirkt wie eine schlecht verwischte Schultafel auf der nachträglich Graffitis eingeritzt wurden. In der Mitte leuchtet eine blaue Fläche, die, von einem dunklen Rahmen aus Teer umrandet, einen eigenen Raum bildet. Es ist, wie bei Rothko, der Raum der Farbe. Hier entsteht allerdings kein rein meditativer Raum, denn das Graffiti und auch der Teer holen den Raum in die Realität zurück. Man könnte sagen, dass die Grundstimmung dieses eher minimalistischen Bildes eine Poesie des Alltags beschwört.

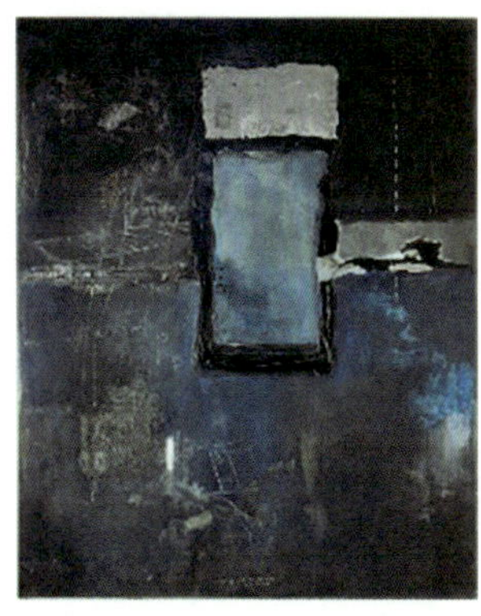

Abb. 1

Die immer wiederkehrende Integration von artfremden Materialien rückt die Werke Rainer Dissels auch in die Nähe der großformatigen Assemblage; da gibt es Stühle oder ganze Fensterrahmen, die in das Bild gesetzt werden und nicht selten, wie schon bei NOCTURNAL EMISSION, Arbeiten mit Teer bzw. Pech. Manchmal reißt der Künstler den Teer als noch warme, fließende Substanz wieder weg, was Verletzungen in den Malschichten und der Grundierung verursacht. In solchen Combines entstehen dadurch an manchen Stellen raue Oberflächen – sie sind zugleich malerische Decollagen, die ob der Wahl des Mittels Teer auch palimpsestartige Einblicke in tiefere Ebenen eröffnen und mit diesen in archaische Mythen, was Titel wie DEUS EX MACHINA oder GARDEN OF EVIL MIT SCHUTZMANTELMADONNA erhärten.

Im Laufe der 1990er-Jahre wurden die Arbeiten von Rainer Dissel minimalistischer und der malerische Farbauftrag gewann zunehmend an Bedeutung, der Einbezug artfremder Materialien rückte in dieser Zeit in den Hintergrund. Dafür wurde die Pinselführung gezielt als gestalterisches Mittel eingesetzt. Es entstanden so Arbeiten mit flockiger Oberfläche, die den Eindruck von Durchlässigkeit erwecken. In einem weiteren Schritt wurden die Bilder zudem kleiner. Sie haben ab Ende der 1990er-Jahre oft das Format eines Kabinettstücks. Die Bildfläche wird nun in geometrische Farbfelder unterteilt, die sich voneinander abheben und komplementär ergänzen. Eine hellblaue Fläche mit zarten

Rotwerten wird einer violetten mit Blauwerten gegenübergestellt. Neu ist, dass diese klar abgegrenzten Farbflächen, die weiterhin durch Farbwert und Farbauftrag haptisch und durchscheinig wirken, auch als Bilduntergrund für darauf collagierte, surrealistisch anmutende Figuren, Zeichen oder Objekte dienen. Wo früher die Assemblage ein Thema war, gewinnt nun die Collage an Bedeutung und die Strukturen werden vielschichtiger. Zeitungsausschnitte, Musikpartituren, Eintrittstickets, Papier, Stoff, Pappe werden aufgeklebt, teilweise übermalt, überklebt, wieder übermalt, so dass eine äußerst komplexe, aber dennoch klare Struktur entsteht. In manchen Teilen ist die Farbe transluzent und erlaubt ein Zwiegespräch zwischen den sich überlagernden Schichten. Die unterschiedlichen Informationen – Farben und Schnipsel mit Textinhalten, die im Kleingedruckten teilweise noch wahrnehmbar sind – schaffen im Kopf des Betrachters Assoziationen.
Doch dominiert die klare Abgrenzung der entstehenden Farbfelder und Muster wie es bei den im Katalog abgebildeten Arbeiten zu sehen ist. In den meisten Fällen wird das Bild wie etwa in SALAH AL-DIN von 2014 oder in ALLEGRO von 2013 durch ein sich durchkreuzendes Koordinatensystem von Vertikalen und Horizontalen geprägt. In anderen wie M ODER DARK GREY werden wieder raumschaffende, architektonische Komponenten eingefügt. Doch ihre Verschränkung zwingt das Auge immer wieder zurück in die Bildebene. Die hier genannten Titel und so auch RUN, CABINET und DÜRER sind alle einem Text entnommen, mit dem die Bilder collagiert wurden. Sie suggerieren ganz bestimmte Stimmungen, erwecken Assoziationen mit Musik (Allegro) oder Malerei (Dürer), mit Rennen (Run) oder der Farbe Grau (Dark Grey). Insofern haben sie eine narrative Qualität, dabei ist der Titel selbst immer auch eine Bestandsaufnahme, ein Protokoll über den aus formalen Entscheidungen heraus eingeklebten Schriftzug, der gelegentlich fragmentarisch ist, wie bei RUN, das eindeutig aus der Frankfurter Rundschau herausgeschnitten ist. Viele Titel untermauern die Stimmung des Bildes, wie SUNRISE oder SCHNEE, andere wie RUN, das Dynamik und Hast suggeriert, wirken gegen die statische Bildsprache. So entsteht ein gelungener Dialog zwischen der Poesie der Bildsprache und jener der Schrift. Manche dieser Bilder erinnern in ihrer Komposition und vor allem in der aufgehellten, oft intensiven Farbpalette an die Pop' artigen Bilder von B.J. Kitaj, mit dem sich Dissel zeitlebens immer wieder auseinander setzt.
Man darf die Bildproduktion von Rainer Dissel nicht als geradlinige Weiterentwicklung verstehen. Neben den genannten, komplexen Strukturen, die viele der

kleinformatigen Bilder charakterisieren, greift Dissel gelegentlich immer wieder auf rein minimalistische Ausdrucksformen zurück, wie in einem Kleinformat von 2013, wo die orangene Fläche nur von einem schwarzen Balken und der ebenso schwarzen Rahmung gegliedert ist. Auch das Großformat kehrt wieder.

Mit CIRCUS MAXIMUS von 2011 und die ARGONAUTEN von 2012 sind sie wieder präsent, interessanterweise mit Bezug auf die Antike und Bildthemen aus der römischen Geschichte und der griechischen Mythologie, die beide die menschliche Figur thematisieren. In CIRCUS MAXIMUS sind die Figuren nur in Umrissen zu erkennen. Sie „erscheinen", ohne sich wirklich vom Farbgrund abzuheben, nur durch Konturen angedeutet. Hier und da ragt ein Körperteil hervor – ein Kopf als Oval, der wie ausgeschnitten wirkt und Arme in Form von schwarzen Flächen. Die weiße Bildfläche, die ihnen als Raum dient, wird von Fotoprints überlagert, welche architektonische und skulpturale Details aus den verschiedensten Jahrhunderten darstellen und dadurch einen raumzeitlichen Konnex eröffnen. Formal entsteht eine merkwürdige Verbindung zwischen den schwarz-weißen Fotoprints und der weißen Malfläche in der Mitte, in der sich ein Spiel von Linien und Formen entwickelt, die eine neue Geschichte schreiben. Der Titel CIRCUS MAXIMUS verweist auf das monumentalste Spielfeld aller Zeiten, wo triumphale Wagenrennen und Gladiatorenkämpfe und Wetten stattfanden. Heute sind es Formel 1 und Fußball. Wettspiele und Massen-Unterhaltung haben eben eine lange Tradition. Die Bilder entfalten vor diesem Hintergrund auch ihre kritische Komponente.

Das Bild ARGONAUTEN ist ganz anders aufgebaut. Fast die gesamte Fläche ist mit einem nuancenreichen Weiß überdeckt. An Randzonen und in der Mitte ragen wieder Fotoprints hervor, oftmals sind es wieder antik als auch zeitgenössisch anmutende architektonische Elemente, die sie einfangen. Das Bildmotiv selbst ist in einem liegenden Oval eingezeichnet. Es sind kleingliedrige, bunte, abstrakte Formen, die Landschaftselemente einschließen, vor allem Blau, als würde man durch einen Guckkasten in die Ferne schauen. Ziemlich mächtig wirkt links im Bild eine Gestalt, wohl der Argonaut Jason, der diagonal zur Bildmitte steht. Auch rechts glaubt man, eine in die Landschaft integrierte Gestalt zu erkennen. Der Konjunktiv weist darauf hin, dass wir uns im Reich der Interpretation bewegen, denn eindeutig ist nicht vieles, außer, dass hier eine innere Dynamik das Bild beherrscht, in der das Auge den Strukturen der Bildfläche nachjagt, wie Jason dem goldenen Vlies oder eben auch der moderne technisierte Mensch seinem persönlichen Heiligtum.

Wir könnten noch eine Vielzahl weiterer Arbeiten betrachten und würden zu dem

Schluss kommen, dass jedes Bild für sich andere inhaltliche Bezüge aufnimmt. In der Reihe Blindenarbeiten beispielsweise, in denen Dissel auf von Blinden hergestellten Bodenputztüchern Landschaften malt, ging es ihm nicht primär um die Auseinandersetzung mit einem der Malerei fremden Bildträger, sondern in erster Linie um die Frage, wie man sich die Landschaft ohne Augenlicht vorstellen kann. Mit dieser Fragestellung rückt er unmittelbar in die Nähe der Performance Blindly, die Arthur Żmijewskis zur 55. Biennale von Venedig in 2013 mit Blinden durchführte. Er lud sie ein, sich selbst darzustellen und eine Landschaft zu malen.

Letztlich möchte ich noch Rainer Dissels Notiz- und Kunstbücher erwähnen, denn diese sind äußerst aufschlussreich in Bezug auf den Entstehungsprozess seiner Bilder. Der Künstler verwendet alte Buchhaltungsbücher und skribbelt darauf, was ihn gerade beschäftigt. Es kann ein Kopf, eine Bewegung, ein Ornament sein, es kann vorgefundenes Material sein, das er einklebt und kommentiert oder neu betitelt, alles ist Denkmaterial für Rainer Dissel und einer gestalterischen Auseinandersetzung wert. Manches findet sich in seinen Bildern wieder. Konsequent über Jahre entstanden, erlaubt diese singuläre Werkgruppe wie eine Art Tagebuch Einsicht in den Werkprozess und in die sukzessiven Interessen dieses vielschichten Menschen und fokussierten Malers.

Zur Autorin

Dr. Danièle Perrier arbeitet als unabhängige Kuratorin, Kunstkritikerin und Kunstberaterin. Von 2004 bis 2012 war sie geschäftsführende künstlerische Leiterin am Künstlerhaus Schloß Balmoral sowie von 1999 bis 2004 Geschäftsführerin des Künstlerhauses. Zuvor leitete sie das Ludwig Museum im Deutschherrenhaus, Koblenz. Perrier ist in einer Vielzahl von Gremien vertreten, u.a. ist sie Vizepräsidentin der AICA Deutschland, dem internationalen Kunstkritikerverband.

RAINER DISSEL — PALIMPSEST AND PAINTING

Dr. Danièle Perrier * with the kind support of Dr. Julia-Constance Dissel

Vingt fois sur le métier remettez votre ouvrage
Polissez-le sans cesse et le repolissez;
Ajoutez quelquefois, et souvent effacez.
Nicolas Boileau, L'art poétique

Return to your workpiece twenty times
File away at it again and again;
add something and above all reduce things!
Nicolas Boileau, L'art poétique

Rainer Dissel is a painter in the truest sense of the word. Since his days as a student in the 1980s at the renowned academy of visual arts, the Staedelschule, in Frankfurt, he has felt attracted to abstract painting, which is self-referential. His oeuvre thus comes fully under the sign of exploring the reach of painterly forms of expression. But painting is not just form, but always also expression and statement, and to convey these Dissel relies not only on the canvas as the basis for the paint, but also to historical cash ledgers and art books, not to mention blindly made floor cleaning clothes, and integrates found objects from his own everyday life as well as fragments of text that enter into an alliance of signification with the painting.
In the pieces he made in the 1980s and early 1990s, Rainer Dissel preferred very large canvases, a trend that started in the US, where Dissel spent much time after graduation, with Abstract Expressionism and endured until well into the 1980s. However, he opts for classical compositions: The canvas is prepared with a grounding, primed, and then coated with various thin layers of paint. The final result is an additive mixture of colors with an in part diaphanous effect. Dissel prefers self-made tempera paints and oil resin glazes, a technique used by the Old Masters that not only favors consistency in the colors but above all their intensity and the sense of depth created. The technique imbues Dissel's surfaces with a touch of lightness, as if they were breathing. This can be discerned especially with NOCTURNAL EMISSION (ill. 1): The grey grounding seems like poorly wiped school blackboard onto which subsequently graffiti were scratched. In the middle, a blue surface gleams that is embraced by a black framing in tar to form a space of its own. It is, as with Rothko, the space of color. However, no purely meditative space is created, as

the graffiti and the tar, too, bring the space back into reality. One could say that the underlying mood of this essentially minimal image evokes a poetry of everyday life.

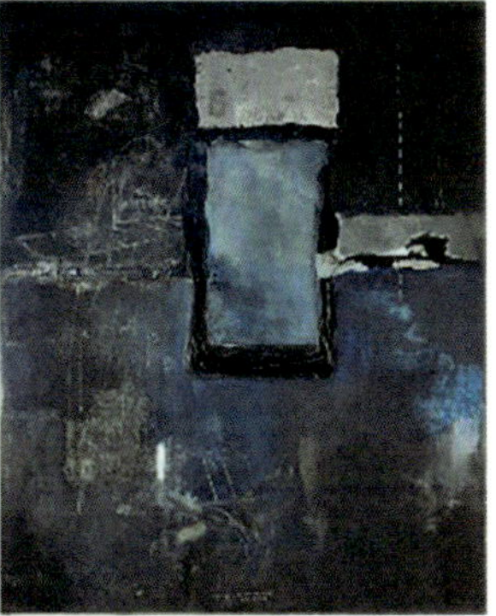
ill. 1

The recurrent integration of materials alien to art also means Rainer Dissel's work can be related to large-format assemblages; there are chairs or entire window frames set into the images and not rarely, as with NOCTURNAL EMISSION, works with pitch or tar. Sometimes he tears the tar off again while it is still a warm, liquid substance, causing damage to the layers of paint and the grounding. In such combines the result is in some places rough surfaces that are at the same time painterly decollages, which thanks to the medium of tar also offer palimpsest-like insights into deeper levels and thereby into archaic myths, something borne out by titles such as DEUS EX MACHINA or GARDEN OF EVIL MIT SCHUTZMANTELMADONNA.

In the course of the 1990s, Rainer Dissel's work became increasingly minimalist and the application of the paint became ever more significant, the incorporation of non-art materials started to recede into the background. To this end, he consciously deploys the brushwork as a creative medium. The result were pieces with a flaky surface that give the impression of permeability. In another step, he then started opting for smaller formats. As of the end of the 1990s they often have the size of display cabinet items. He starts subdividing the picture's surface into geometrical color fields that stand out from and complement one another. A bright blue field is juxtaposed to a violet one with blue tones. What is new is that these clearly distinct color fields that continue to seem haptic and translucent thanks to the color tones and brushwork, also serve as the backing for collages of seemingly Surrealist figures, symbols or objects. Where once it was assemblage that interested him, now it is collage and the structures become more polyvalent. Newspaper cuttings, music scores, entrance tickets, paper, fabric, card are glued onto this backing, partly pained over, glued over, painted over again, to create a highly complex and yet nevertheless clear structure. In some sections, the paint is translucent and triggers an animated dialog between the superimposed layers. The different information, colors and snippets of text, some of which can still be perceived in the small print, trigger a mass of associations in the viewer. However, it is the clear demarcation of the color fields that arise and the patterns, as with the images reproduced in the catalog which predominates. In most cases the image, as with SALAH AL-DIN (2014) or Allegro (2013) is defined by a grid coordinate system of verticals and horizontals. In others, such as M OR DARK GREY he again adds, expansive, architectural elements. But the way they interweave constantly forces the eye back to the pictorial level. The above-mentioned pieces and likewise RUN, CABINET AND DÜRER, are all gleamed from a text with which the pictures were collaged. They bring to mind very specific moods, conjure up associations with music (Allegro) or painting (Dürer), racing (Run) or the color grey (Dark Grey). To this extent they possess a narrative quality, whereby the title itself always takes stock of the process, is a record of the line of writing glued on for formal reasons, and on occasion it remains fragmentary, as in RUN, which was clearly cut out of the Frankfurter Rundschau daily. Many of the titles underscore the image's atmosphere, as with Sunrise or Schnee; others, such as RUN, allude to dynamism and haste, go against the static pictorial language. Thus, Dissel forges a successful dialog between the poetry of the pictorial idiom and that of the written word. Some of these images are reminiscent in terms of composition and above all the brighter, often intense color palette of the Pop-like paintings of B.J. Kitaj, with whose oeuvre Dissel has repeatedly concerned himself.

One should not construe Rainer Dissel's image output as some straight linear development. Alongside the afore-mentioned, complex structures that characterize many of the small-format images, Dissel on occasion repeatedly resorts to purely minimalist forms of expression, as in the small-sized painting of 2013, where the orange surface is structured only by a black bar and the likewise black framing line. Large formats also come back into focus.

In the form of CIRCUS MAXIMUS (2011) and ARGONAUTEN (2012) they are present again, interestingly enough referencing Classical Antiquity and pictorial themes from Roman history and Greek mythology, both of which focus on the human figure. In Circus Maximus the figures can only be discerned as outlines. They "appear" without really setting themselves off from the colored grounding, intimated only by outlines. Here and there, a part of a body stands out, a head as an oval that looks as though it has been cut out, or arms in the form of black surfaces. The white pictorial surface that serves as the space, is covered by photoprints that represent architectural and sculptural details from a wide range of centuries and thus create a spatio-temporal context. Formally, a curios connection arises between the black and white photoprints and the white painted surface in the middle, in which lines and shapes playfully evolve, writing a new narrative. The title CIRCUS MAXIMUS references the most monumental playing field of all time, the venue of triumphal chariot races and combat between gladiators, and wagers. Today, grand prix racing and football are the rage. There's simply a long tradition of betting and mass entertainment. In this regards, the images have a critical element, too. The painting entitled ARGONAUTEN is constructed quite differently. Almost the entire surface is covered with a highly nuanced white. On the periphery and in the middle we again see photoprints, and these often again bear seemingly architectural elements that seem to stem from Classical Antiquity or the contemporary world. The pictorial theme itself is drawn in an oval lying on its side. These are small-segment colored abstract shapes that embrace landscape elements, above all blue, as if one were looking through a keyhole into the distance. One figure to the left has a powerful impact and is presumably the Argonaut Jason, standing at a diagonal to the center of the picture. On the right, there also seems to be a figure integrated into the landscape. Here, we are definitely in the realm of conjecture, as little is unambiguous, except that here an inner dynamism prevails, with the eye chasing after the structures of the pictorial surface just as Jason hunted for the Golden Fleece or modern technological man seeks his personal salvation.

We could likewise consider a multiplicity of other works and would still conclude that each image relies on a different set of substantive references. In the series Blindenarbeiten, for example, in which Dissel paints landscapes on floor cleaning clothes made by the blind, he was interested not primarily in the use of a medium alien to painting, but in the question of how one should imagine the countryside to be without eyesight. With this approach, he found himself firmly alongside the Blindly performance that Arthur Żmijewski organized at the 55th Venice Biennale in 2013 with blind participants. He invited them to represent themselves and paint a landscape.

I would like to conclude by mentioning Rainer Dissel's notebooks and artbooks, as they are very informative as regards the process whereby he creates his pictures. The artist makes use of old accounting ledgers and scribbles whatever enters his mind down in them. It can be a head, a movement, an ornament, it may be found material he glues in and comments or gives a new title, all of it is material for thought for Rainer Dissel and worth addressing in creative terms. Some of this is to be discerned in his images. Down through the years he has consistently created them, and this singular group of works functions as a kind of diary, offering insights into the creative process and the successive interests of this profound individual and highly focused painter.

About the author

Dr. Danièle Perrier works as an independent curator, art critic and art consultant. From 2004 to 2012 she was Managing Artistic Director of Künstlerhaus Schloss Balmoral and from 1999 to 2004 Managing Director of the Künstlerhaus. Before that she ran Ludwig Museum im Deutschherrenhaus, Koblenz. Perrier is a member of numerous committees, among other things Vice President of AICA Deutschland, the international Association of Art Critics.

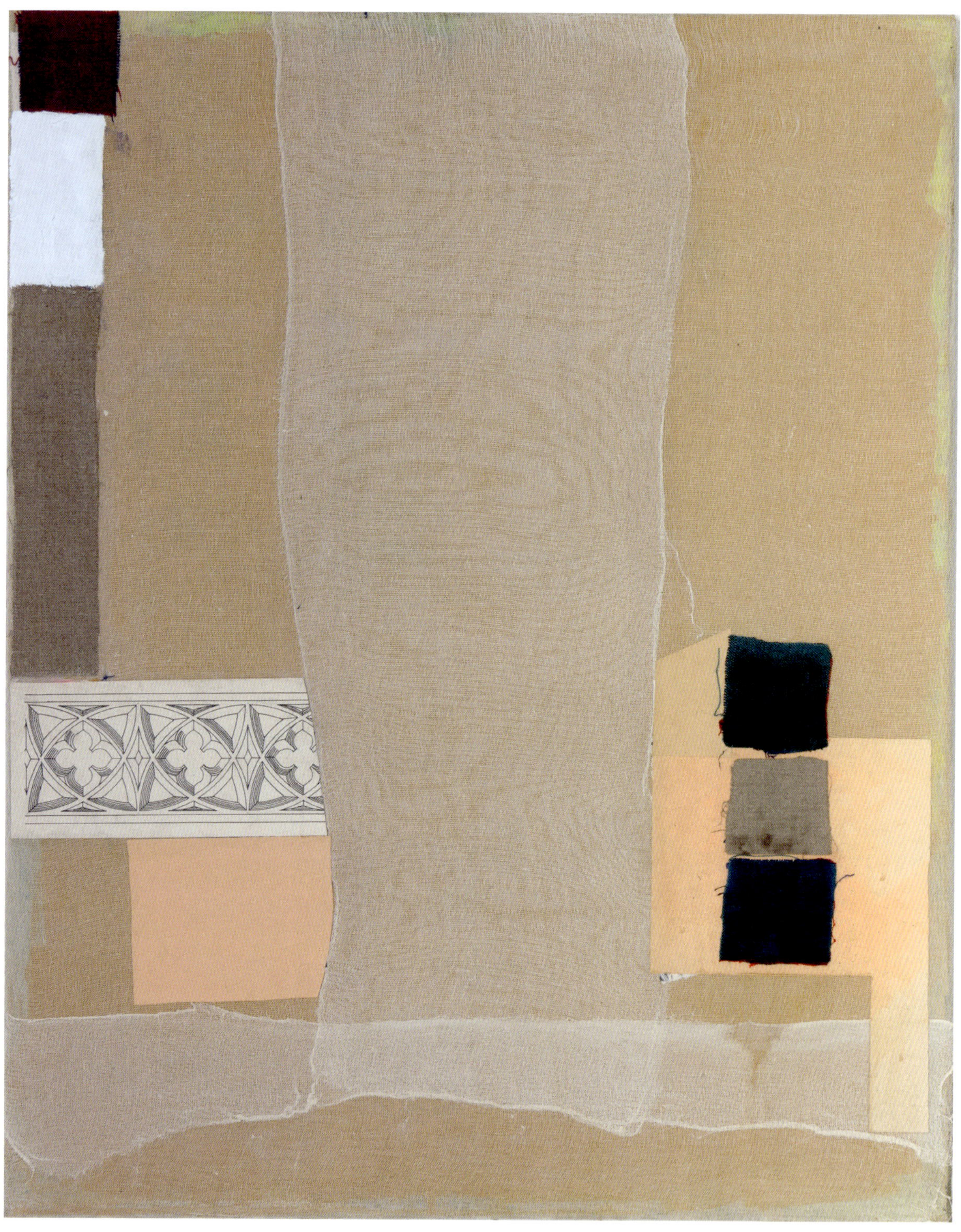

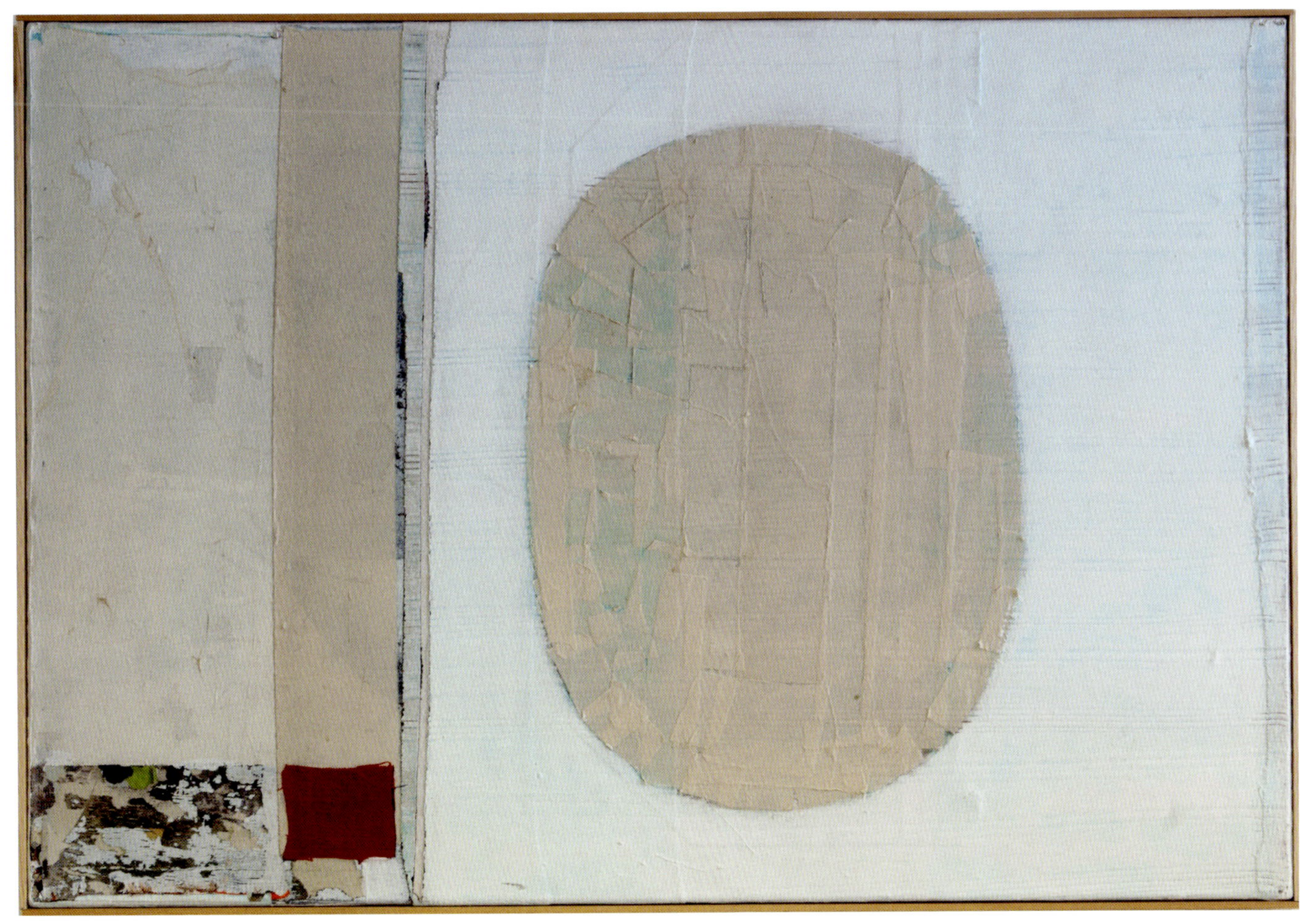

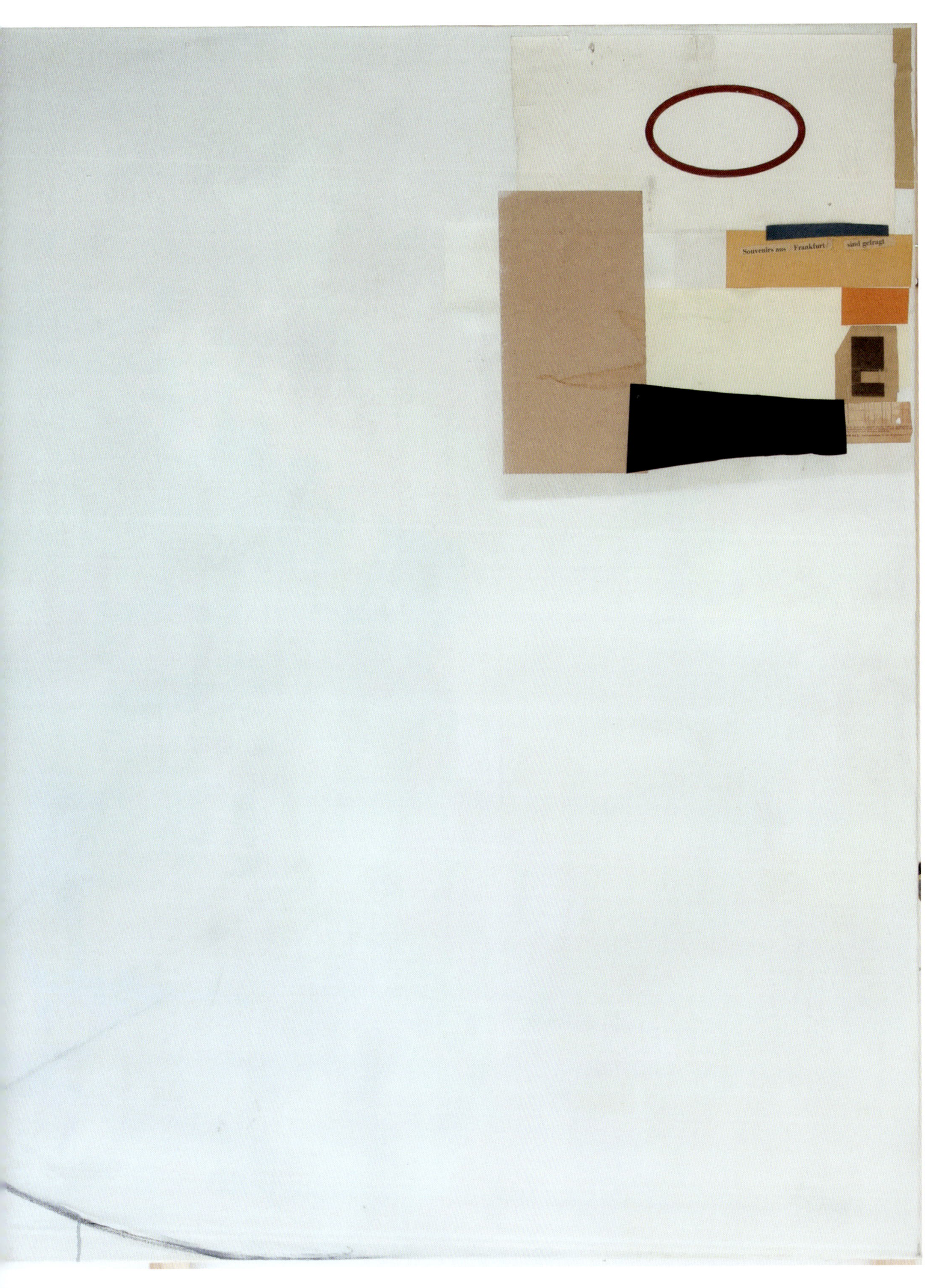
Souvenirs aus Frankfurt sind gefragt

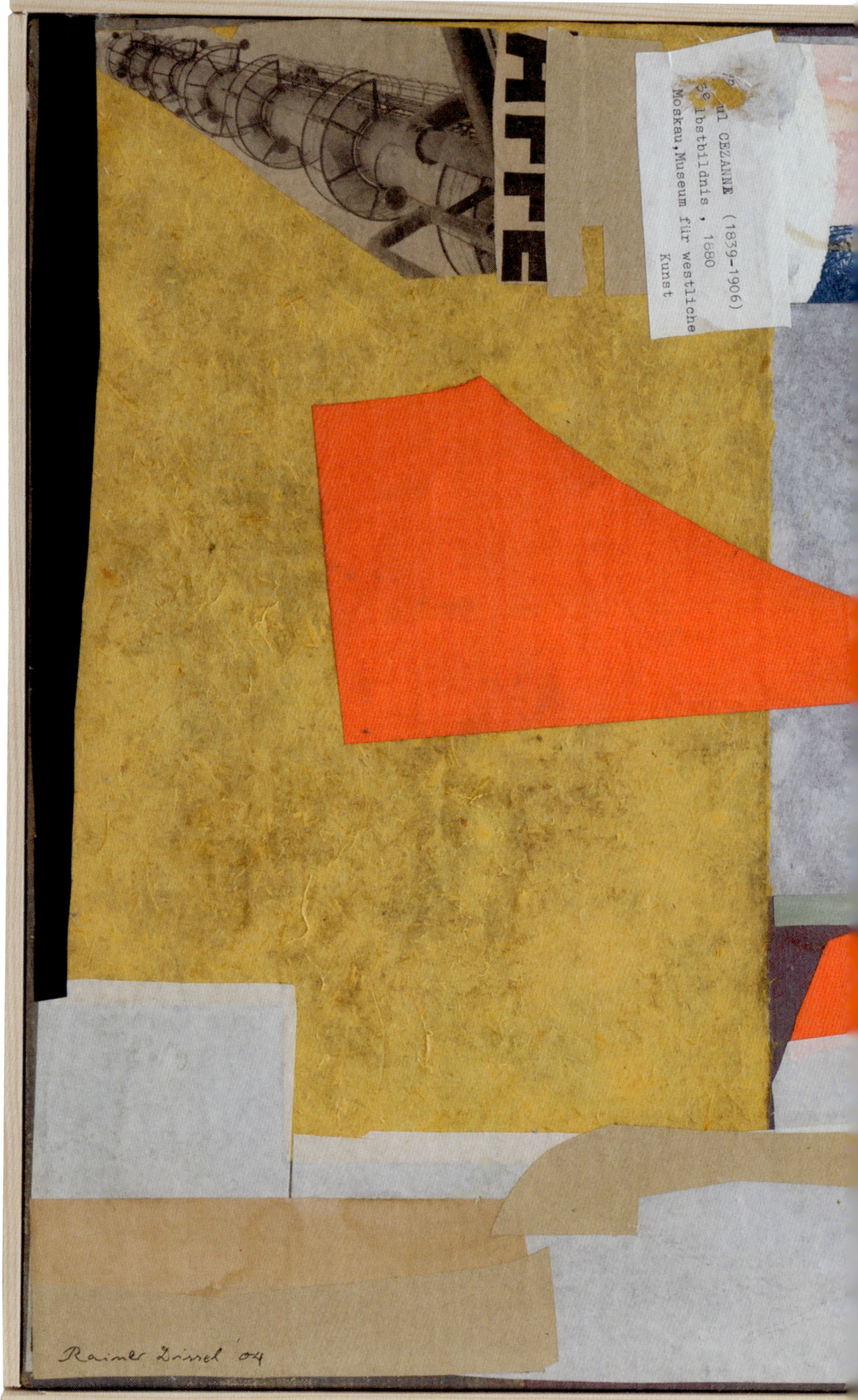
ul CEZANNE (1839-1906)
Se lbstbildnis , 1880
Moskau,Museum für westliche
Kunst

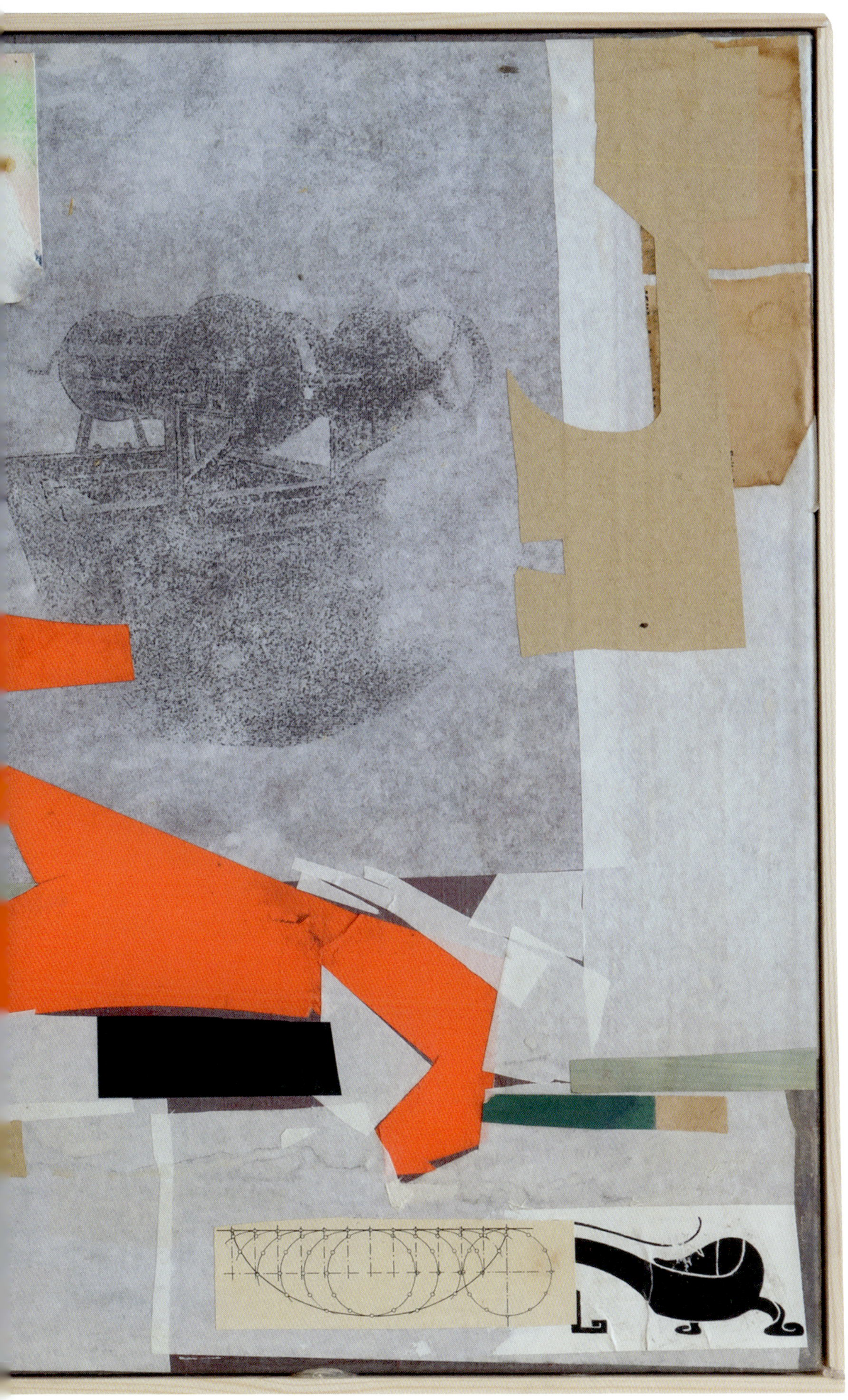

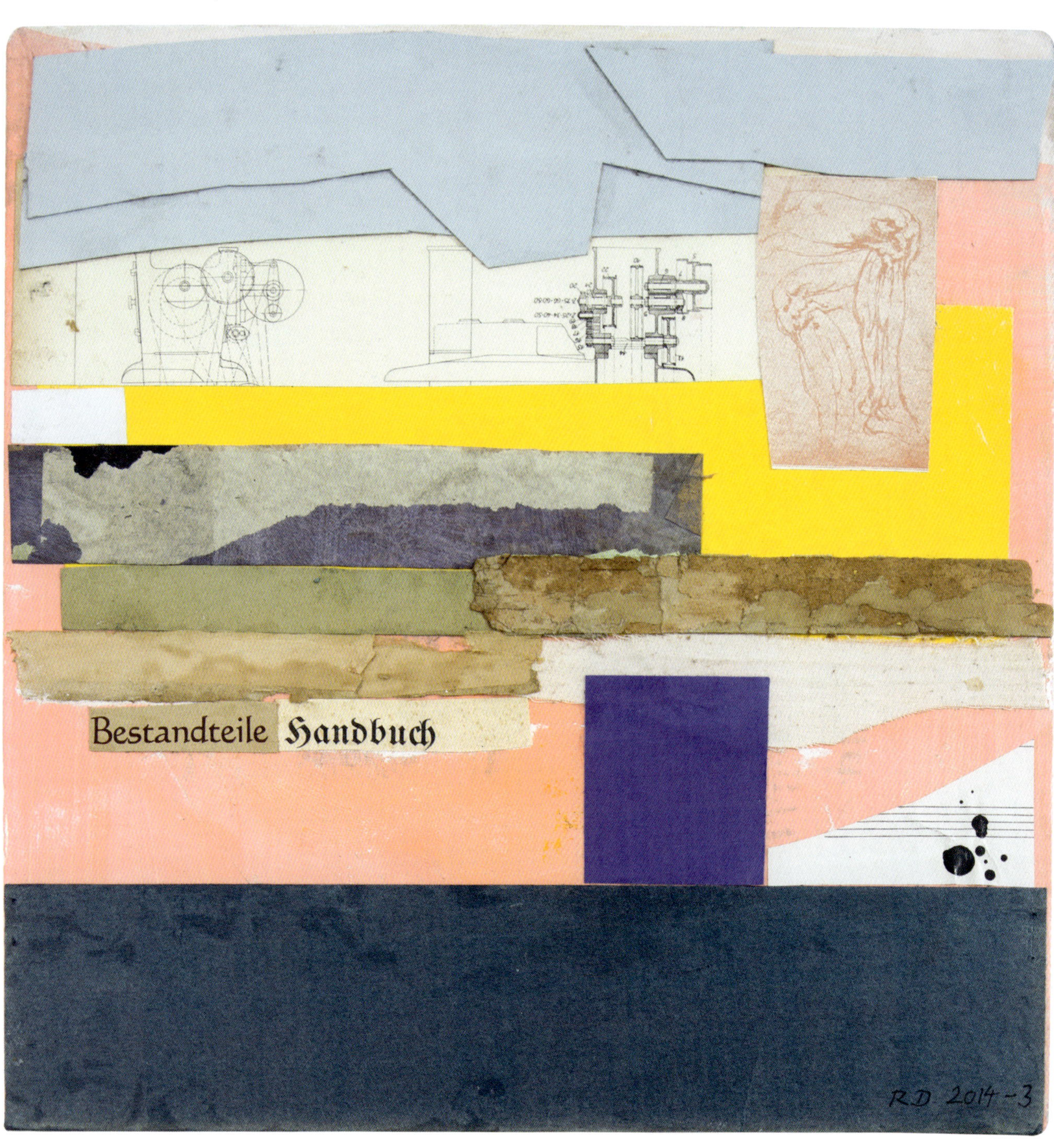
Bestandteile Handbuch
RD 2014-3

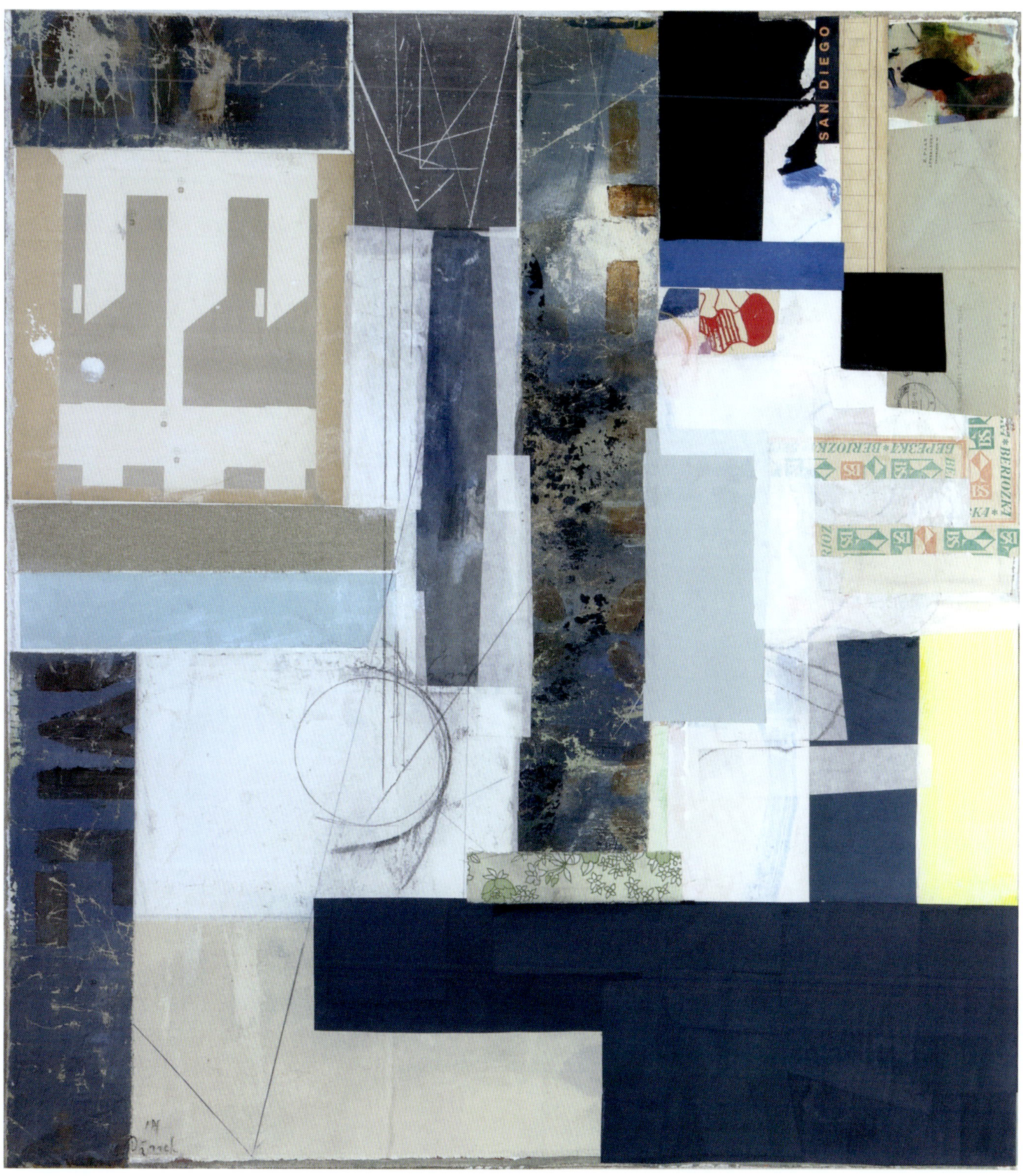
SAN DIEGO

L'ART DÉCORATIF D'AUJOURD'HUI

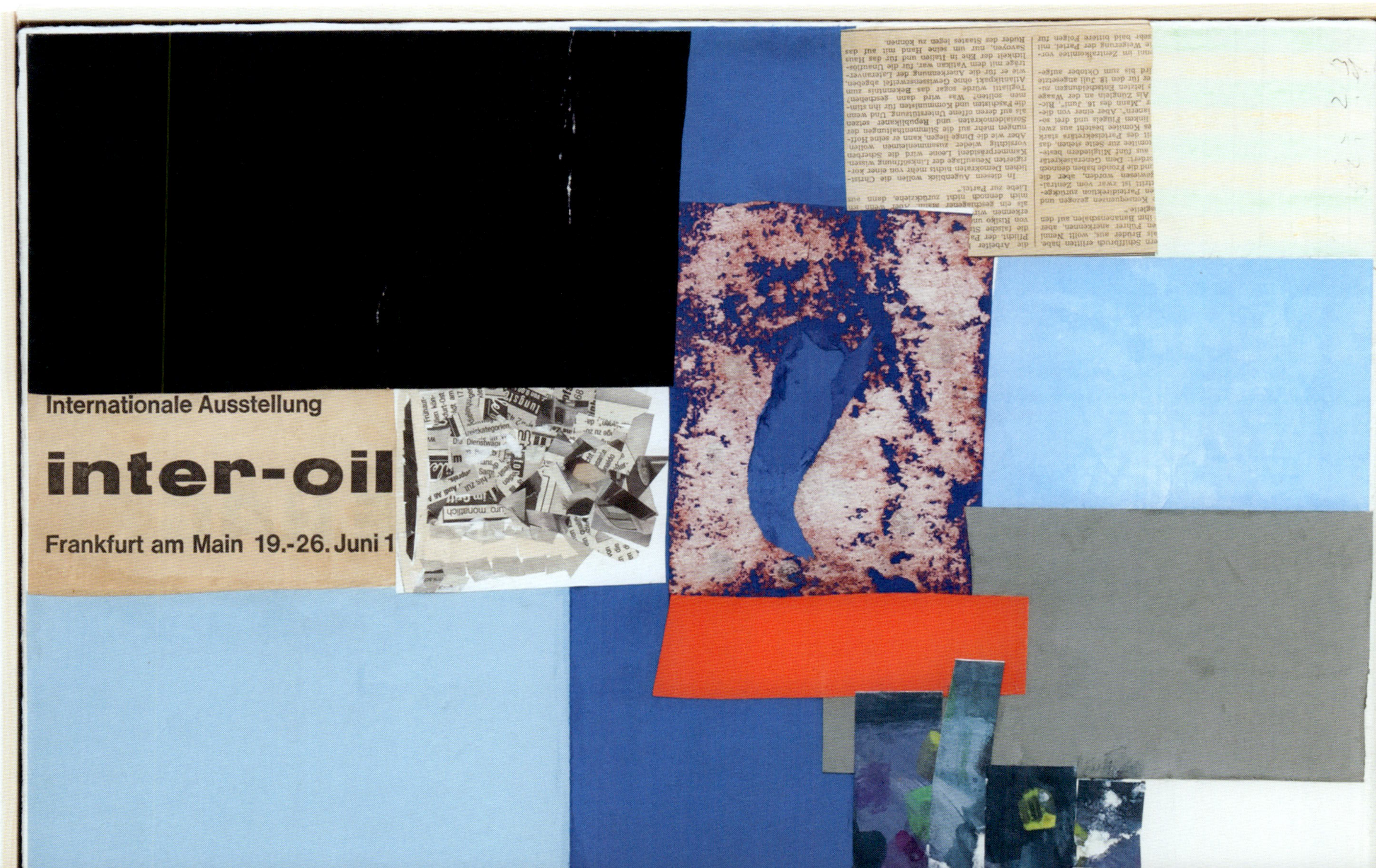
Internationale Ausstellung
inter-oil
Frankfurt am Main 19.-26. Juni 1

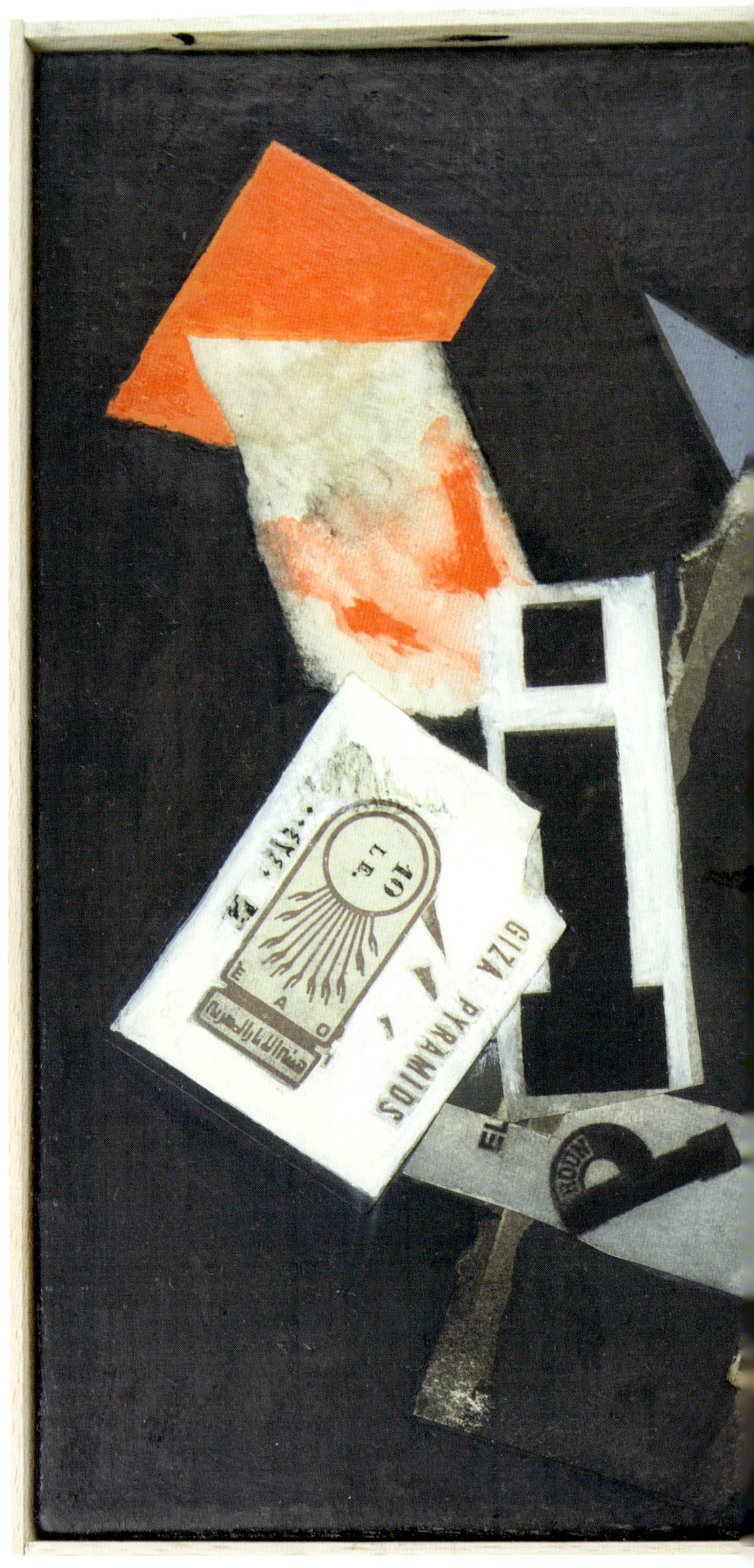
10
L.E.
GIZA PYRAMIDS

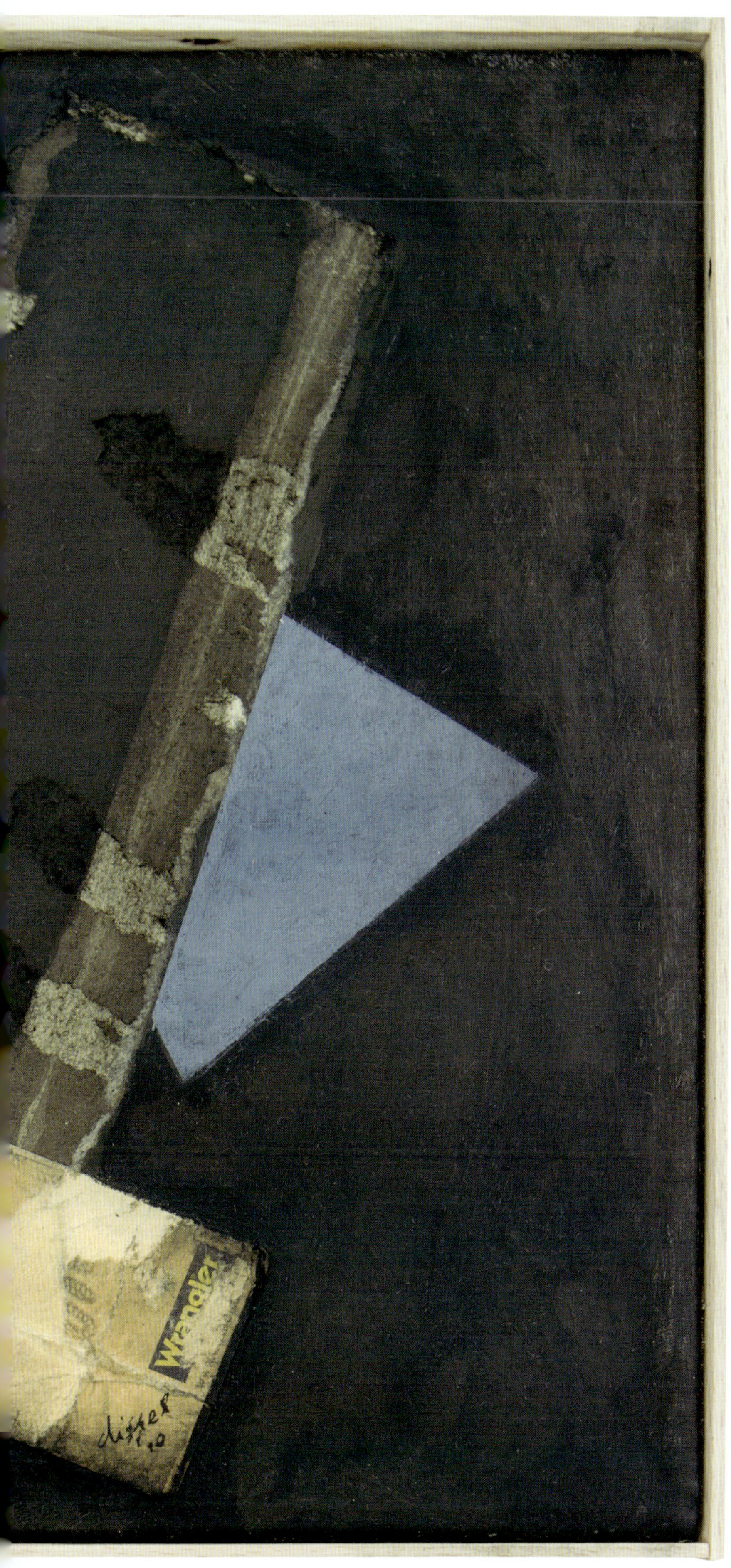
Wrangler

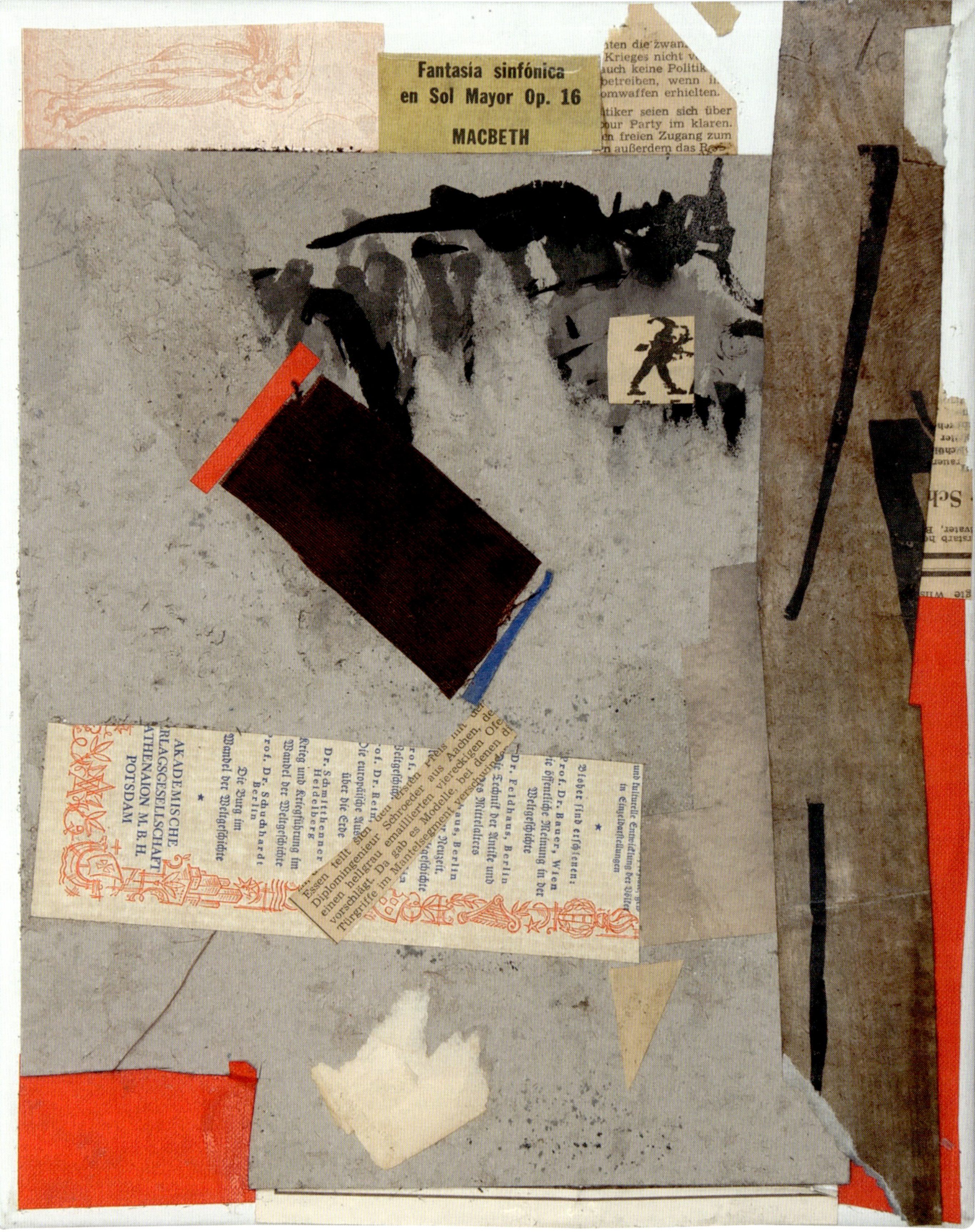
Fantasía sinfónica
en Sol Mayor Op. 16
MACBETH
AKADEMISCHE
VERLAGSGESELLSCHAFT
ATHENAION M. B. H.
POTSDAM

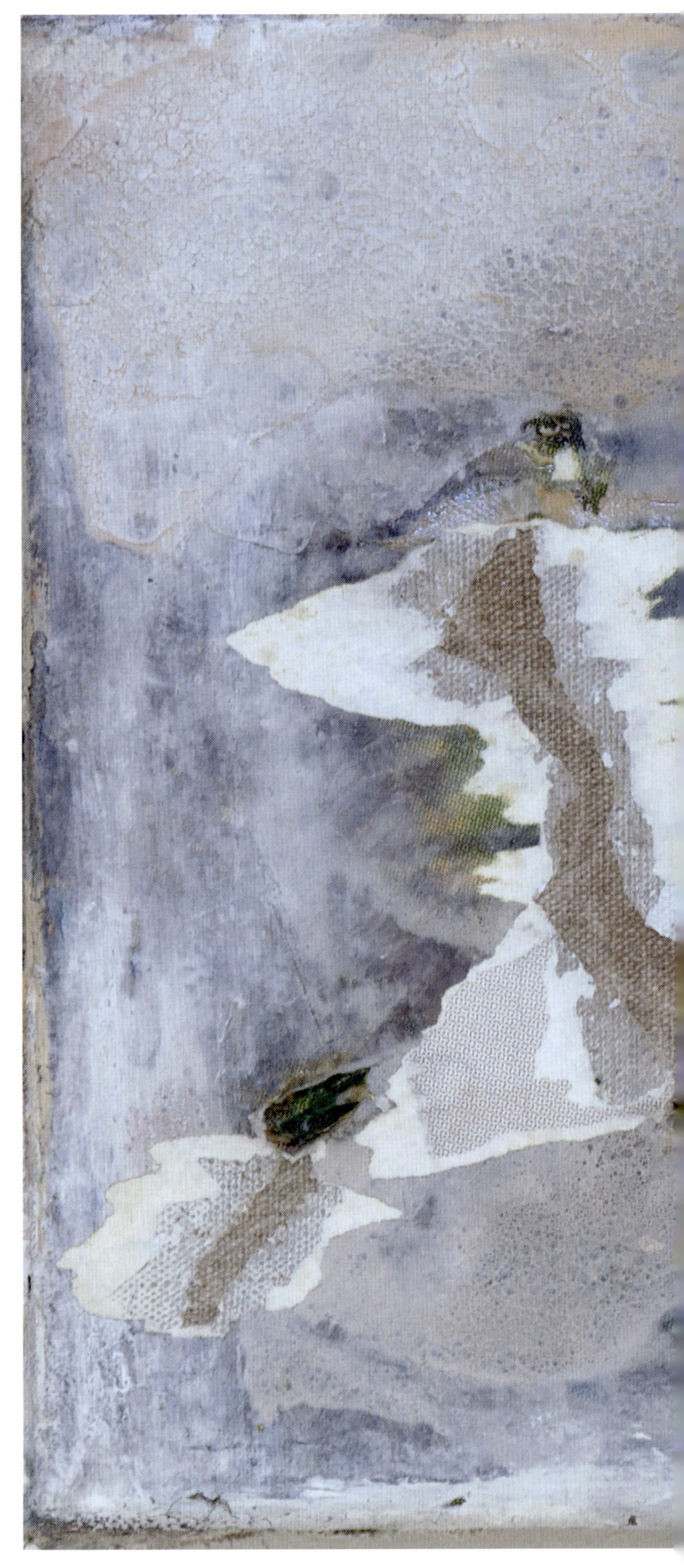

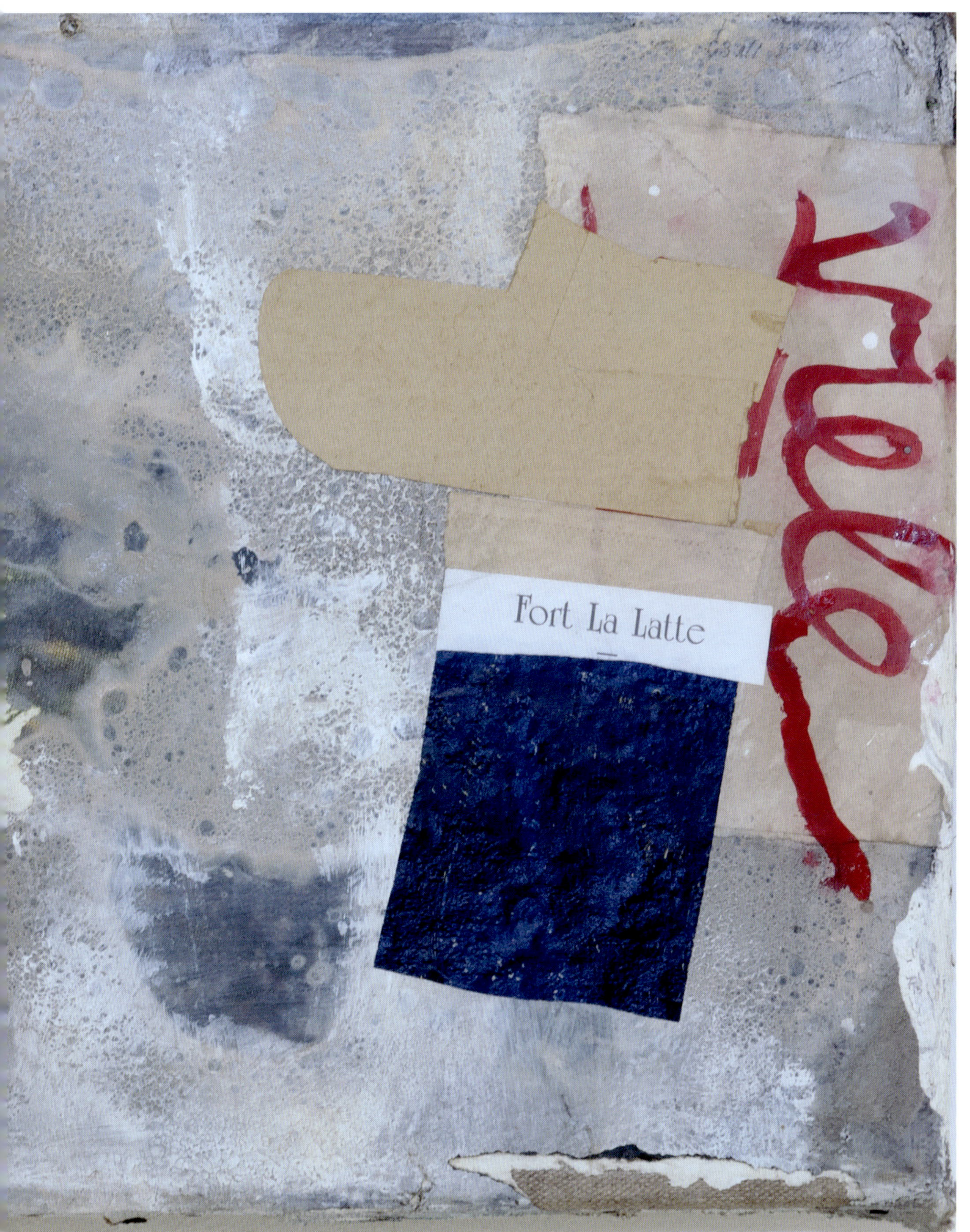
Fort La Latte

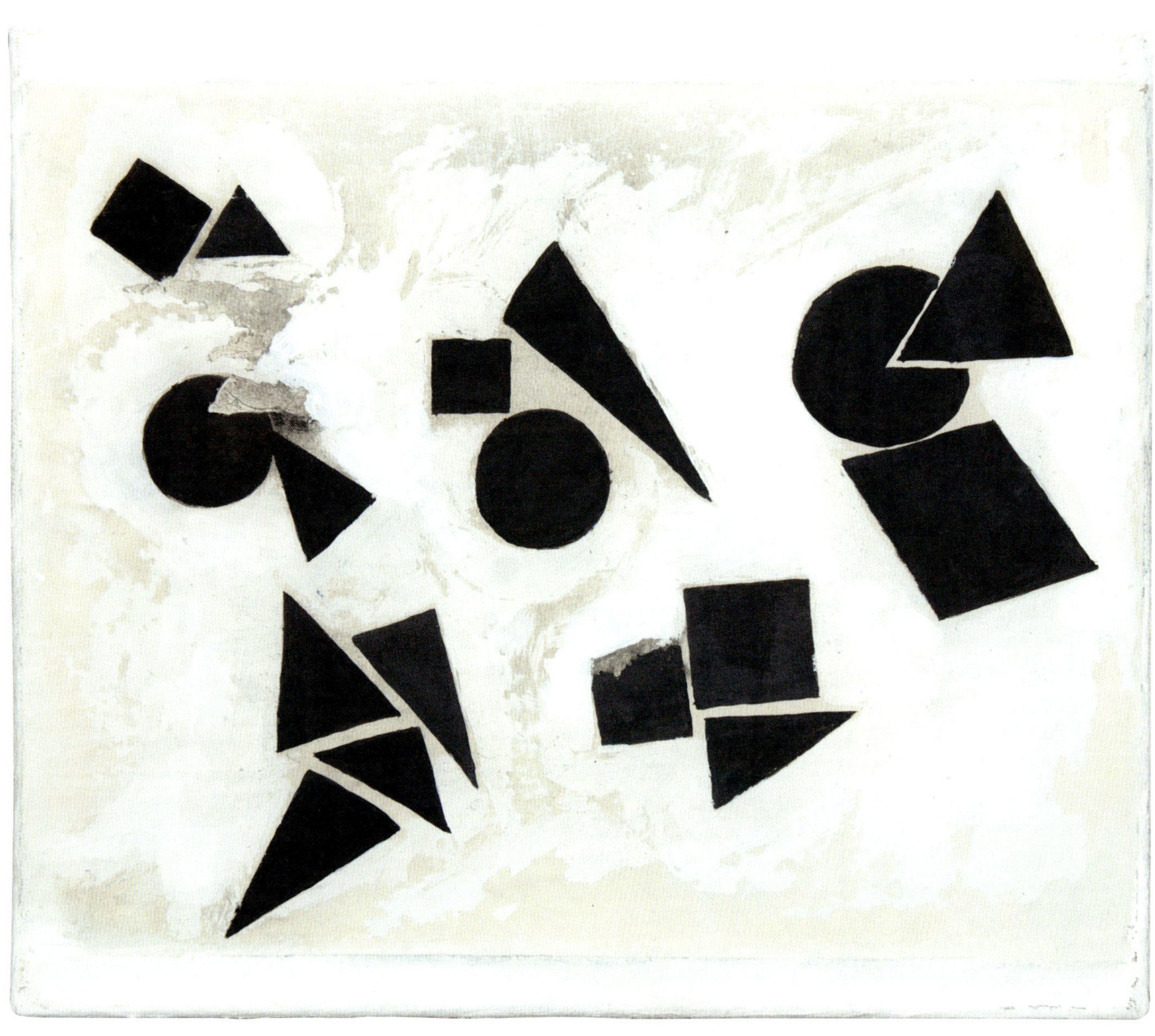

NCENT

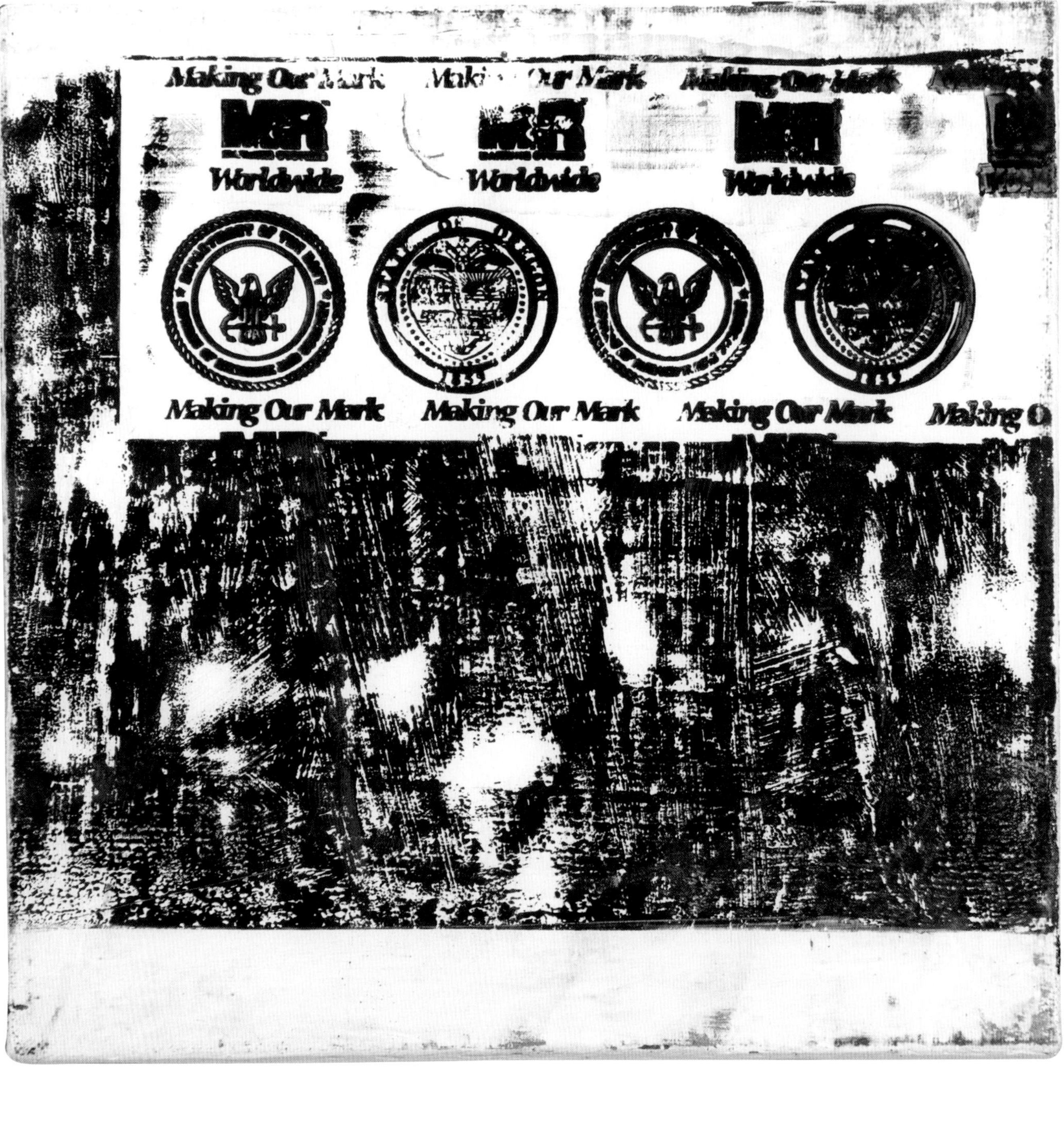
Making Our Mark
Making Our Mark
Making Our Mark
Worldwide
Worldwide
Worldwide
Making Our Mark
Making Our Mark
Making Our Mark

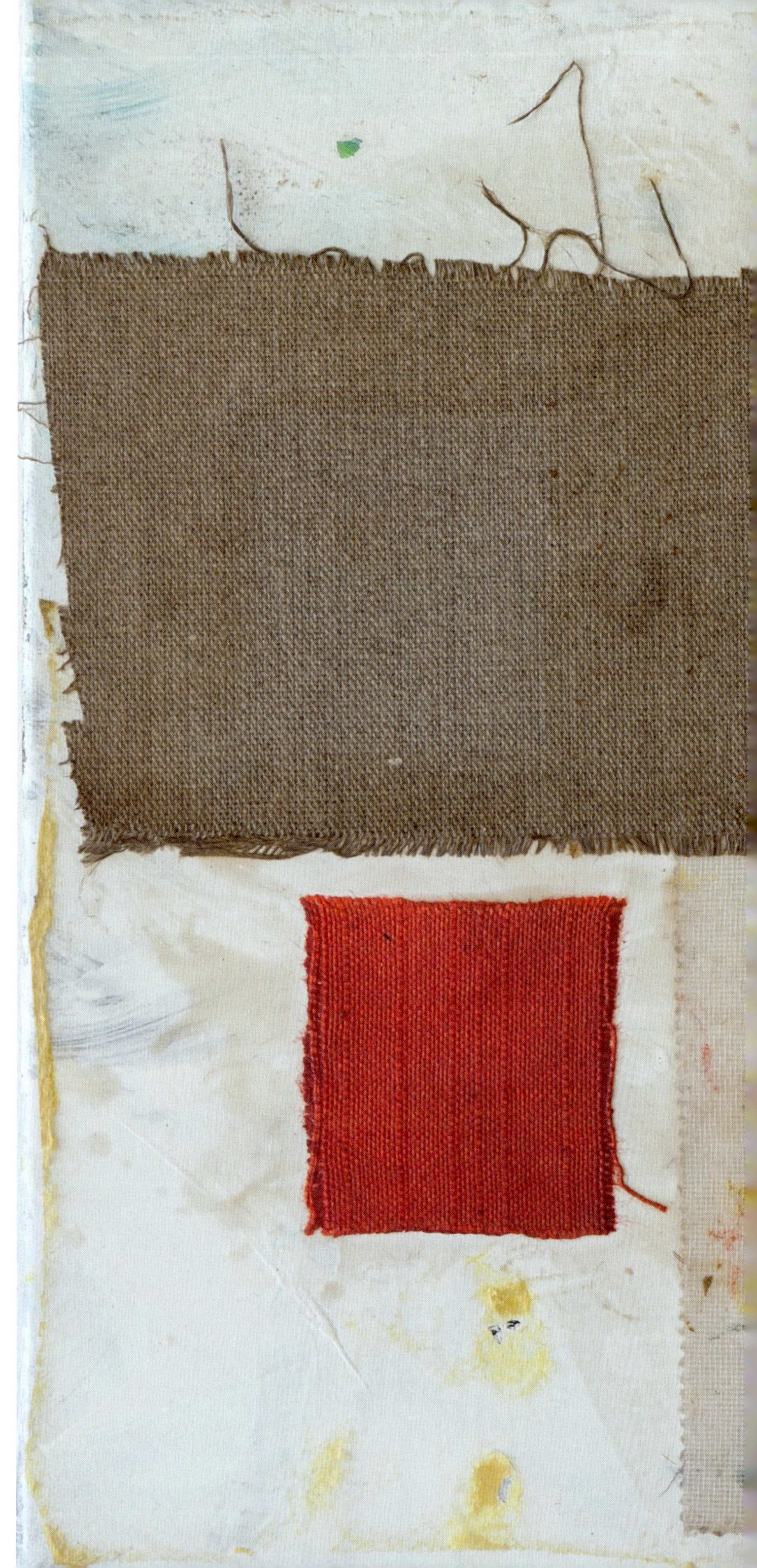

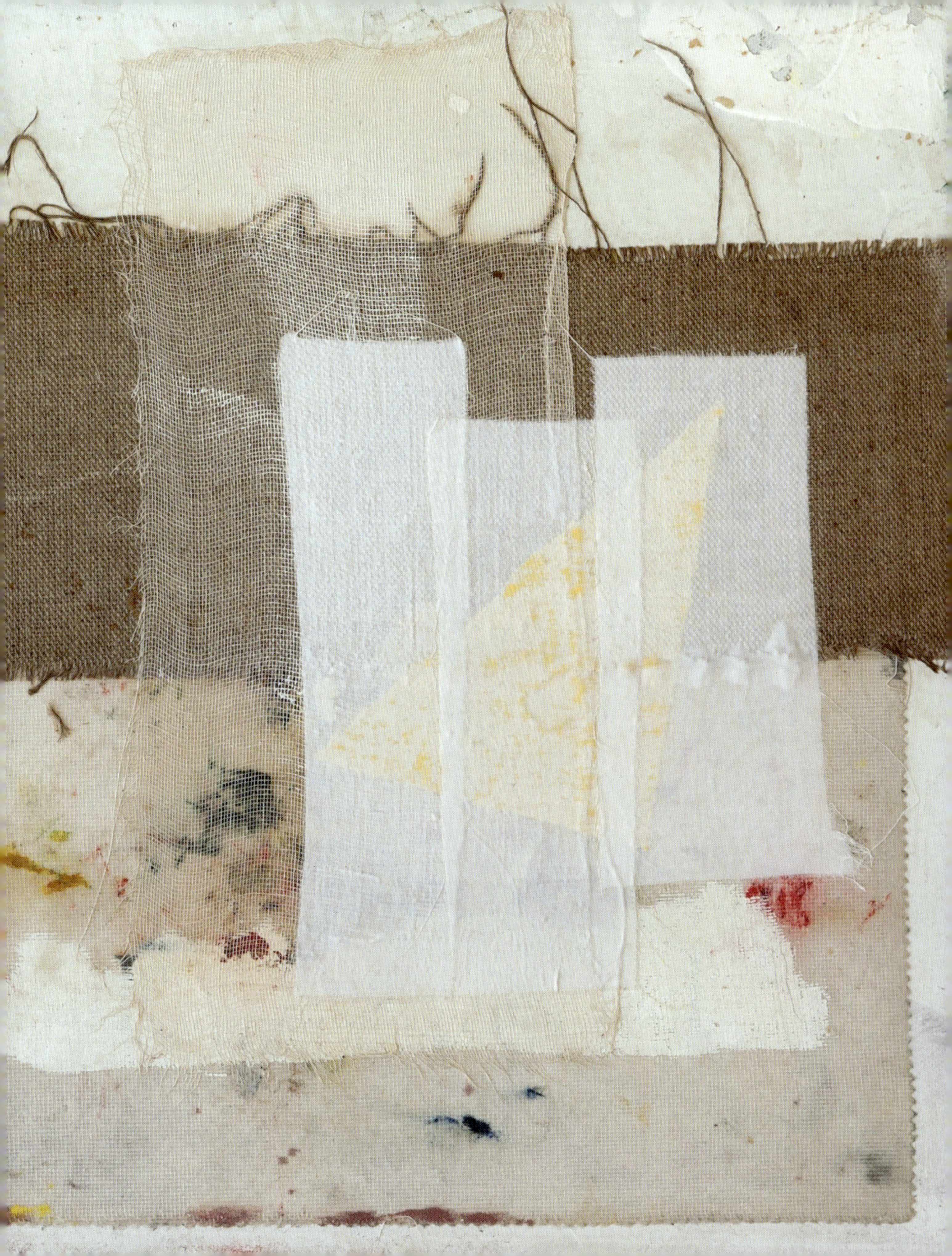

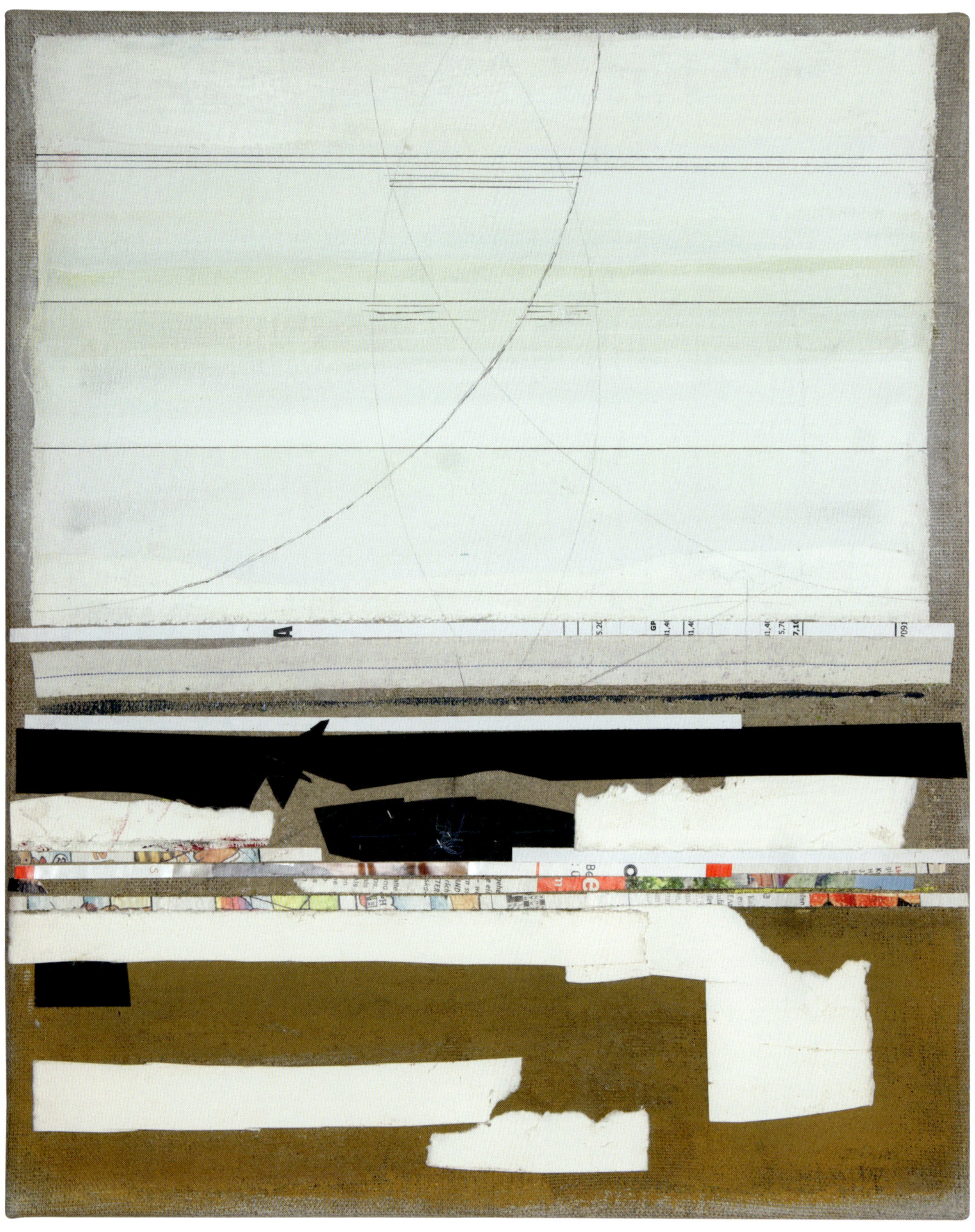

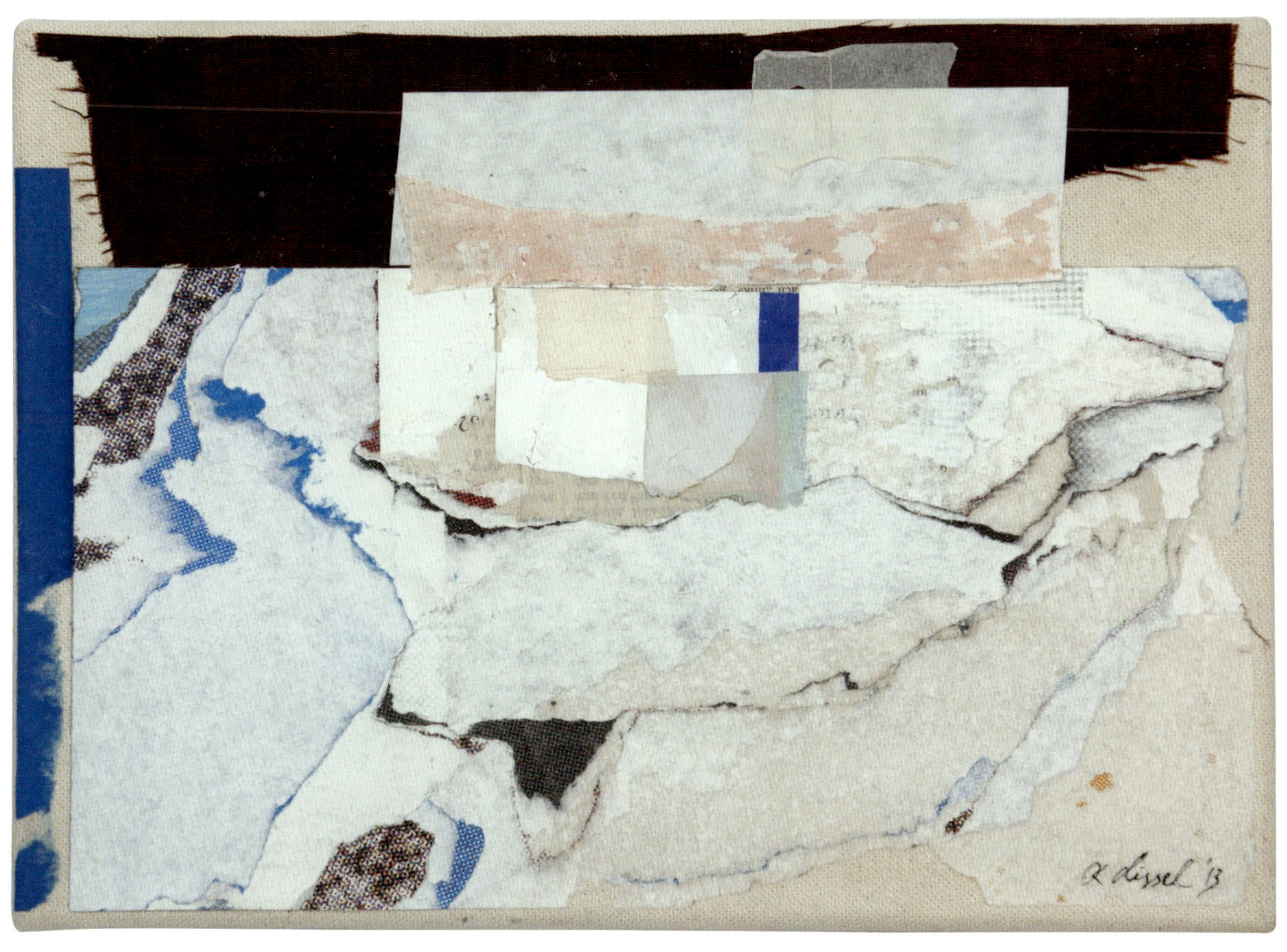

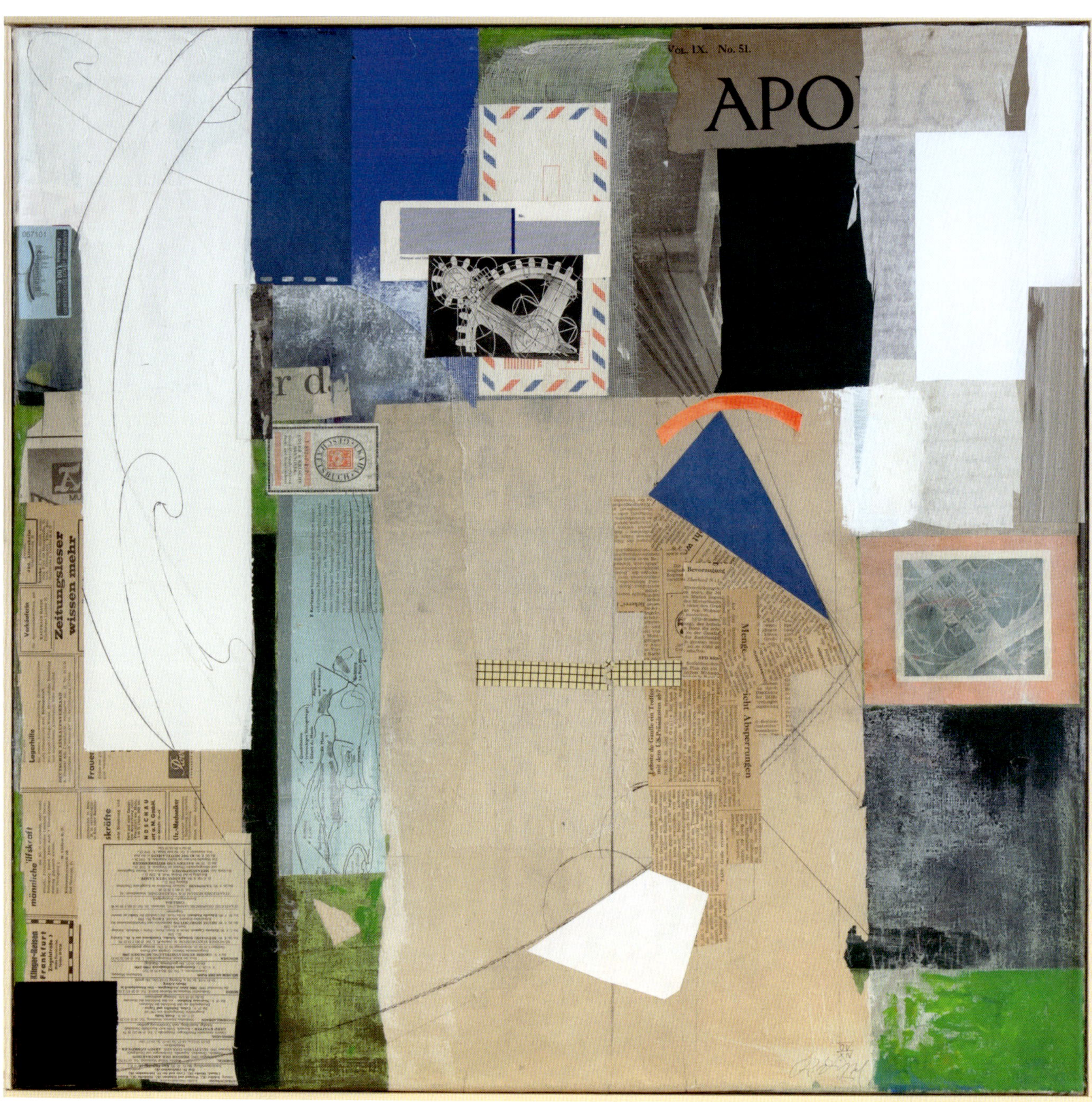
Vol. IX. No. 51.
APO
r d
Zeitungsleser
wissen mehr

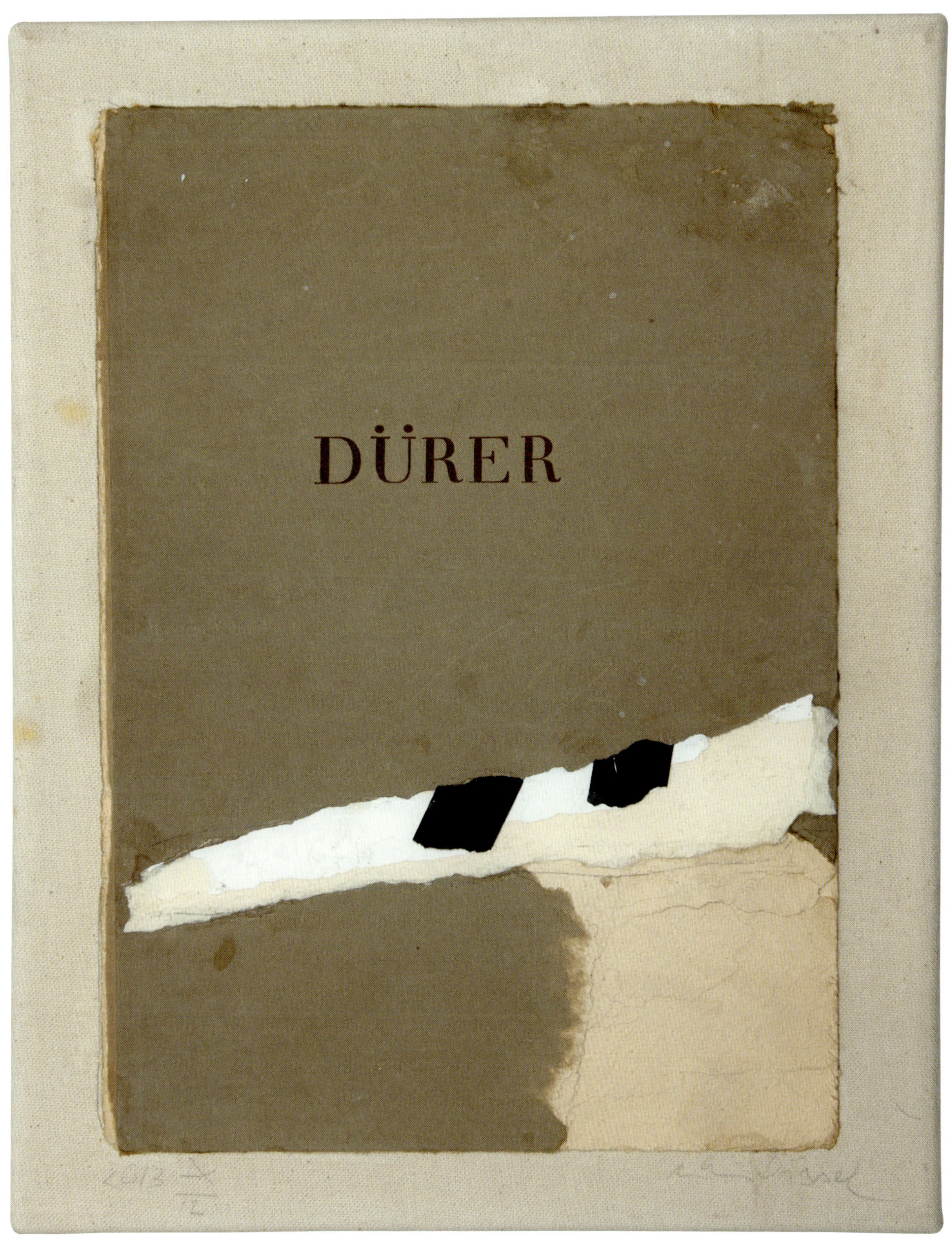
DÜRER

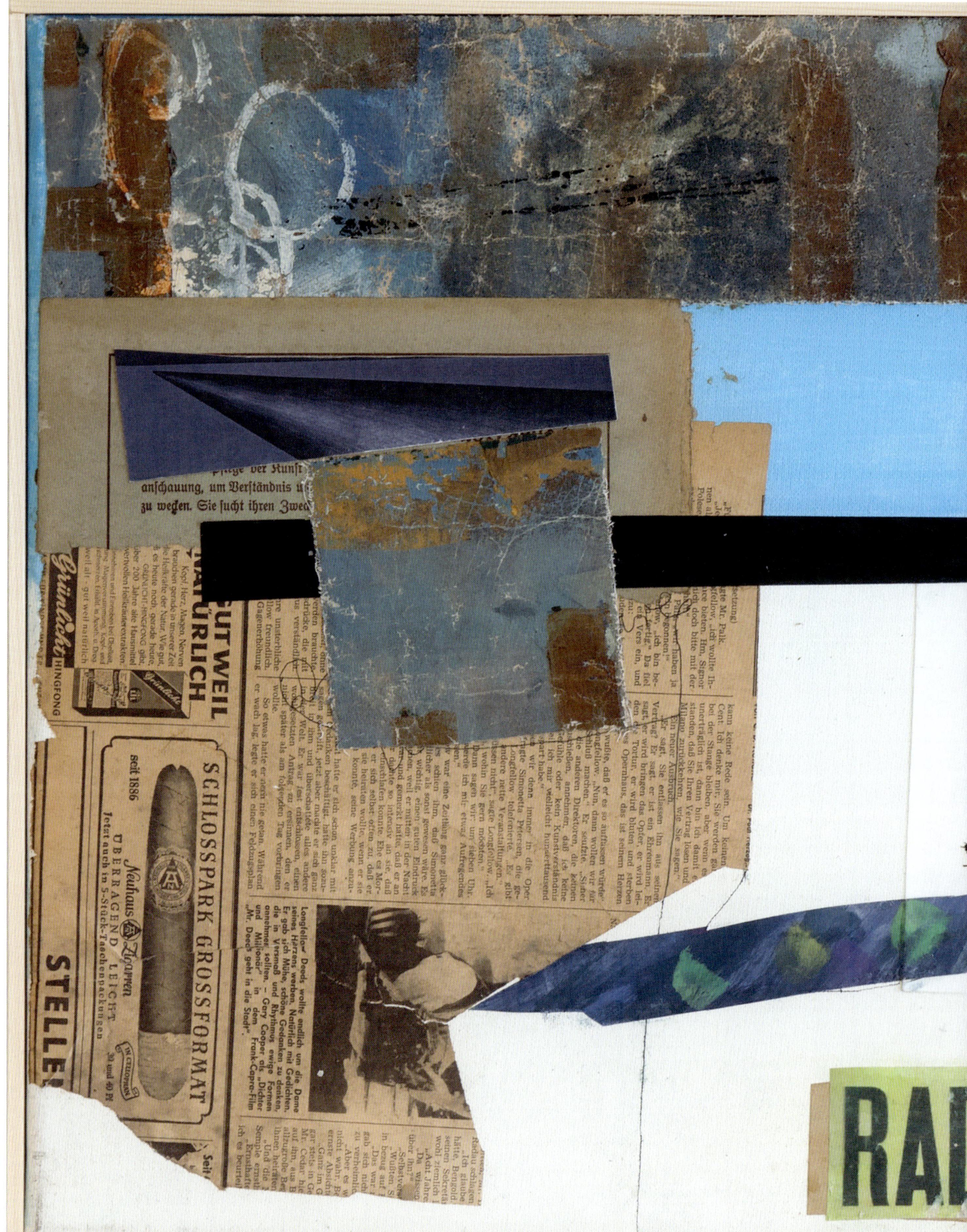
anschauung, um Verständnis
zu wecken. Sie sucht ihren Zwec
GUT WEIL NATÜRLICH
SCHLOSSPARK GROSSFORMAT
seit 1886
UEBERRAGEND LEICHT
Jetzt auch in 5-Stück-Taschenpackungen
STELLE
RA

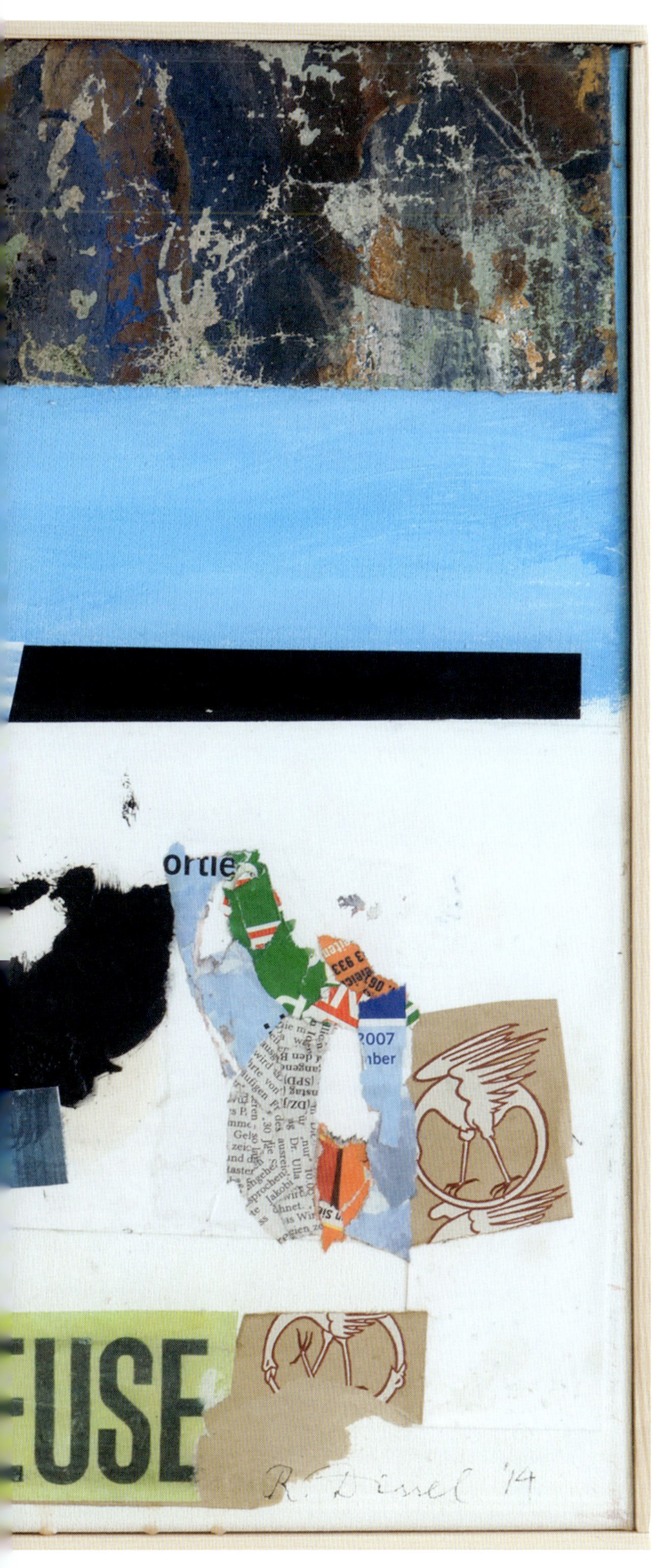
ortie
2007
EUSE

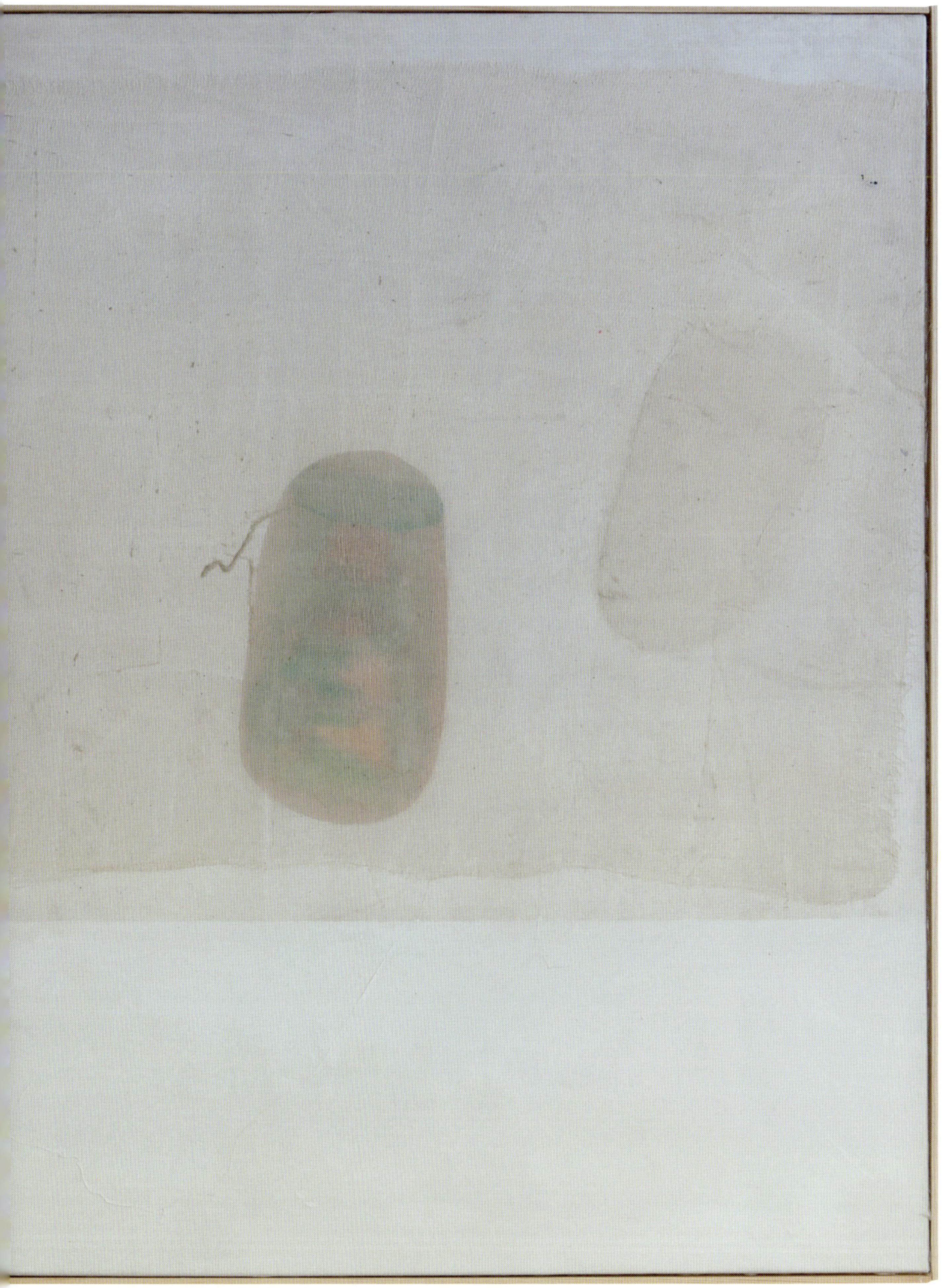

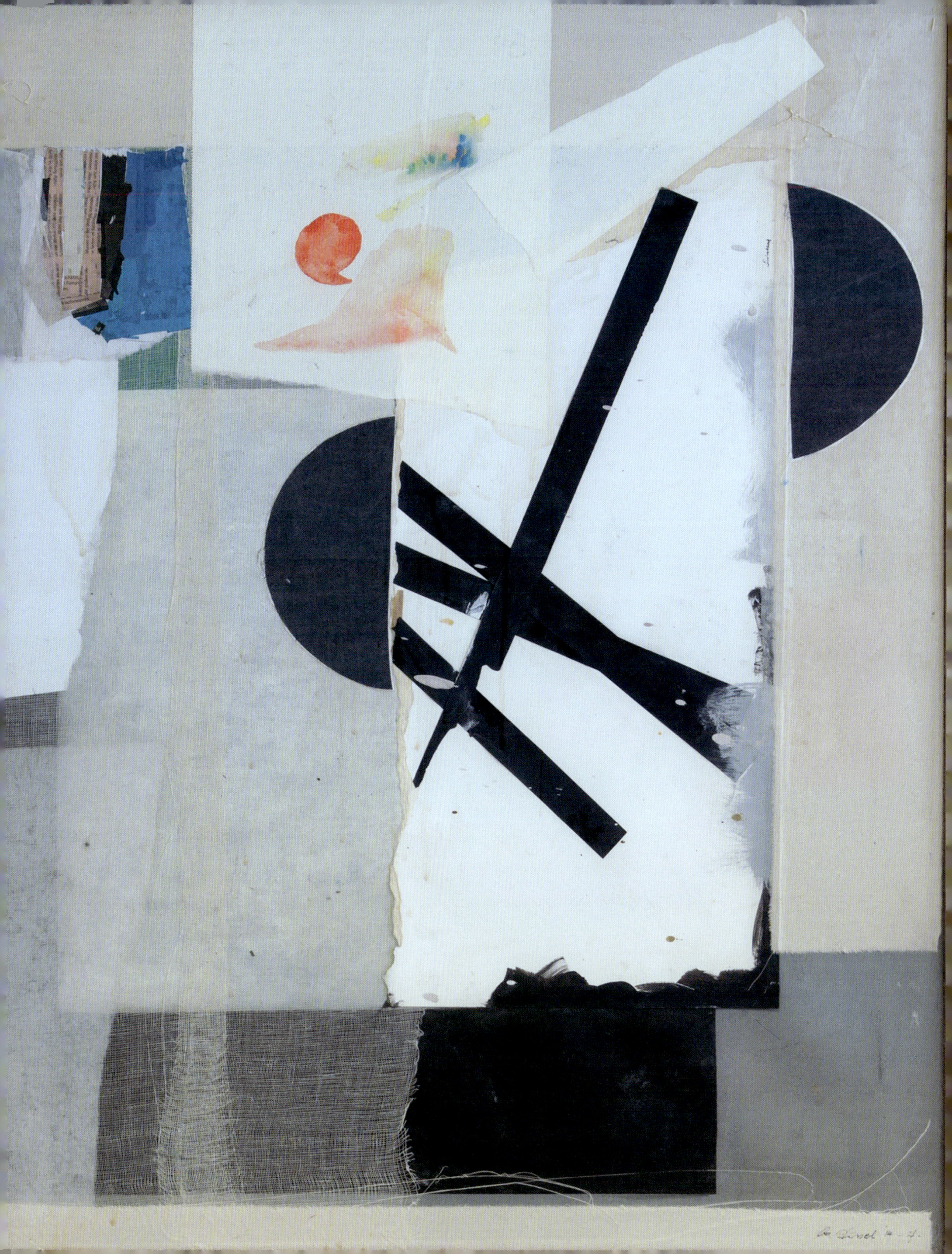

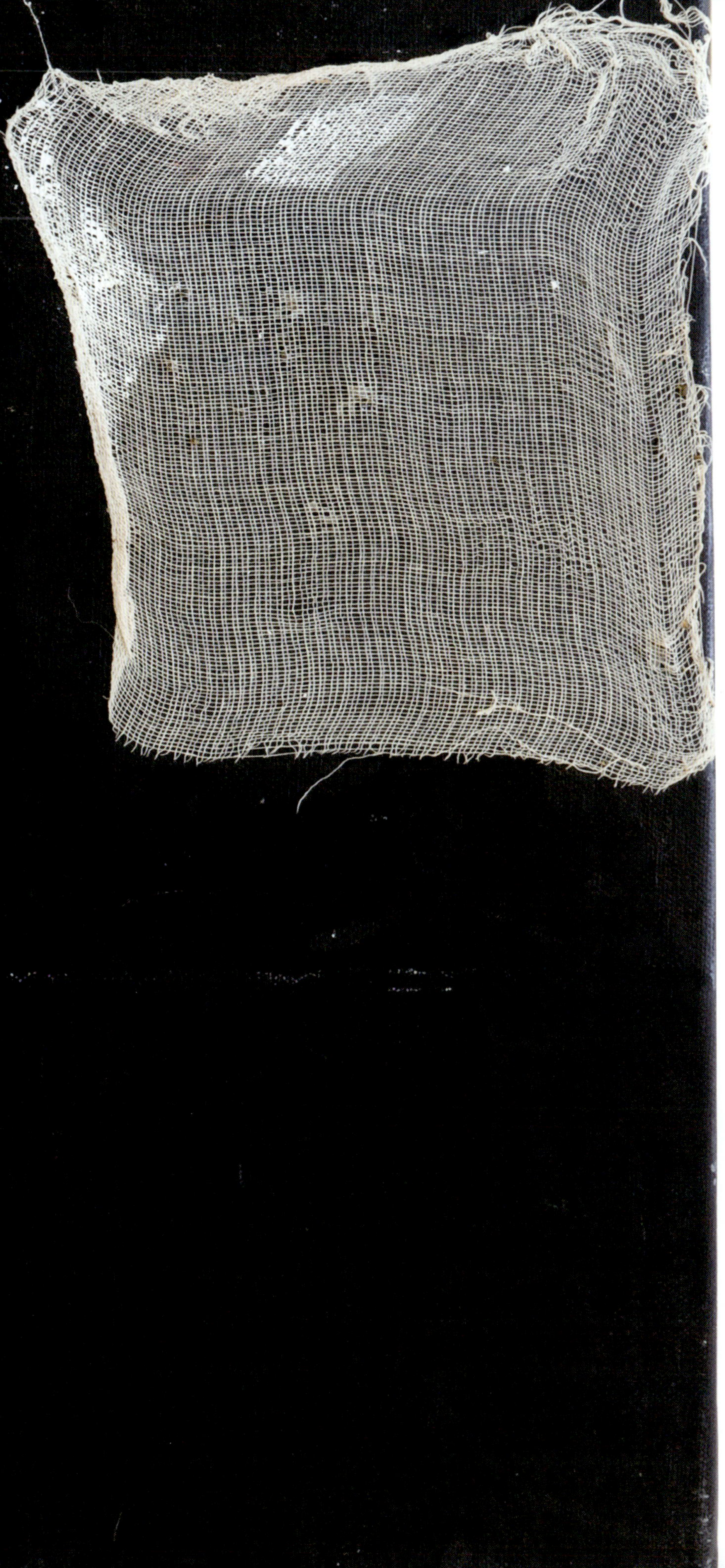

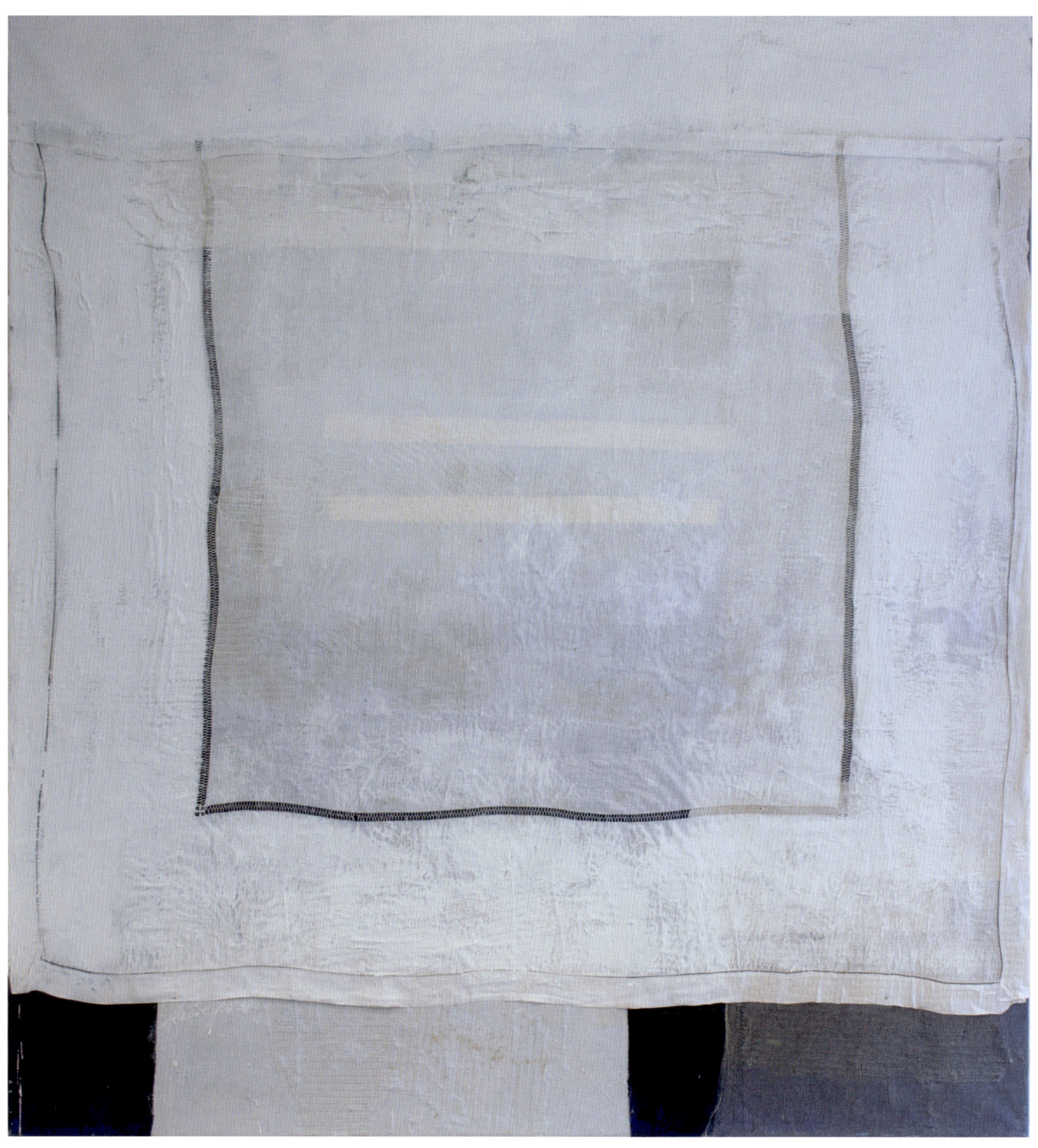

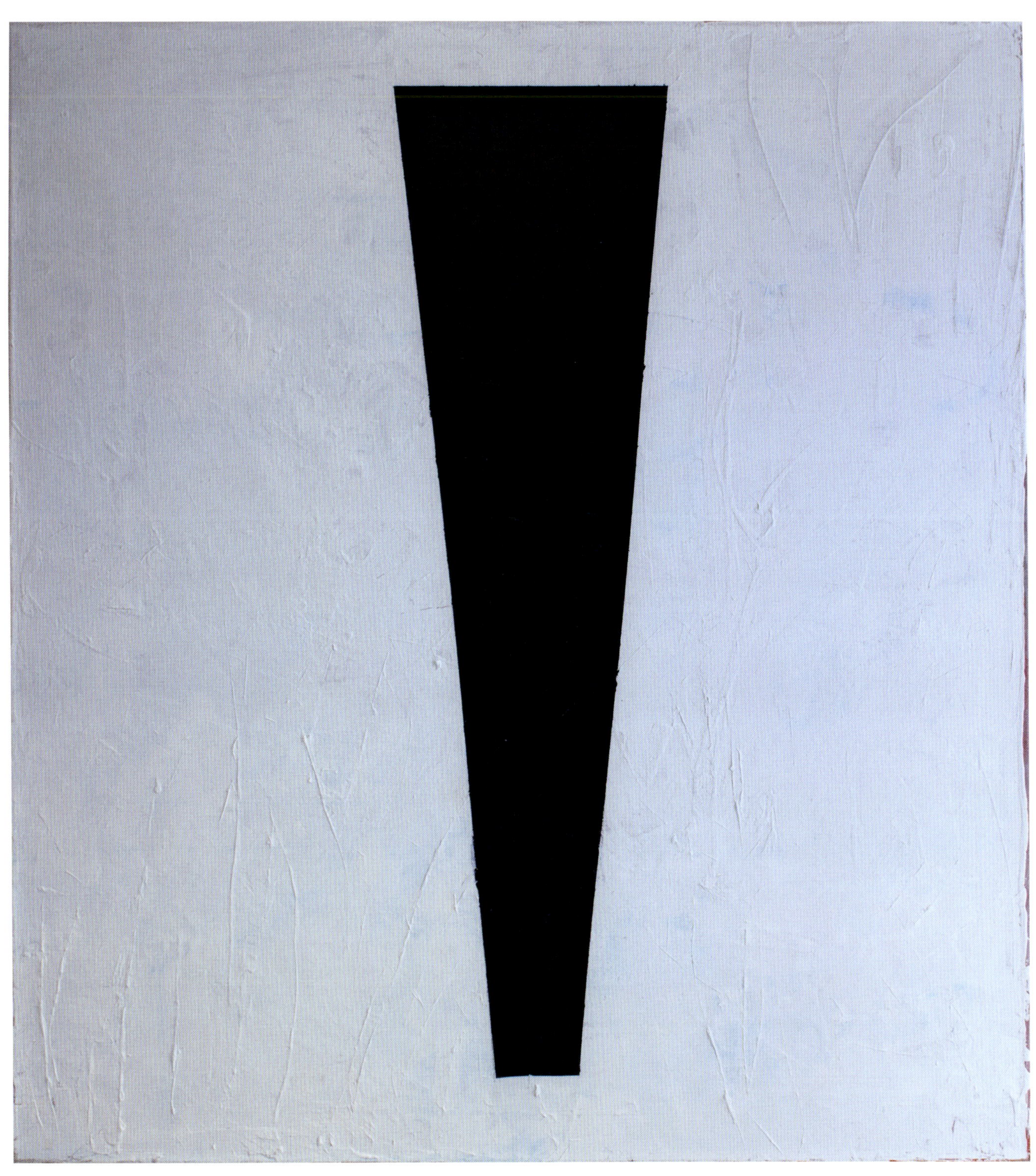

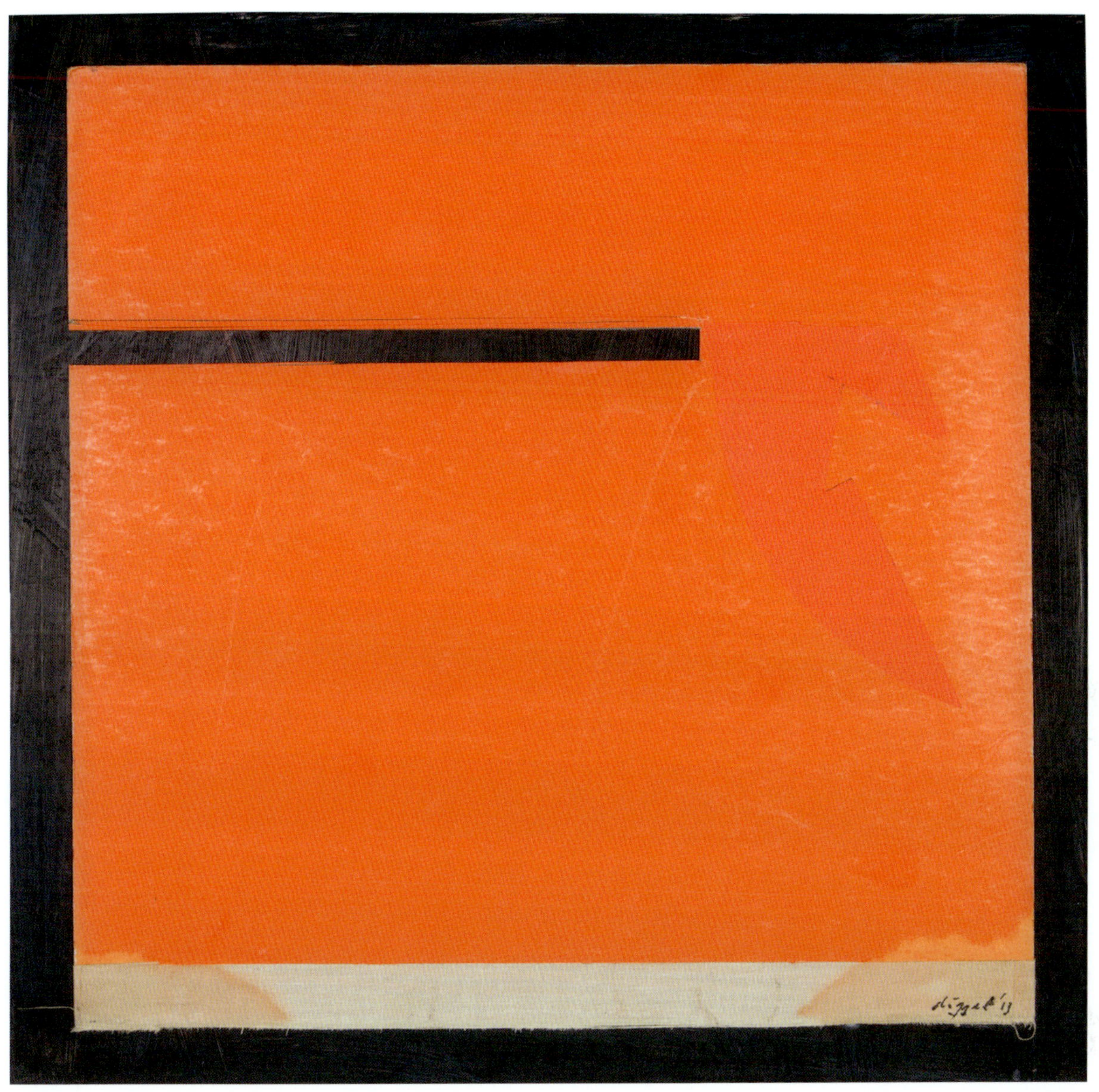

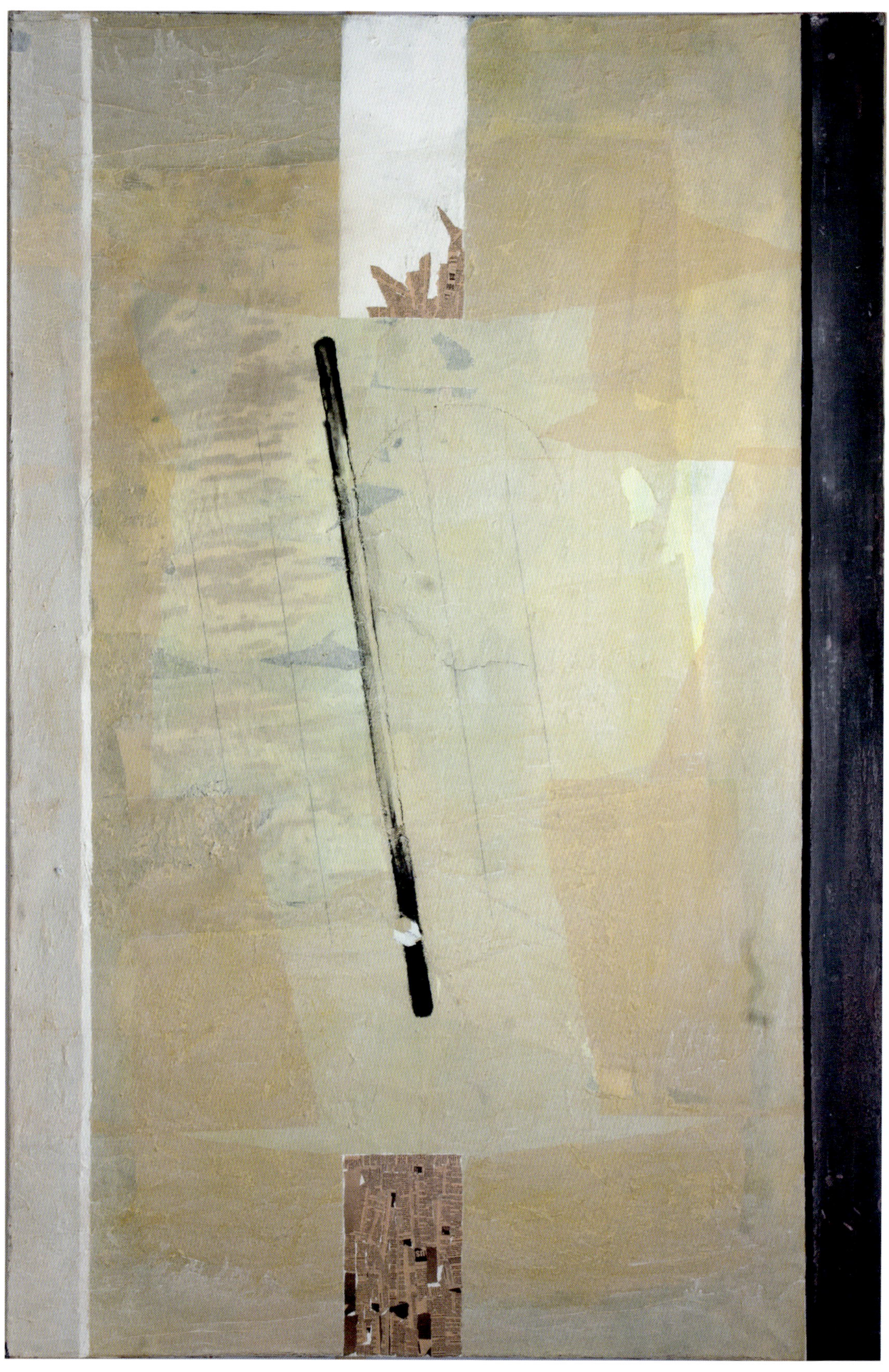

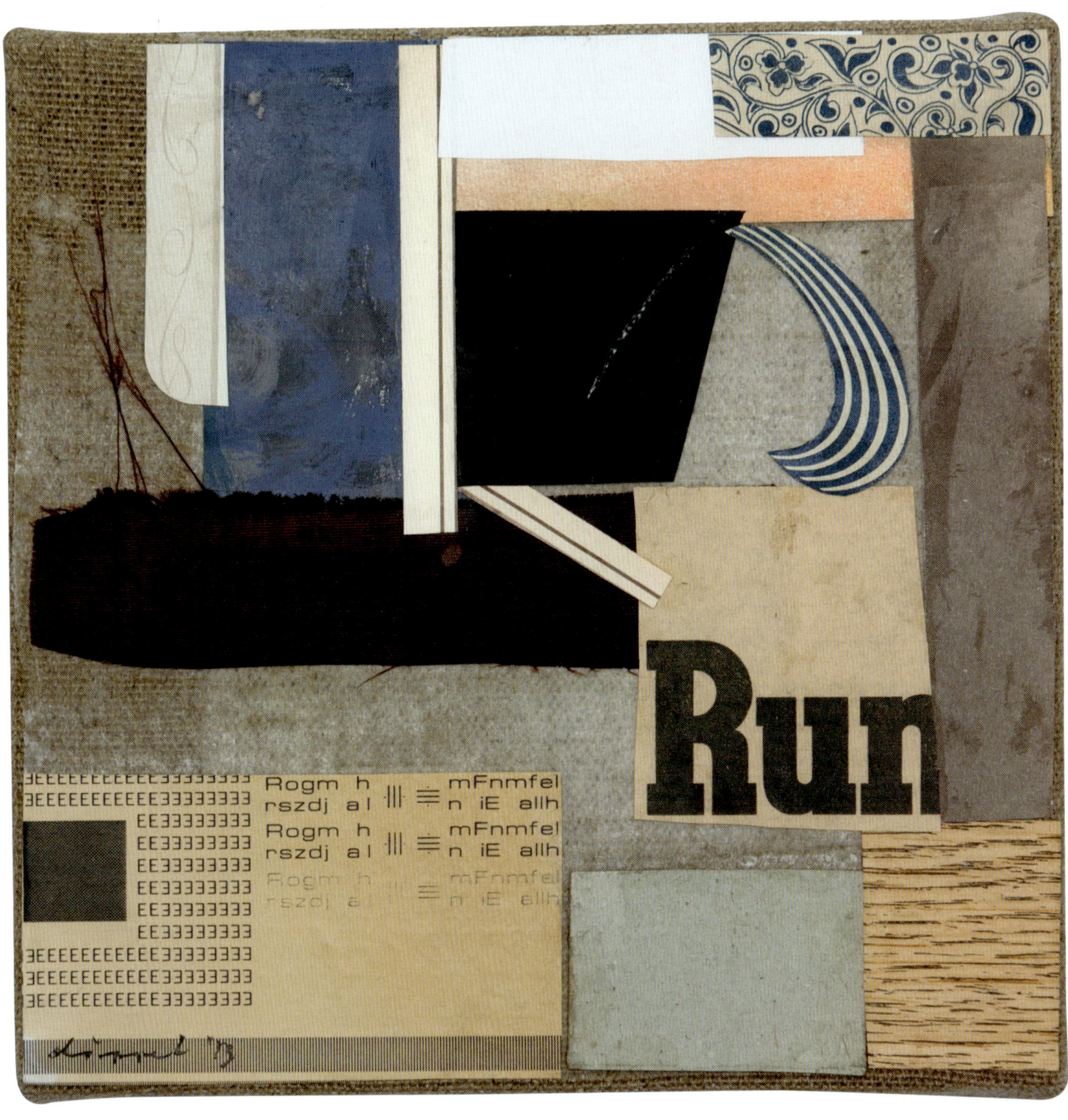
Rogm h mFnmfel
rszdj al n iE allh
Rogm h mFnmfel
rszdj al n iE allh
Rogm h mFnmfel
rszdj al n iE allh
Run

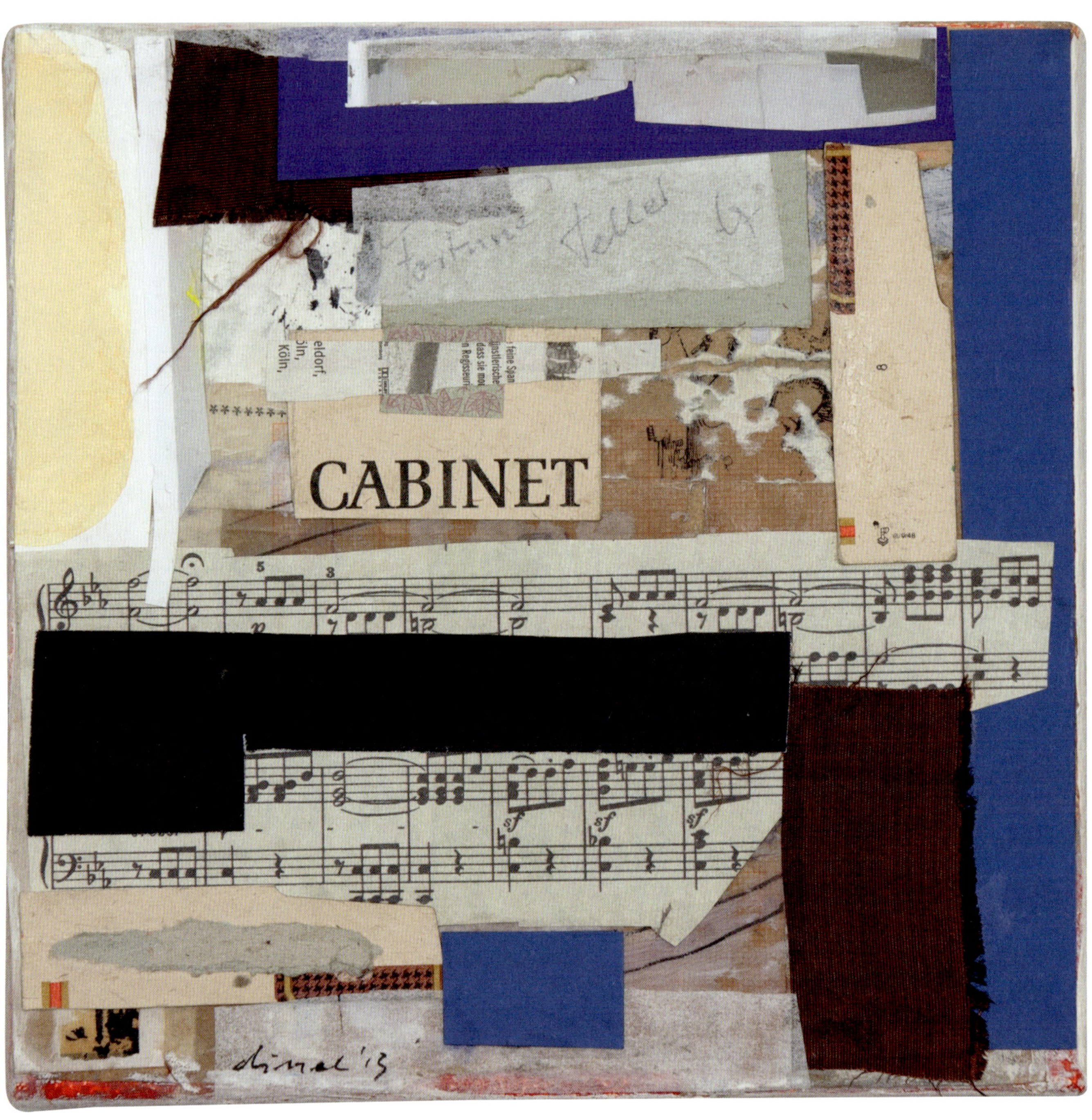
CABINET

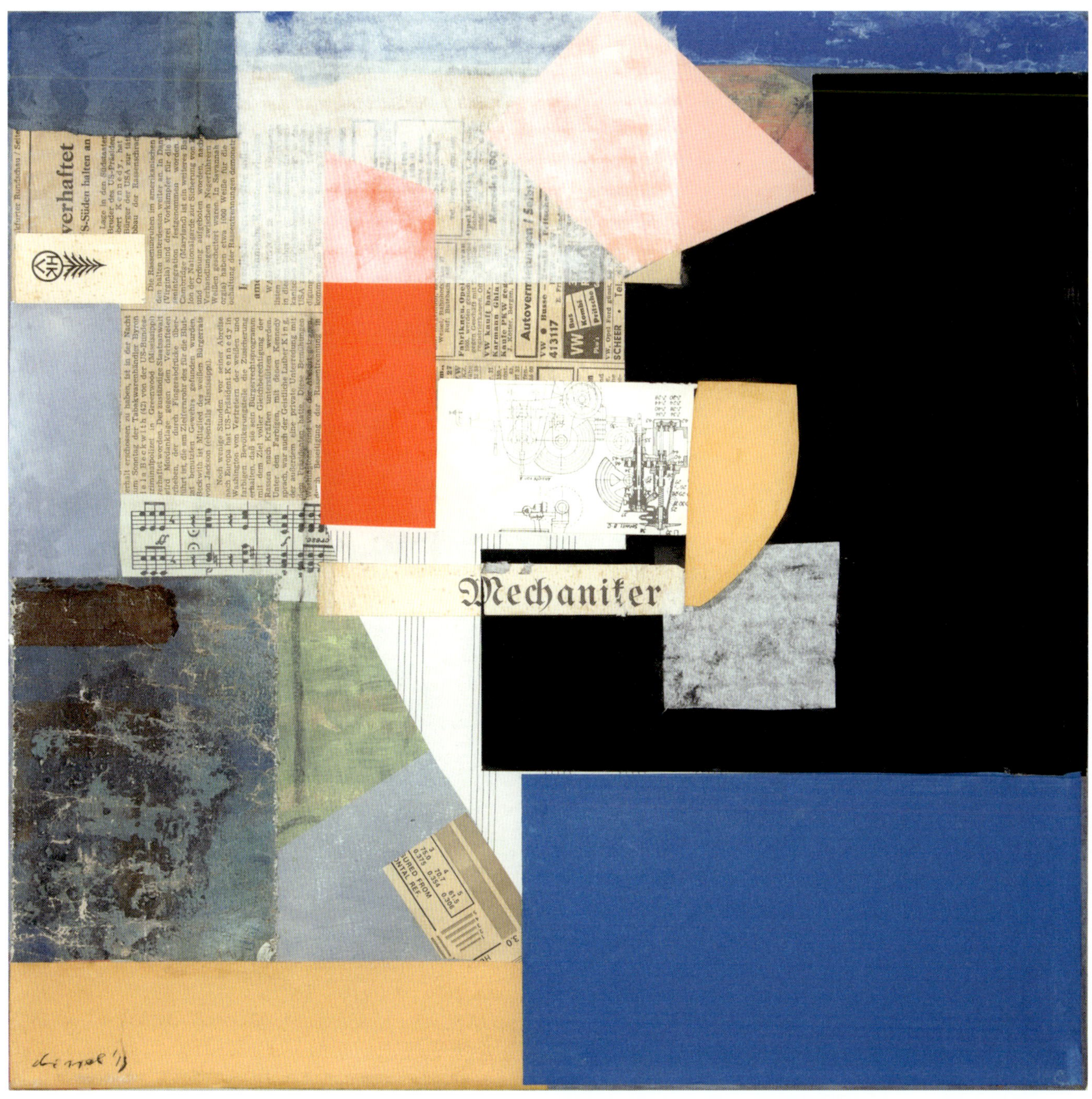
verhaftet
Mechaniker

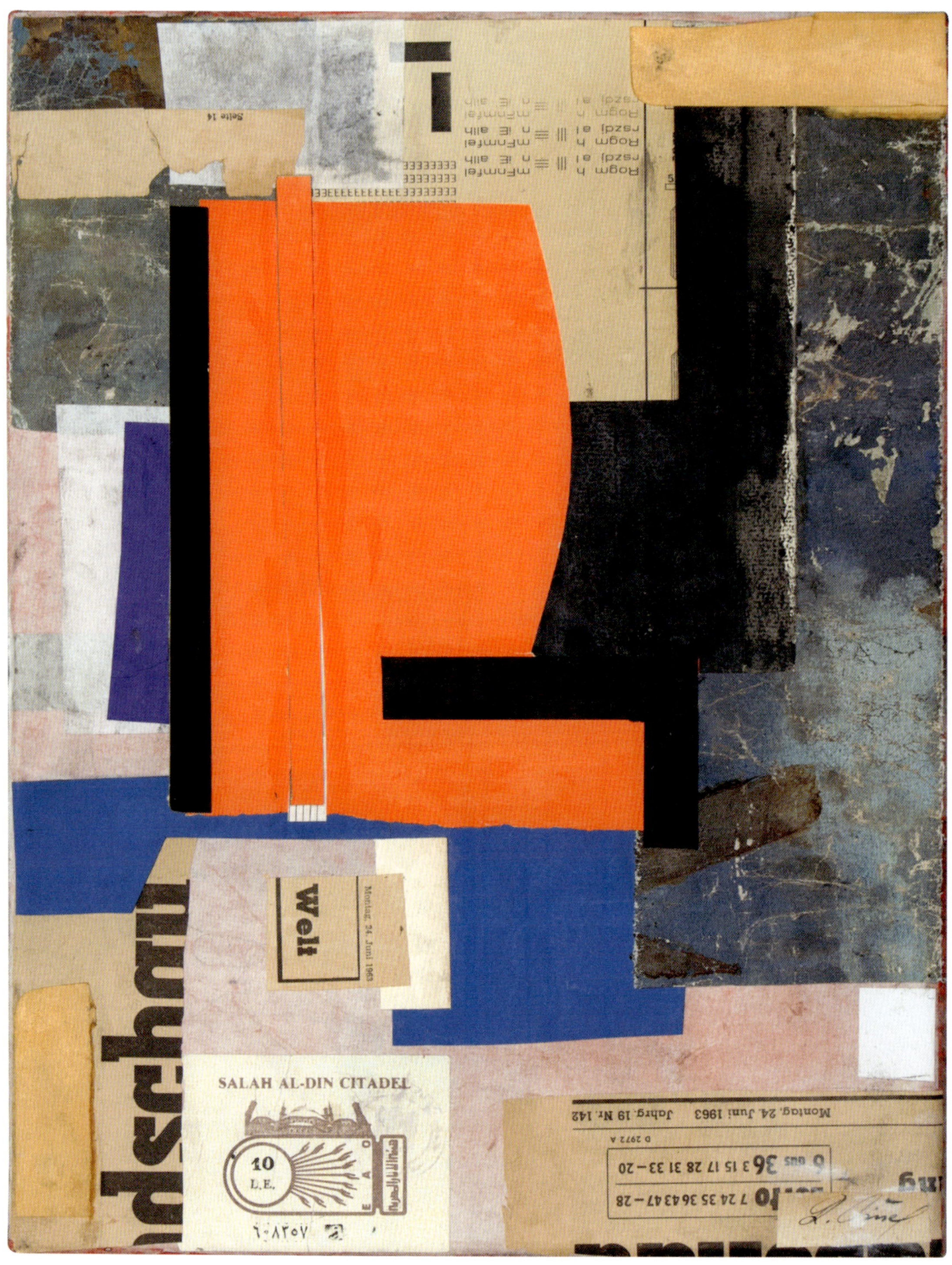
Welt
Montag, 24. Juni 1963
SALAH AL-DIN CITADEL
10
L.E.
Montag, 24. Juni 1963 Jahrg. 19 Nr. 142

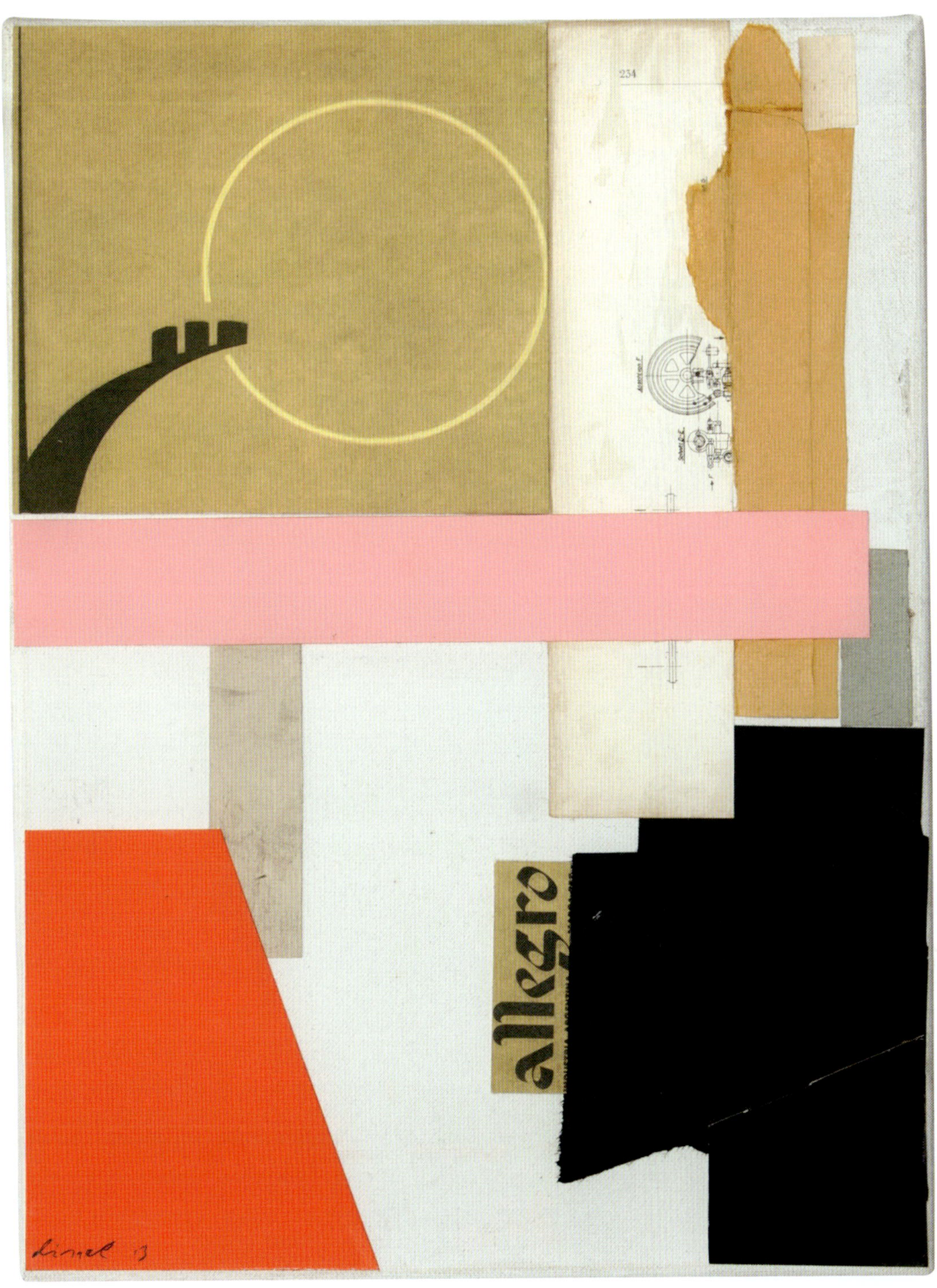
allegro

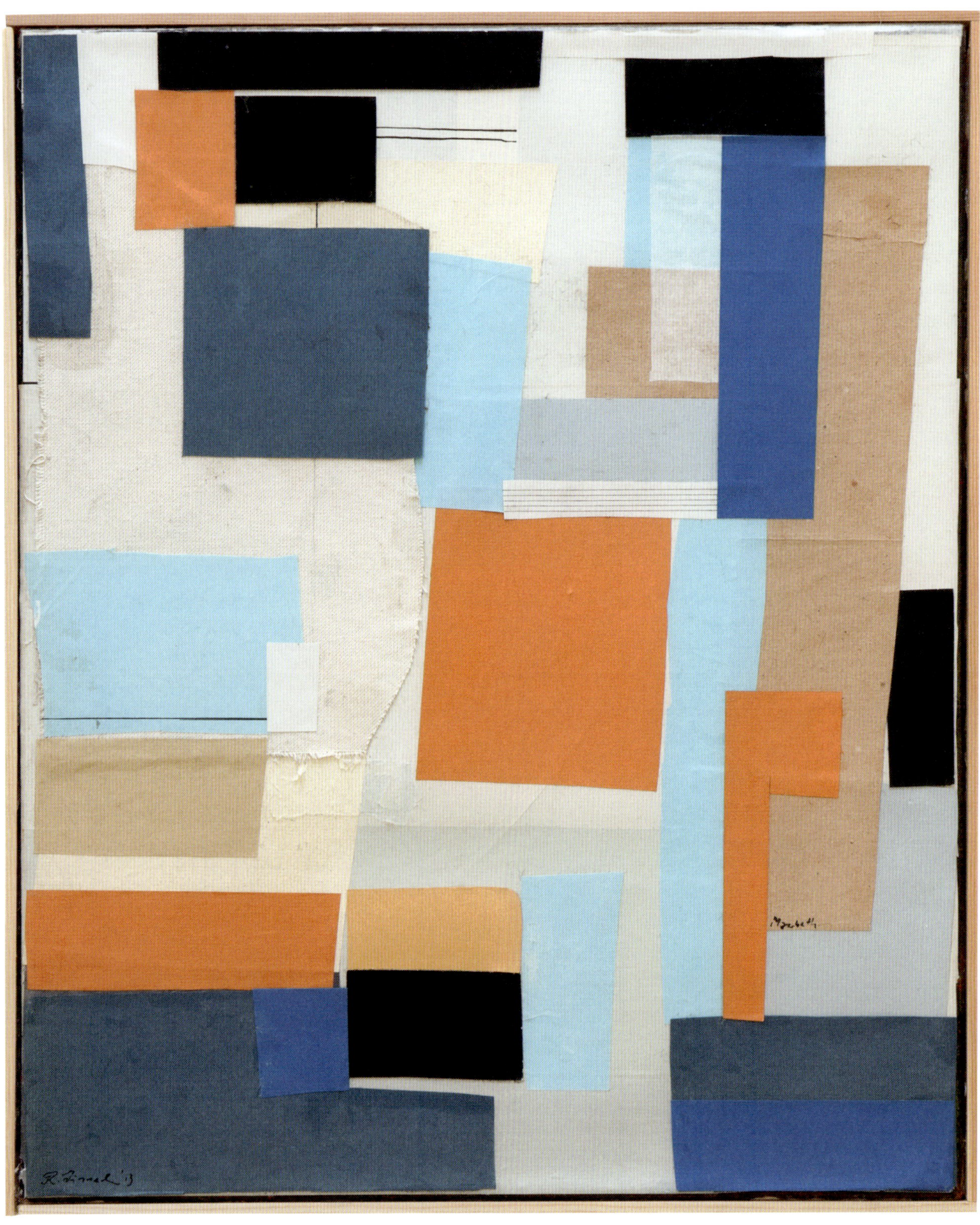

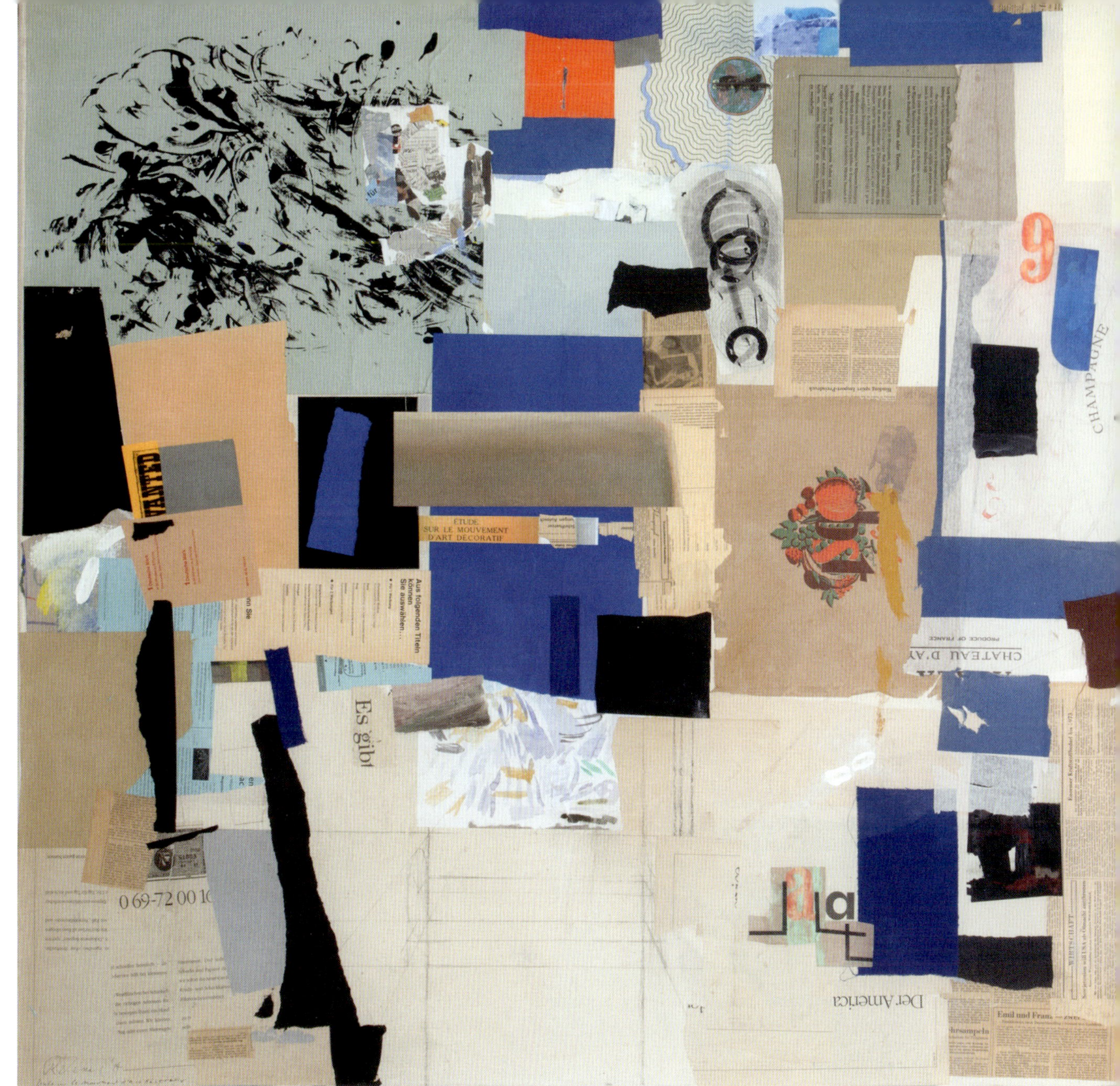
ÉTUDE
SUR LE MOUVEMENT
D'ART DÉCORATIF
Aus folgenden Titeln können Sie auswählen...
Es gibt
CHAMPAGNE
PRODUCE OF FRANCE
Der America

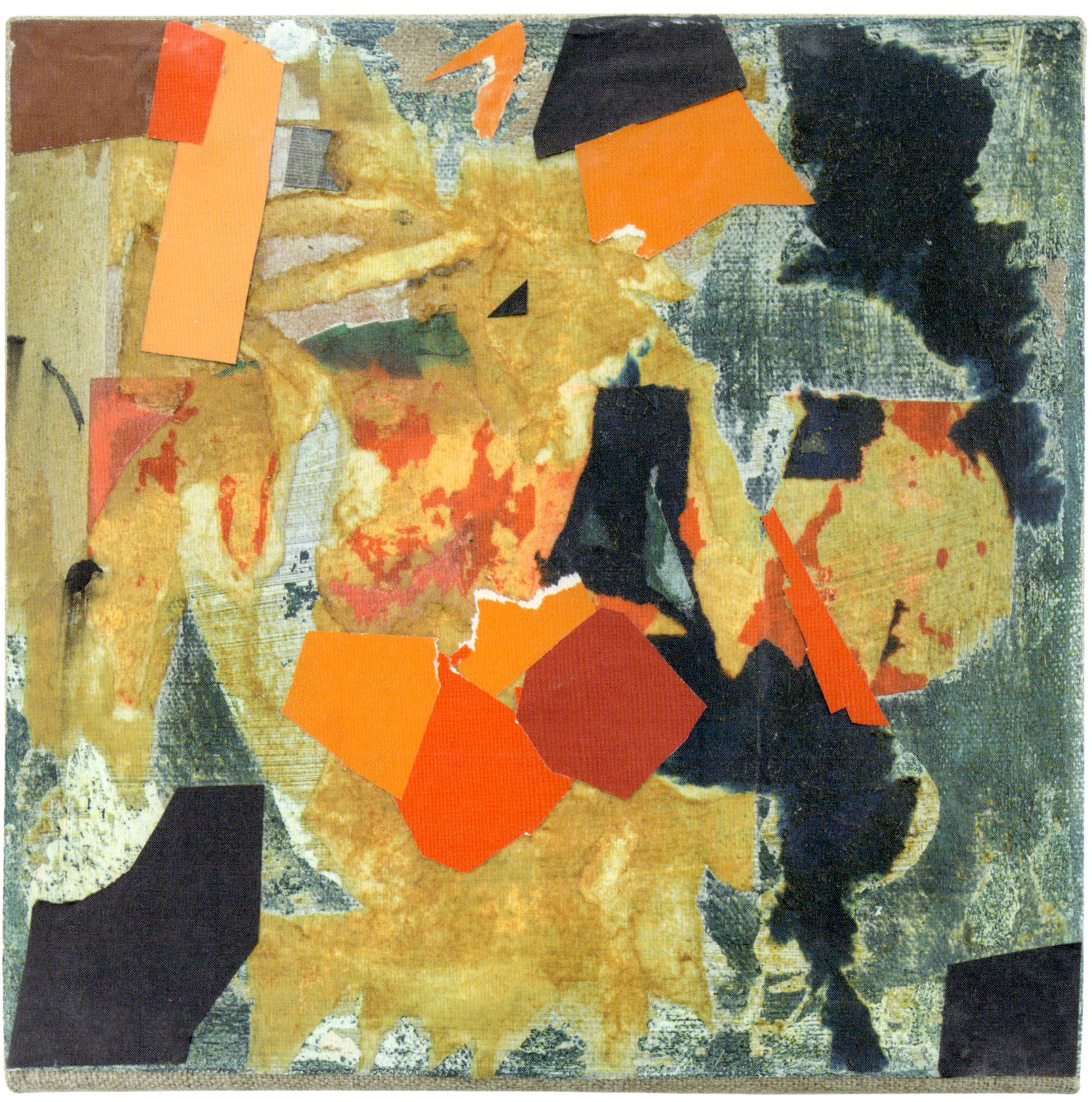

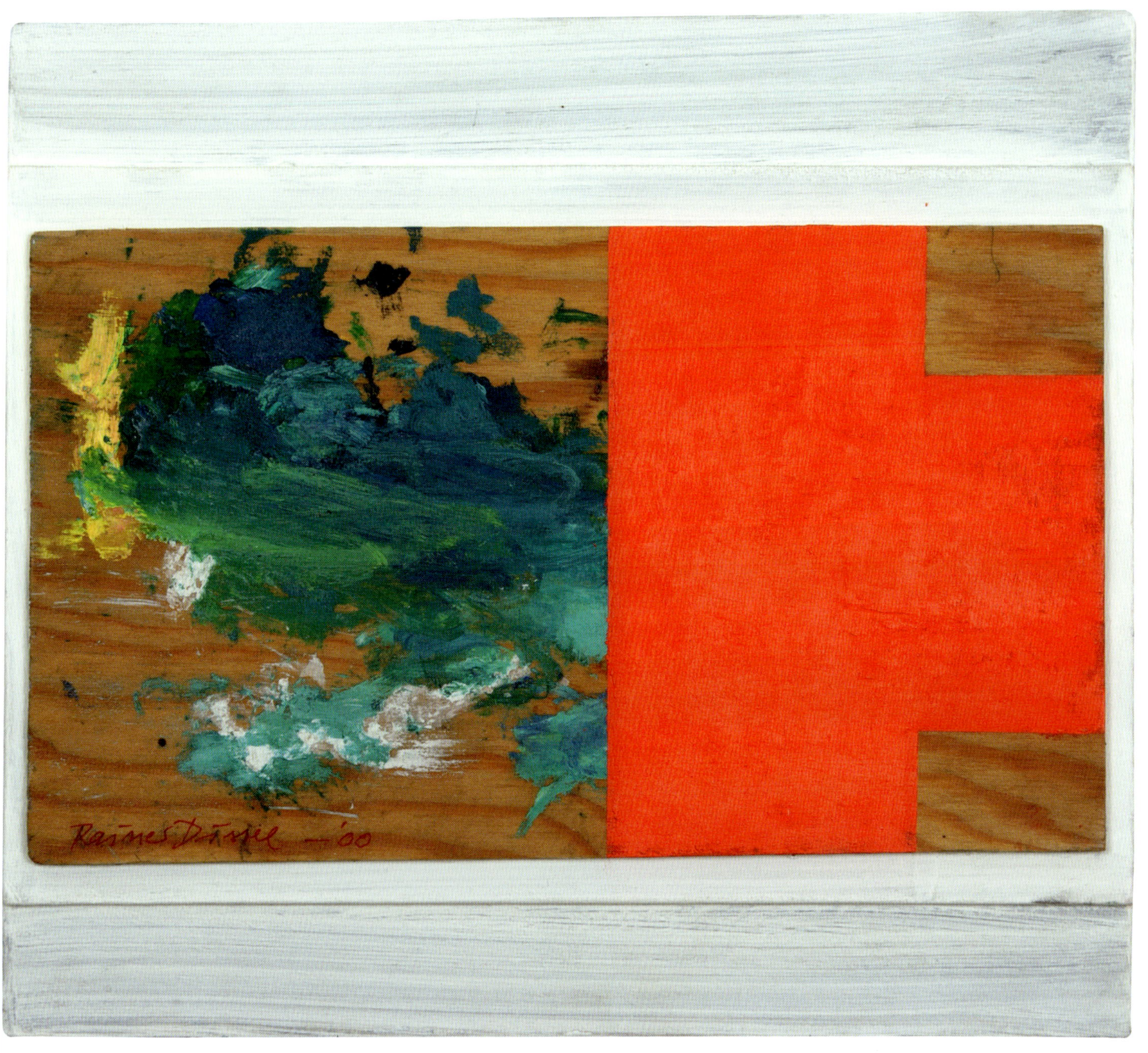

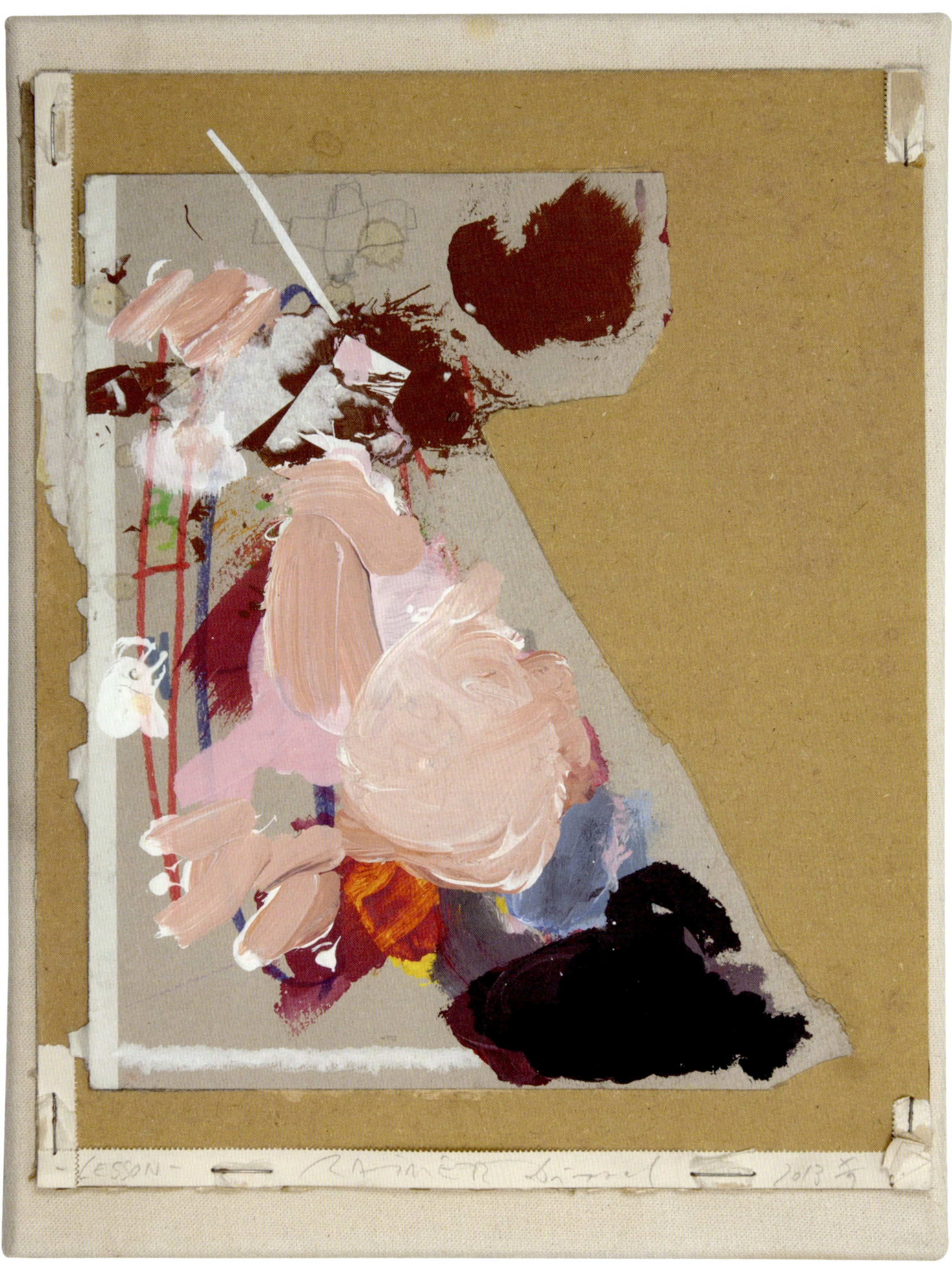
-LESSON-
2013

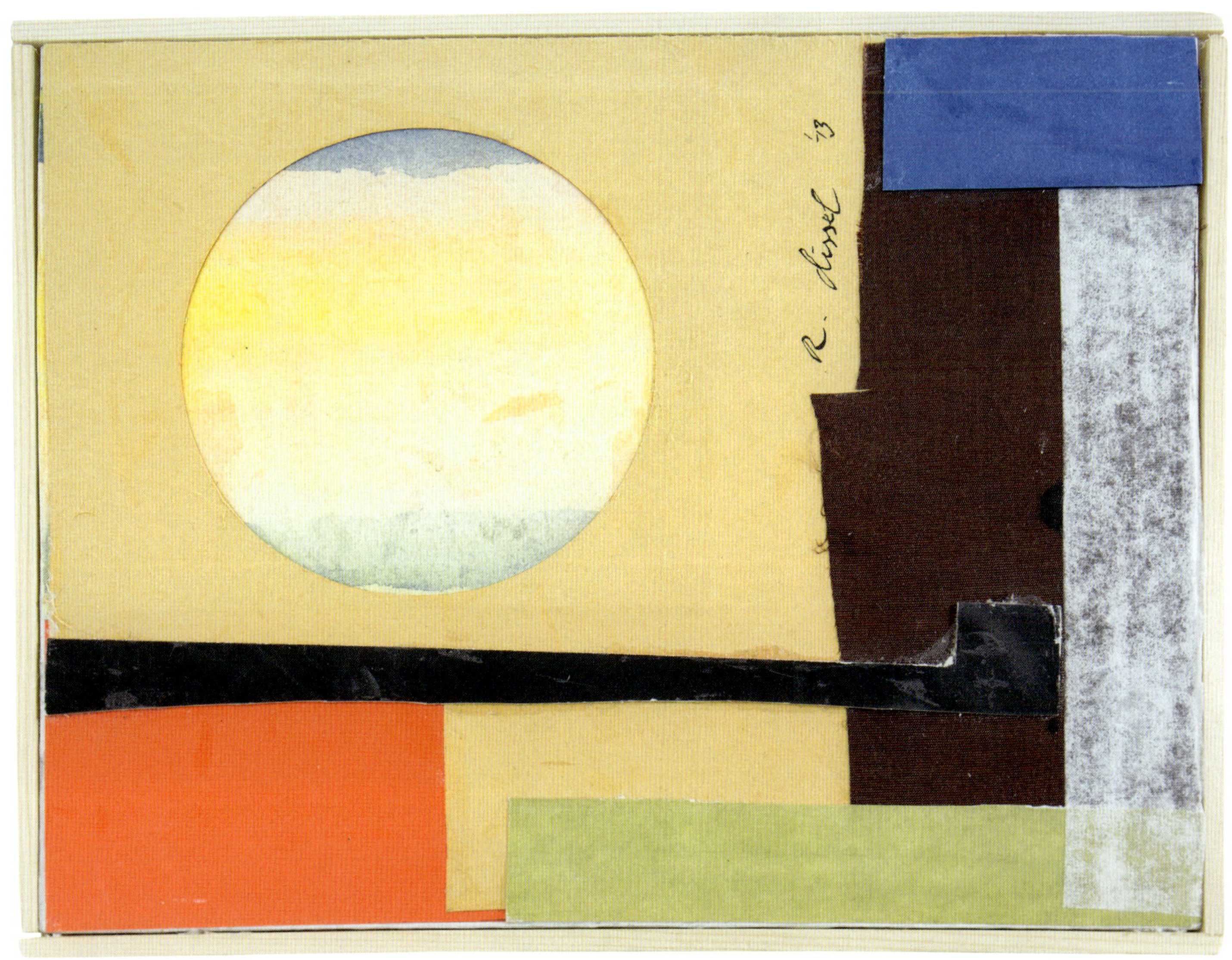

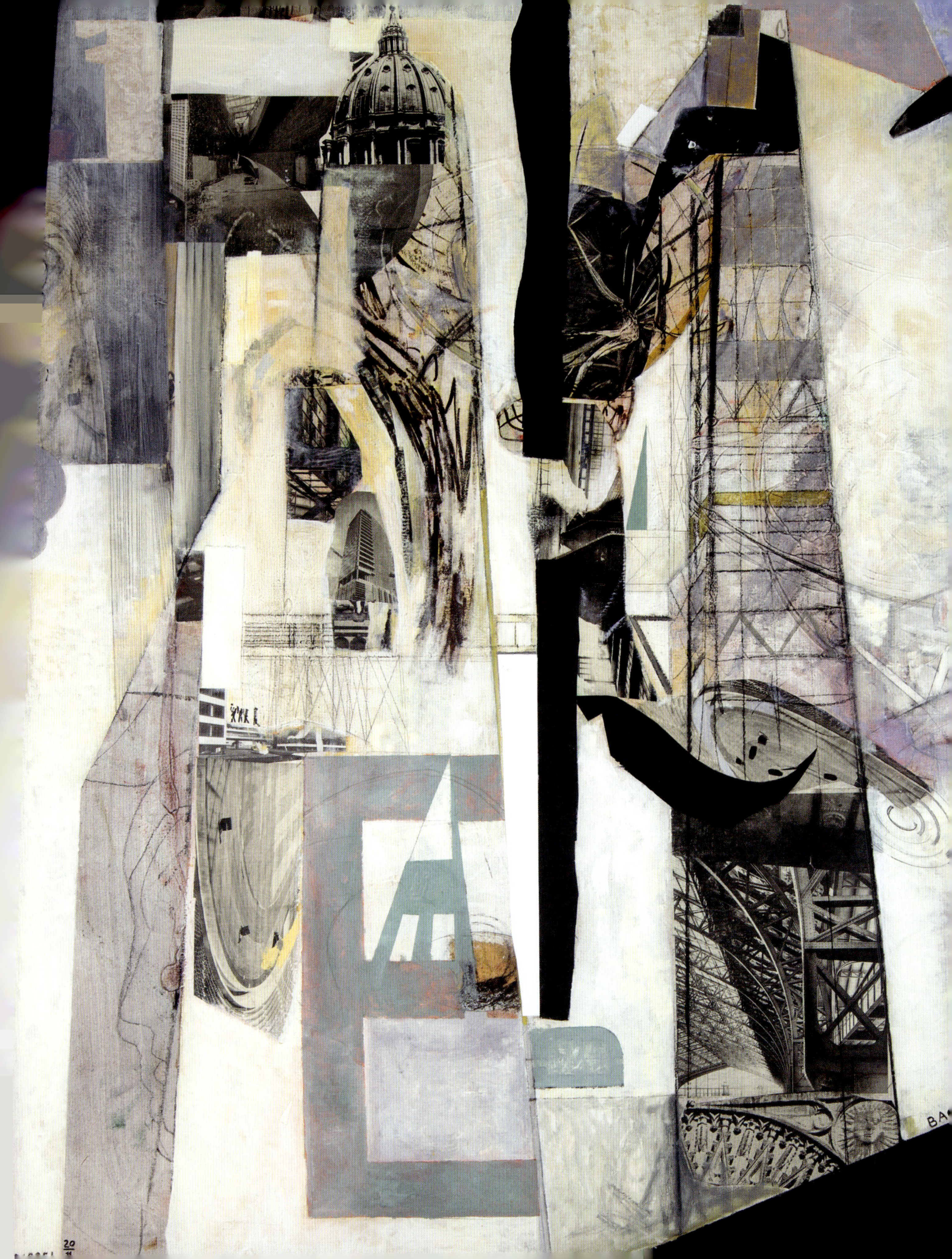

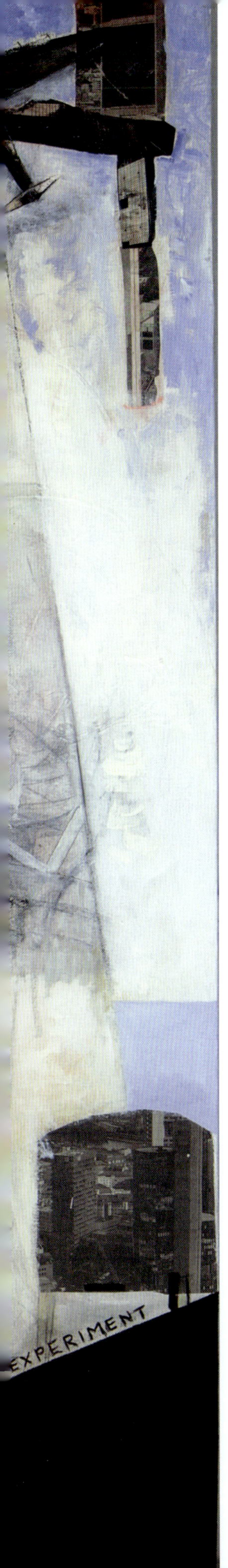
EXPERIMENT

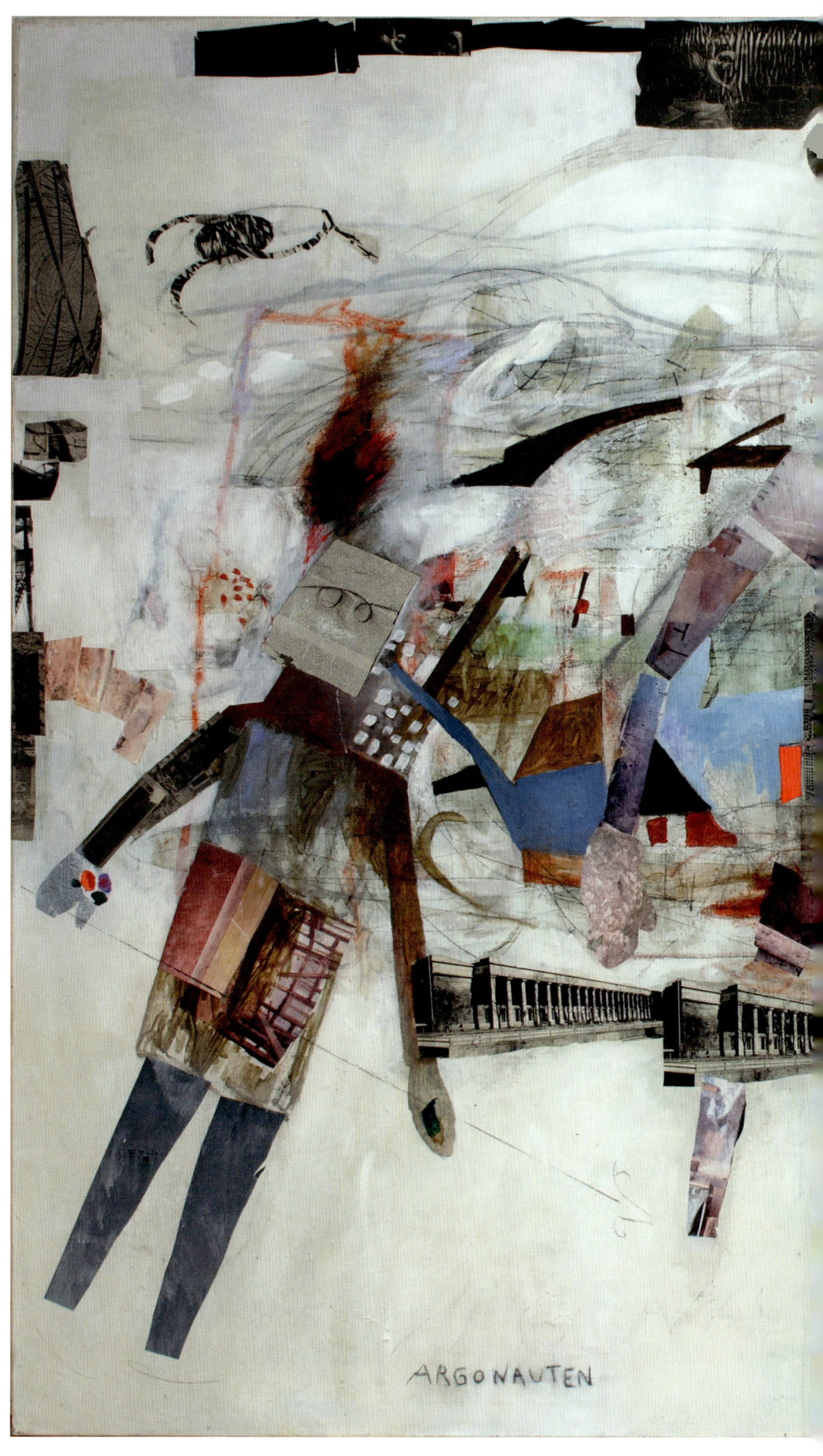
ARGONAUTEN

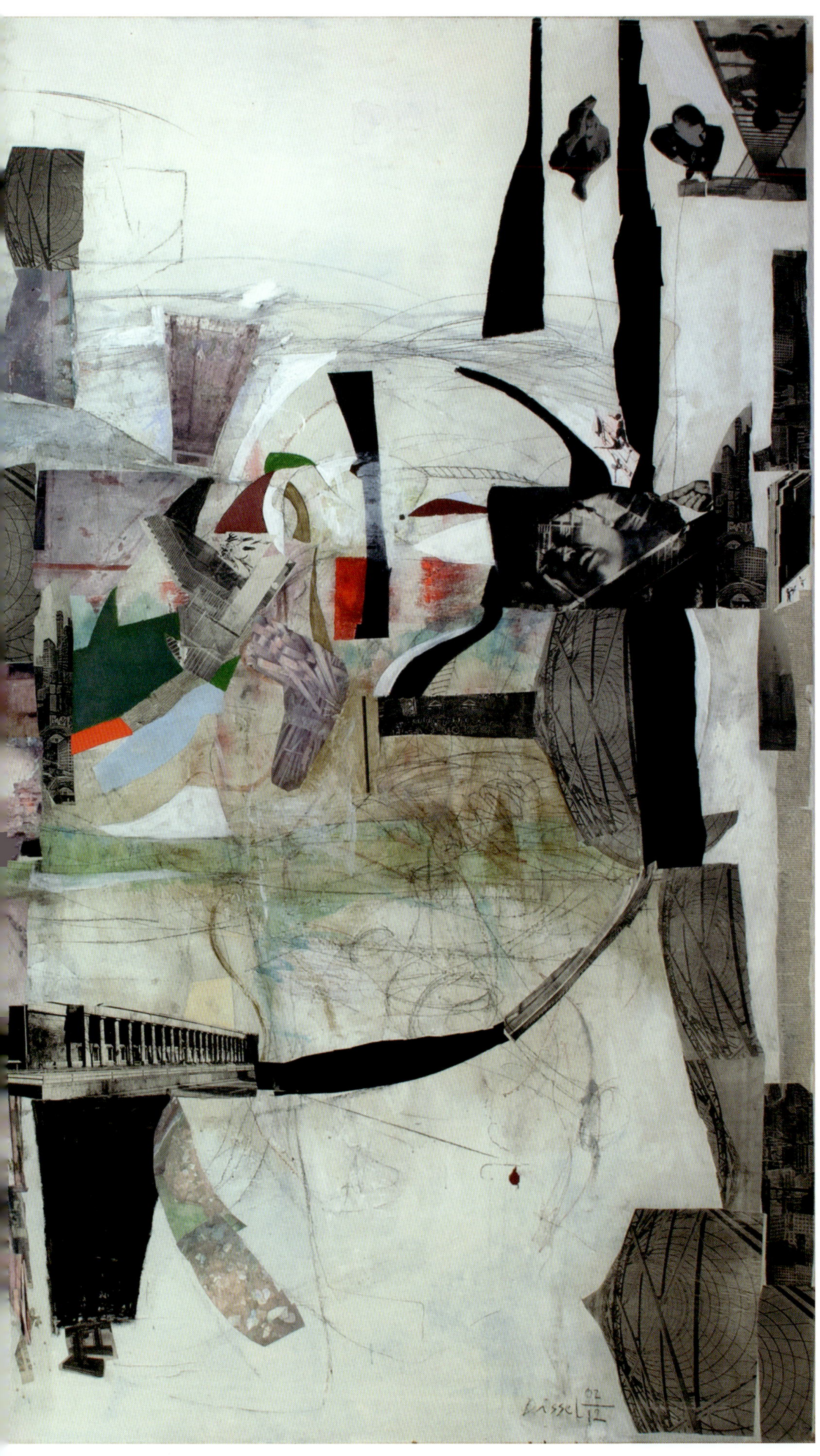

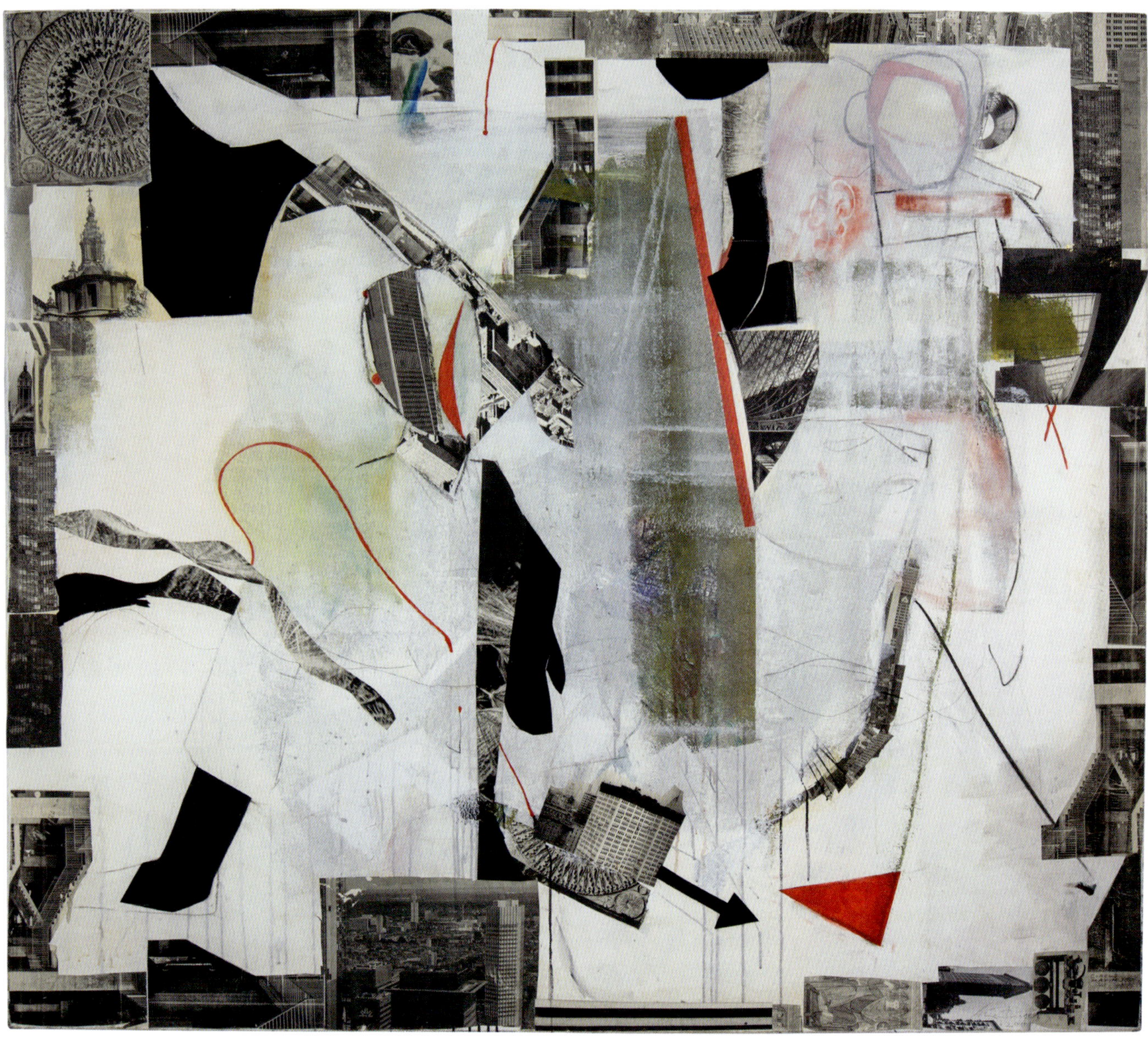

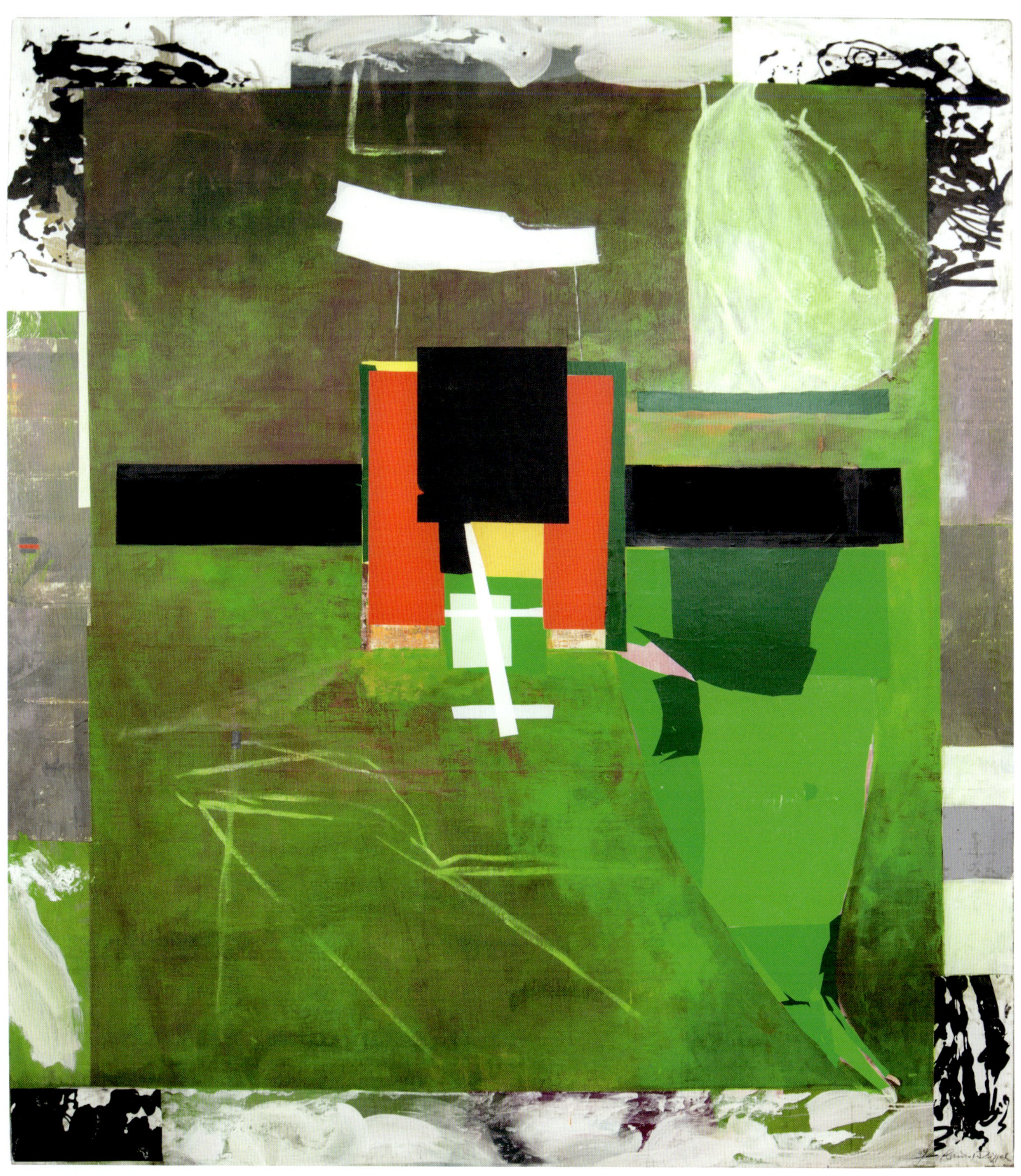

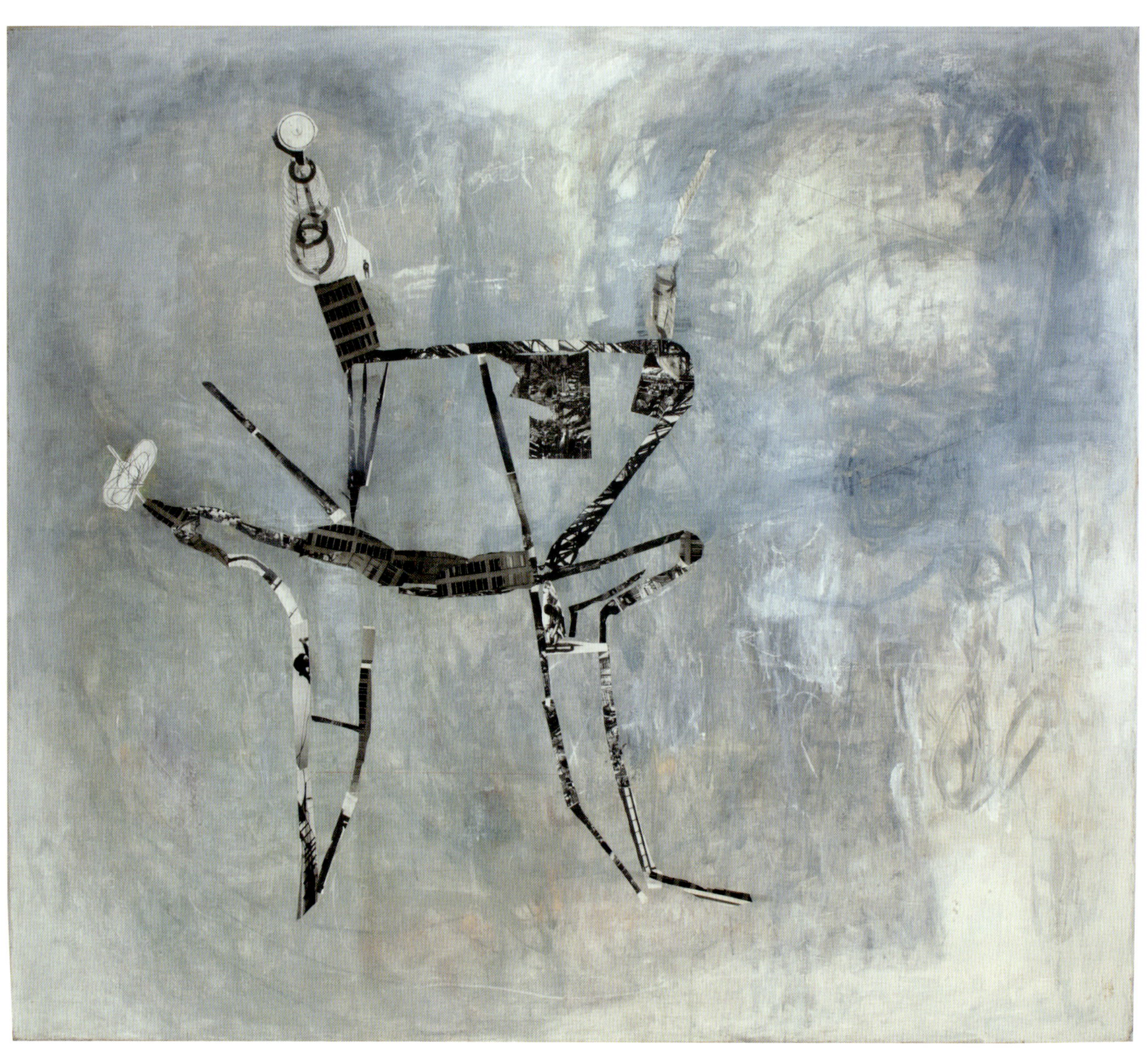

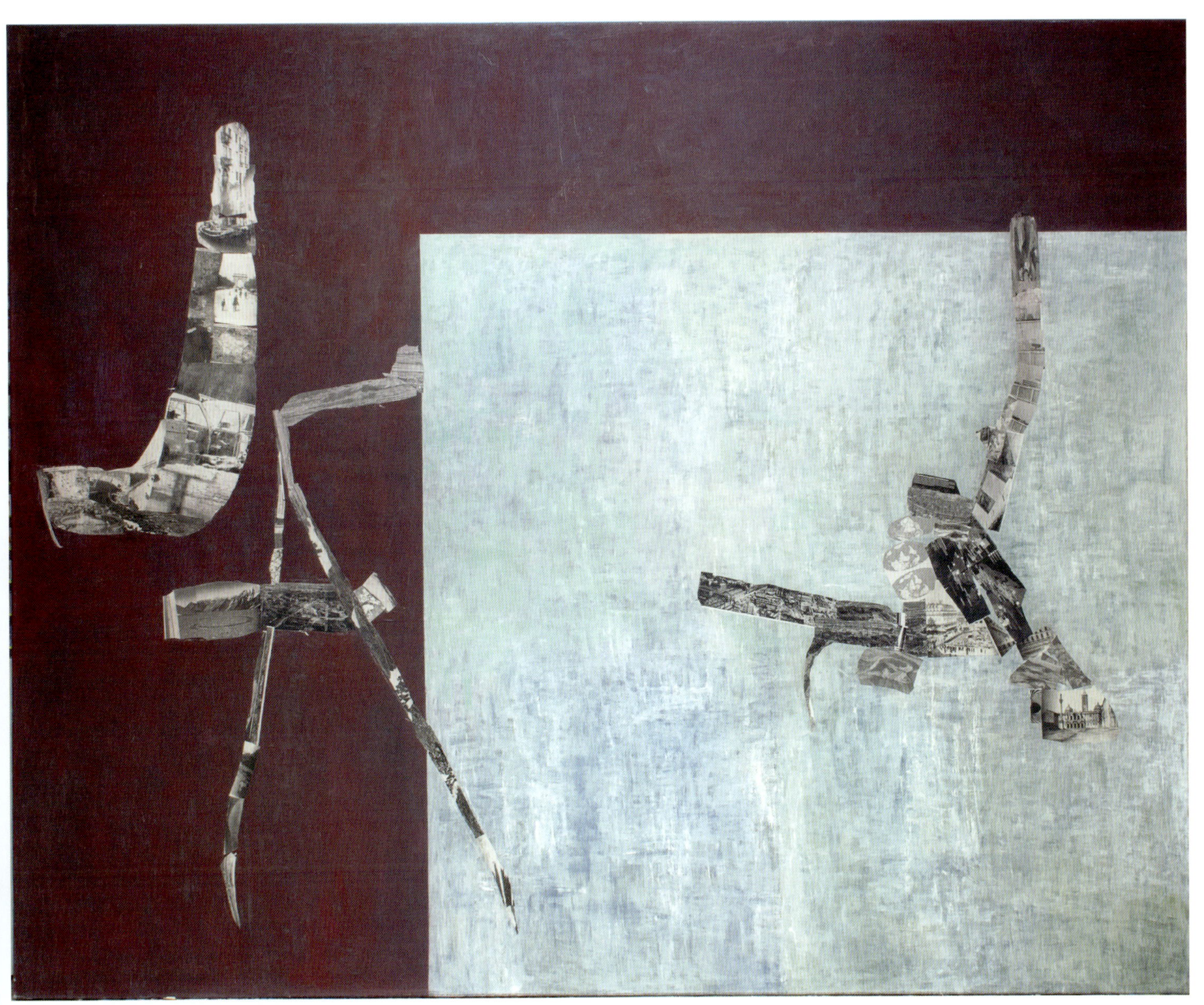

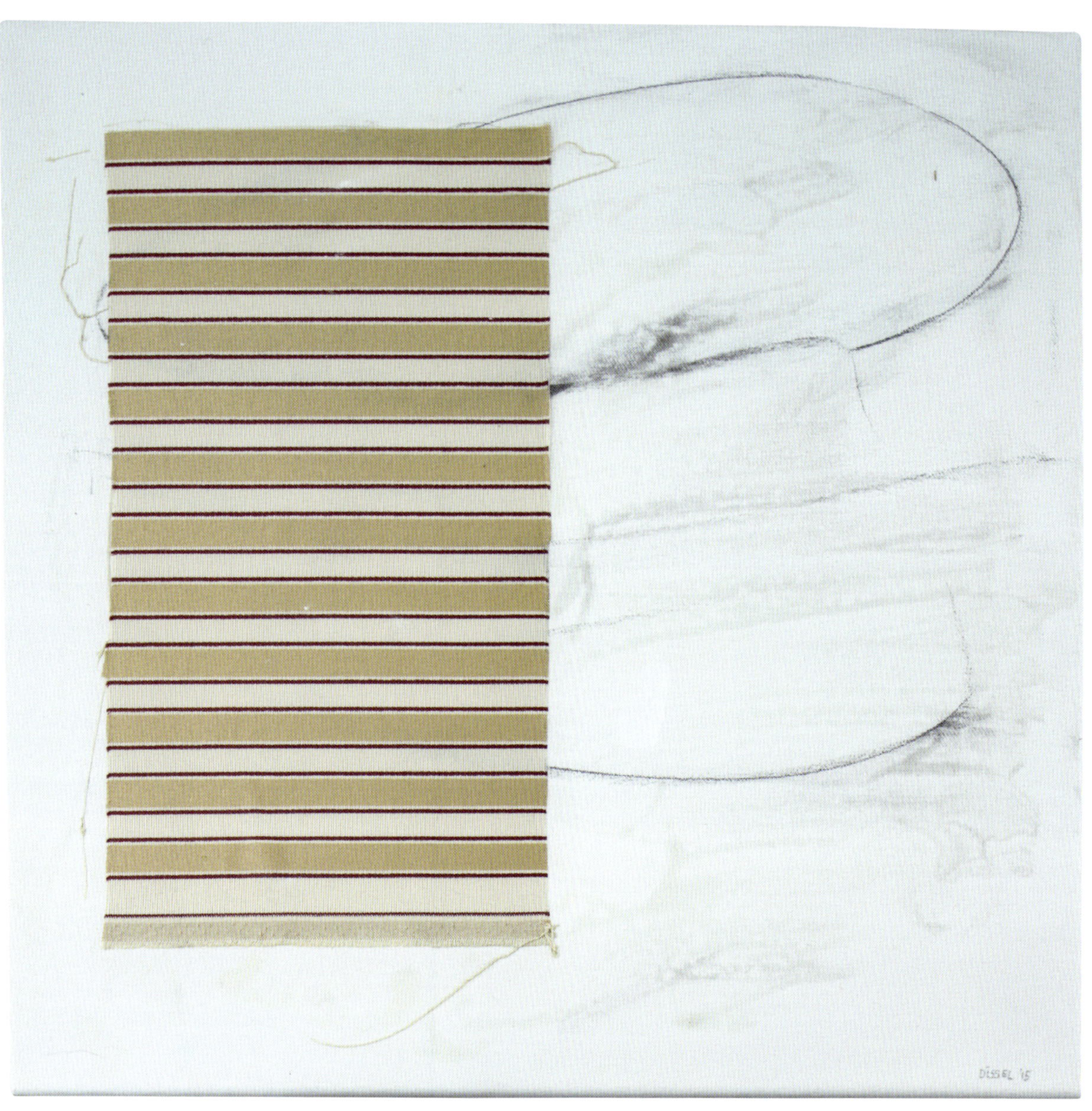

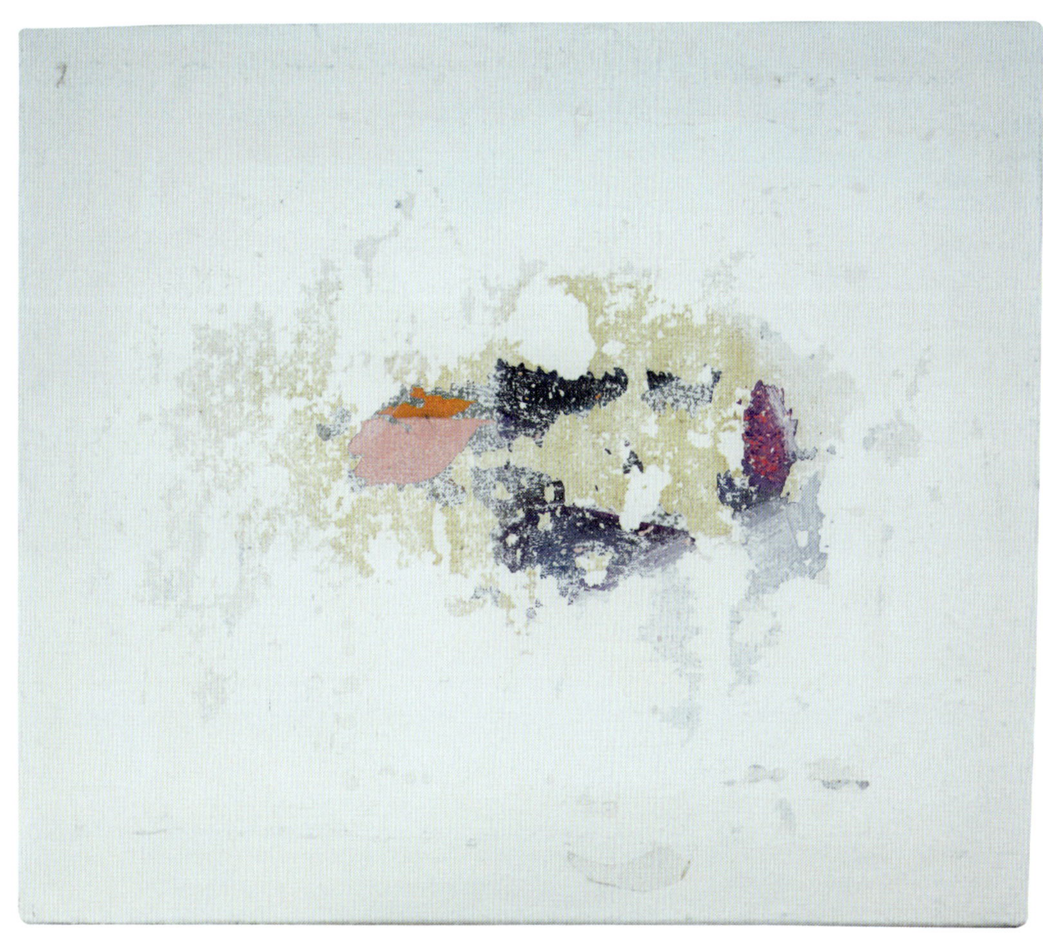

JUGENDSTIL

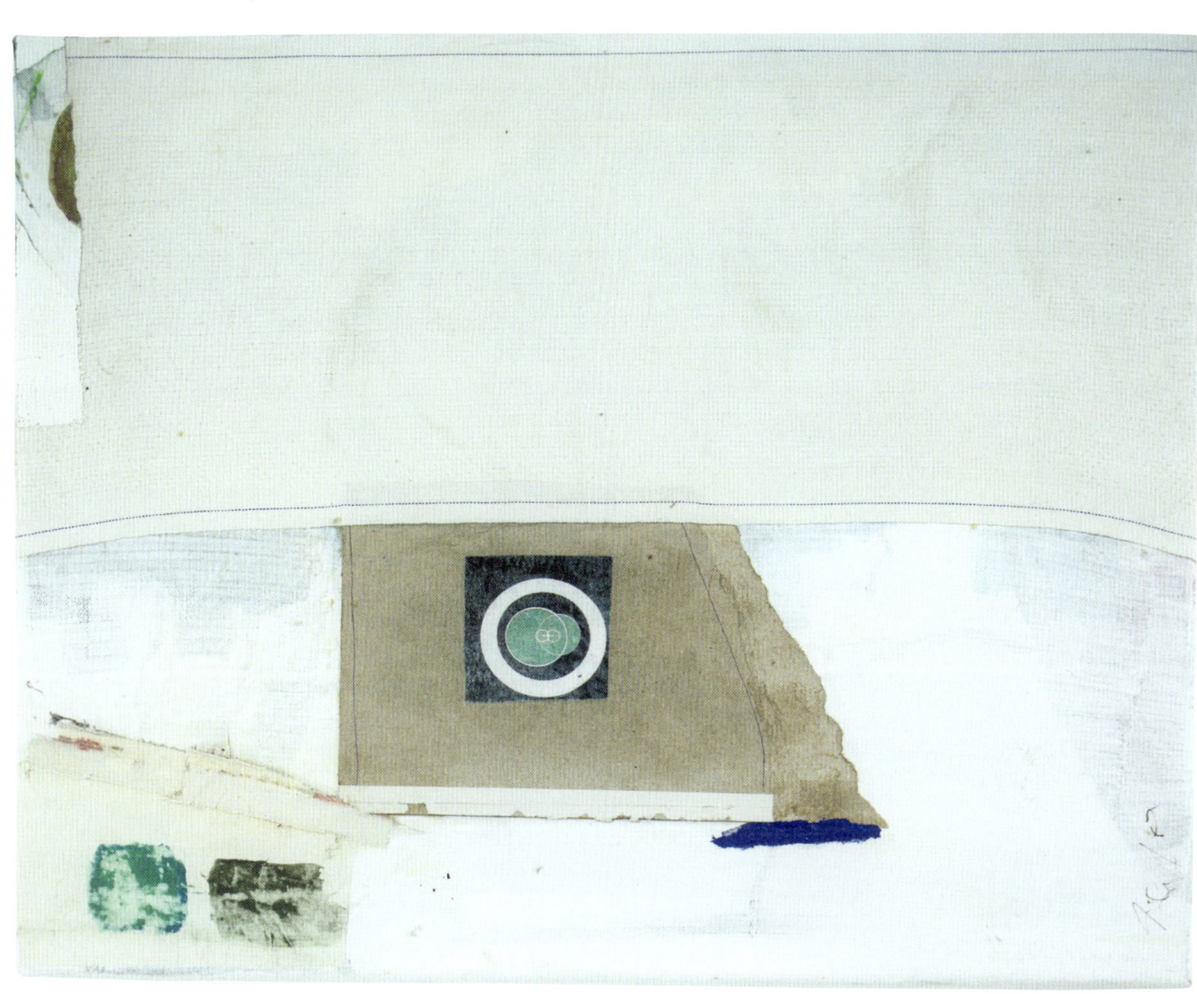

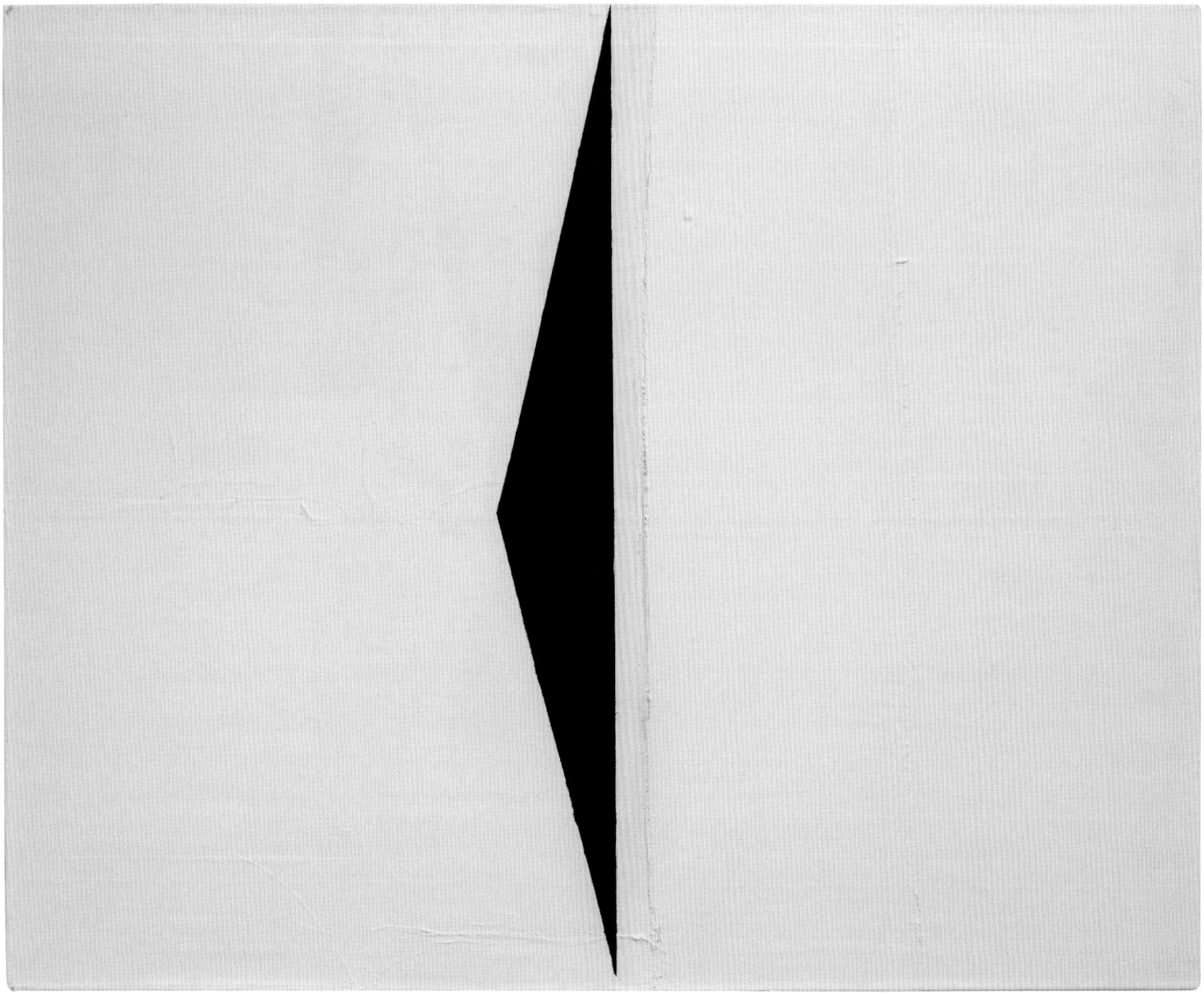

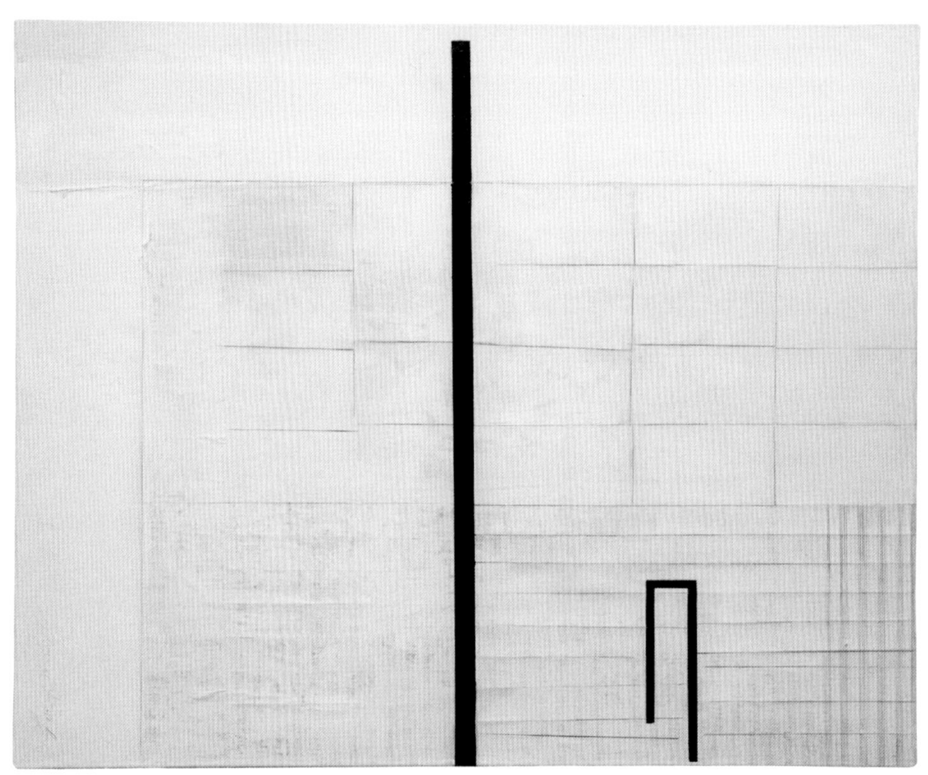

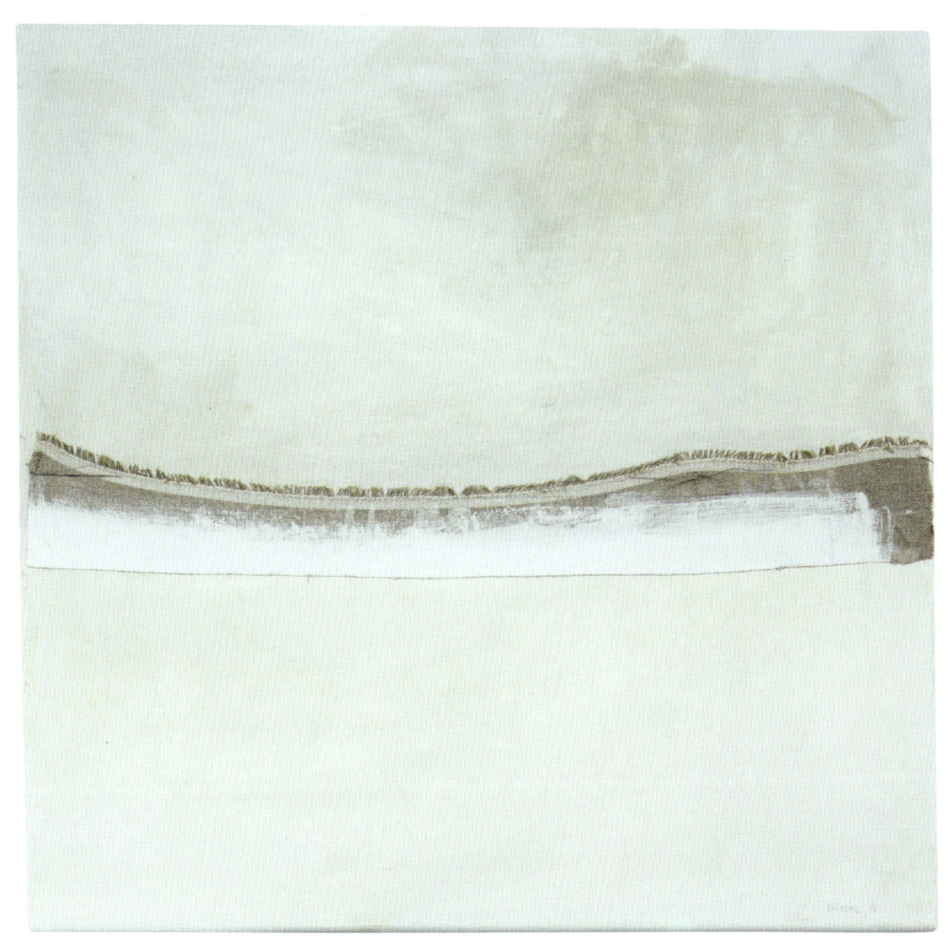

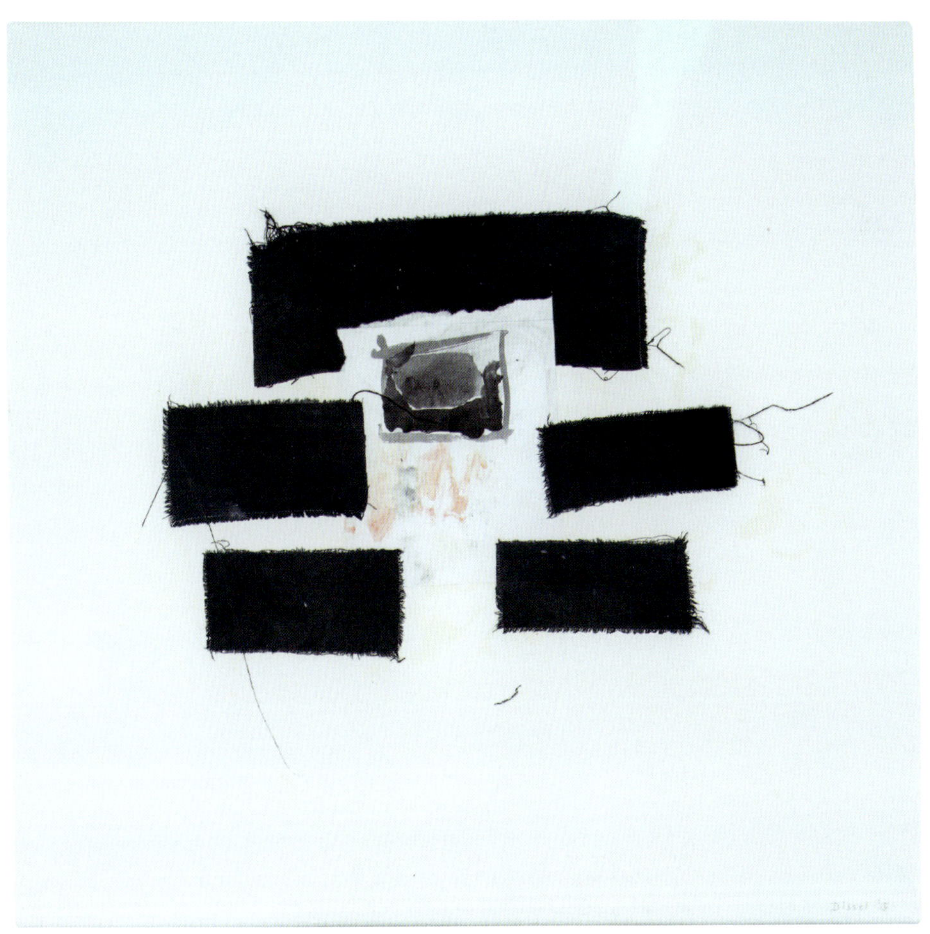

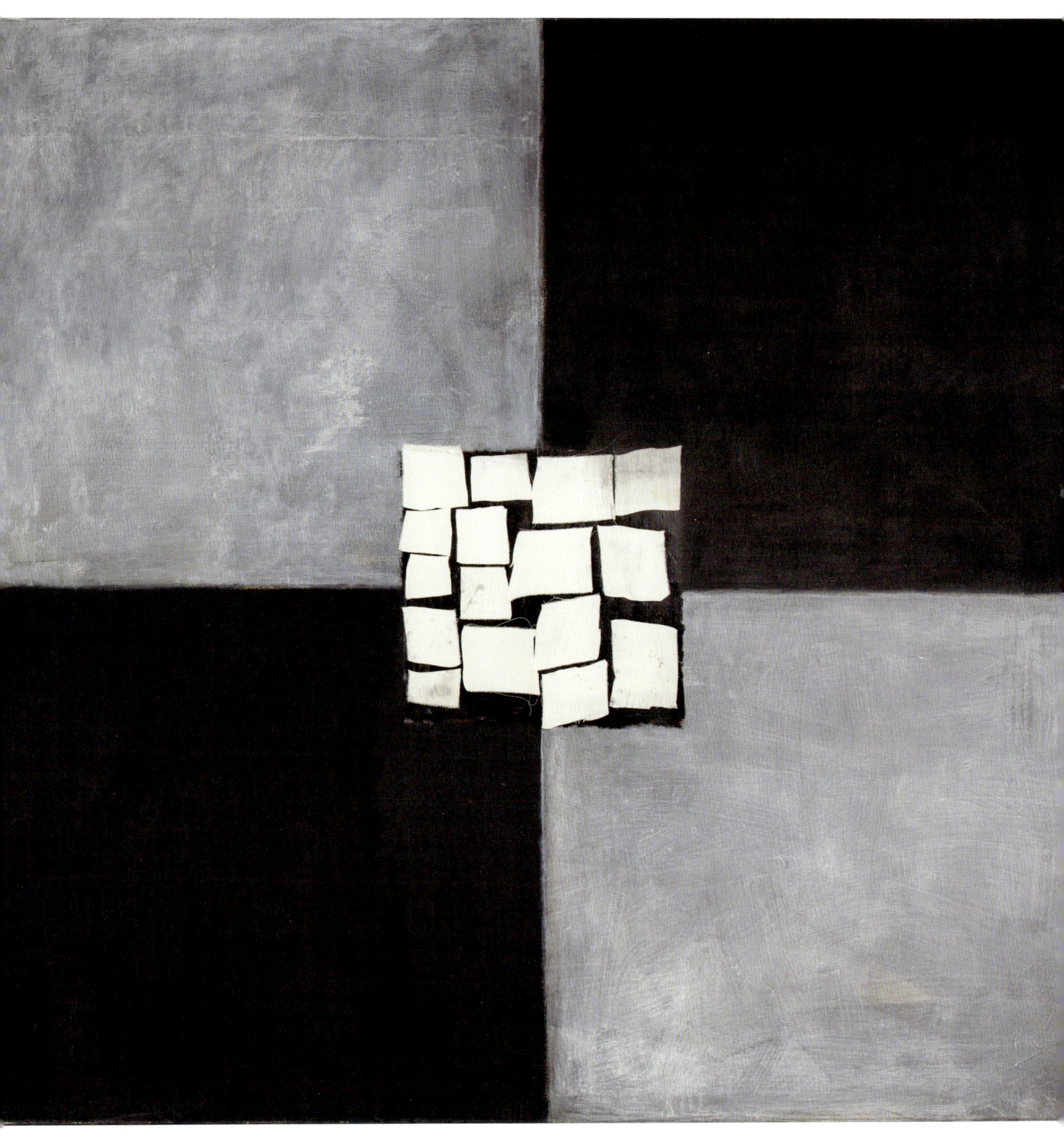

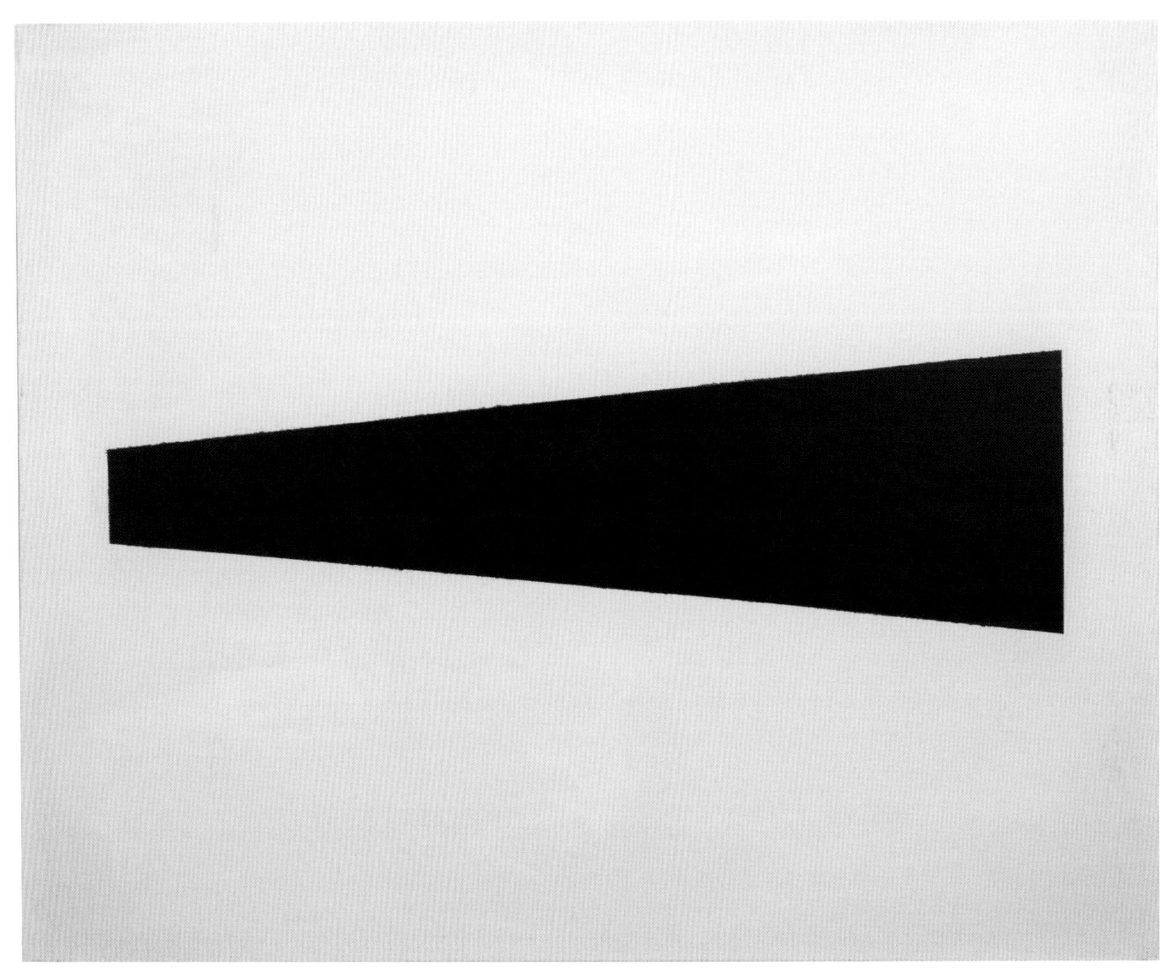

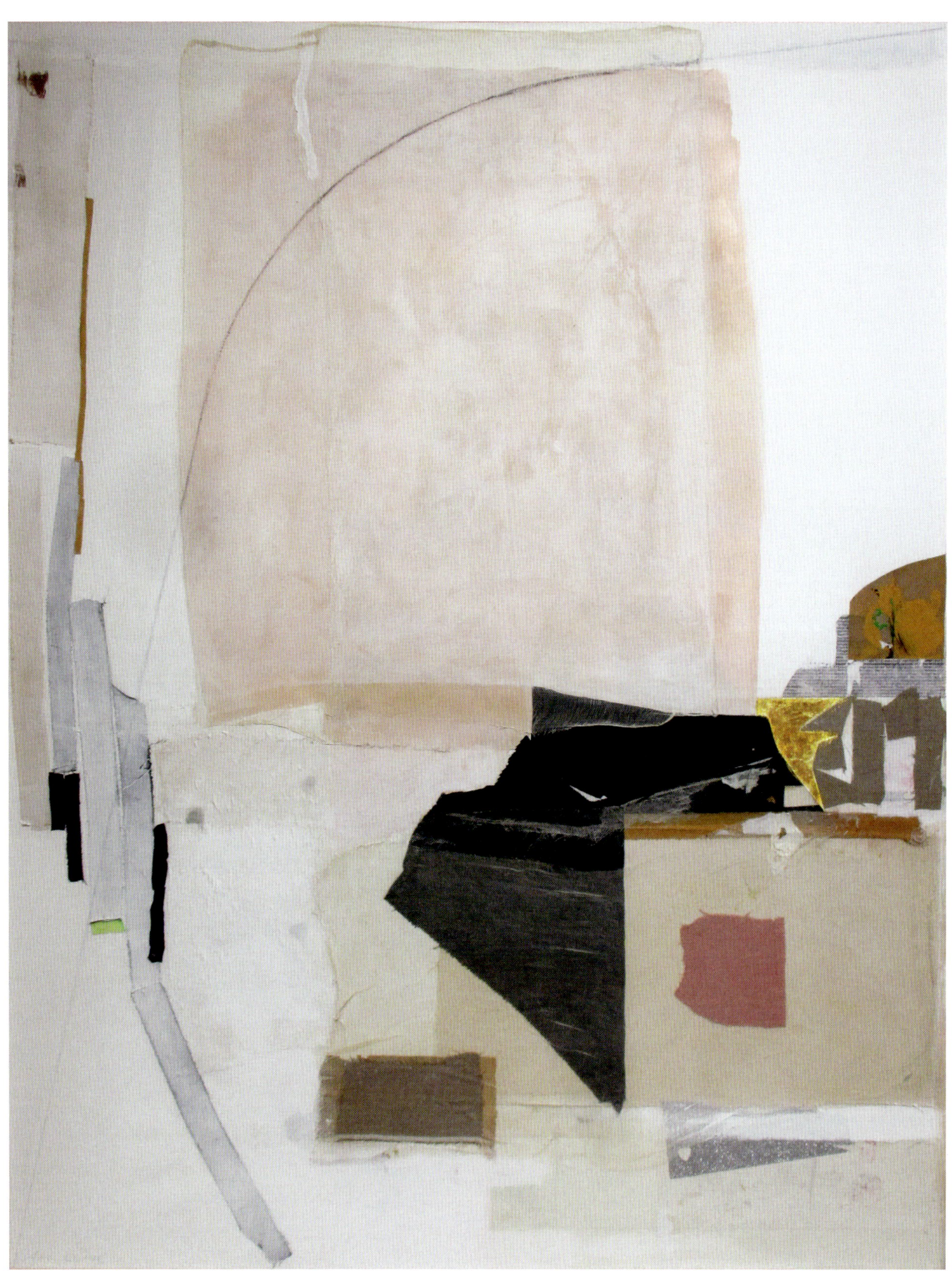

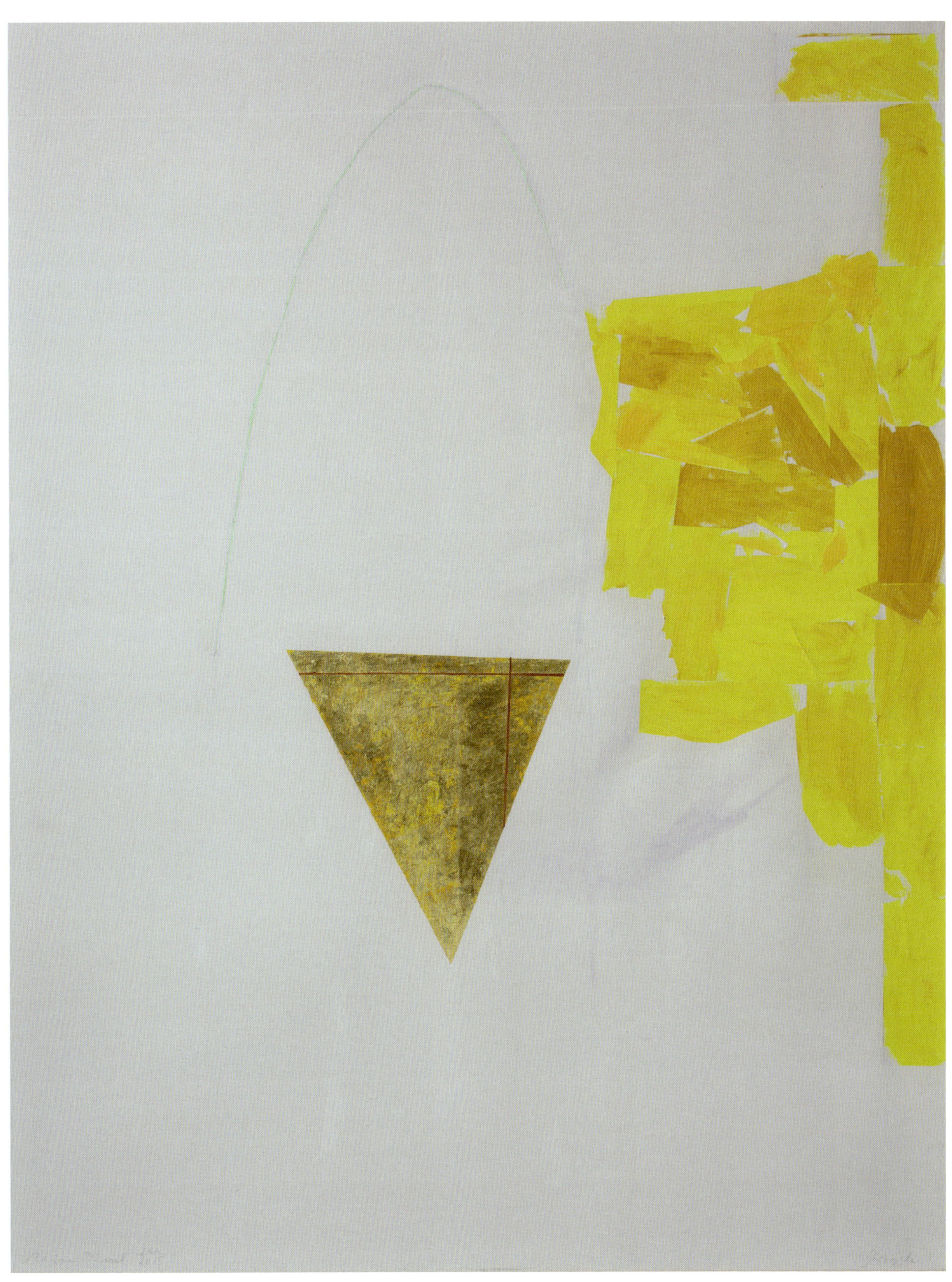

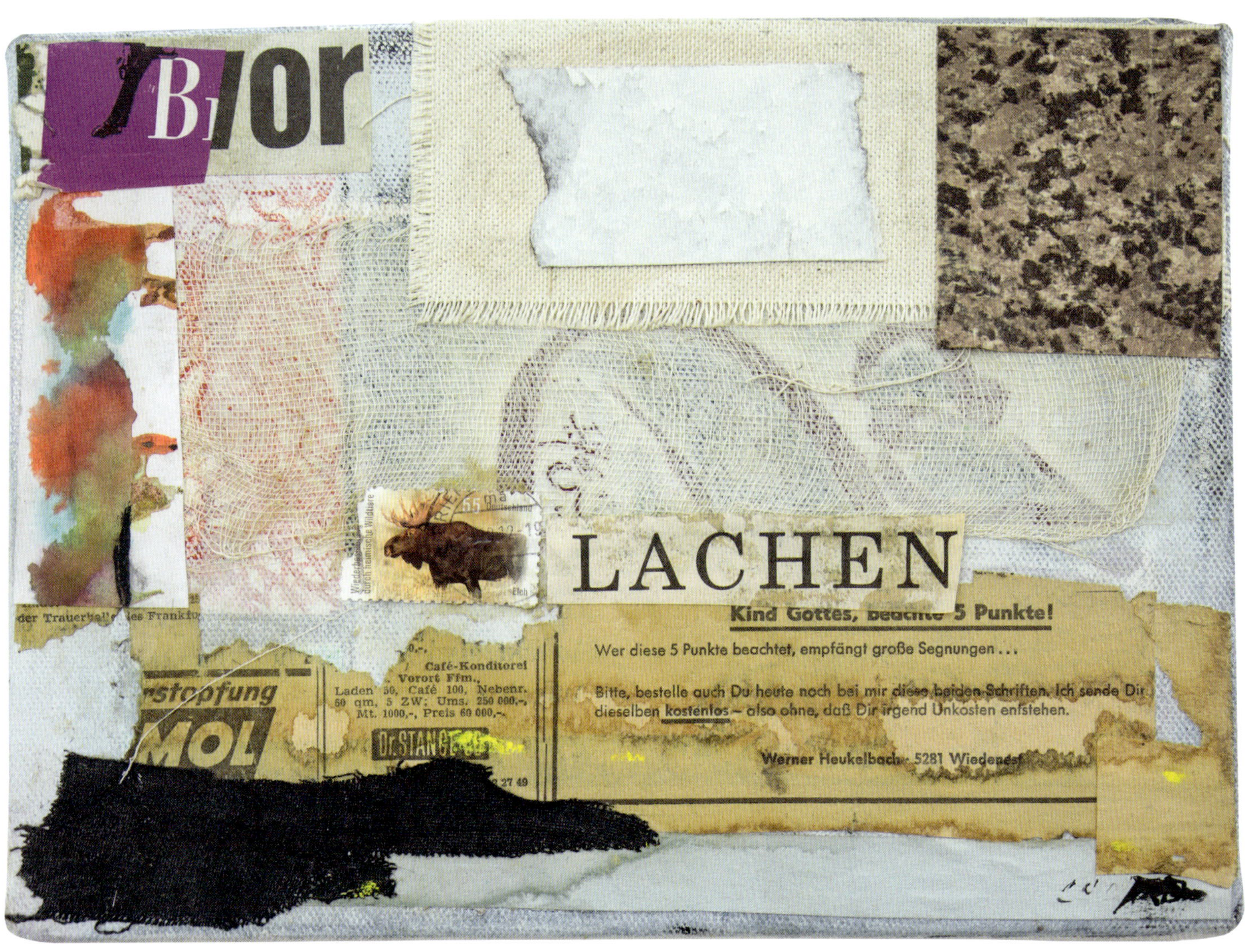
LACHEN
Kind Gottes,
5 Punkte!
Wer diese 5 Punkte beachtet, empfängt große Segnungen ...
Bitte, bestelle auch Du heute noch bei mir diese beiden Schriften. Ich sende Dir
dieselben kostenlos – also ohne, daß Dir irgend Unkosten entstehen.
Werner Heukelbach
Café-Konditorei
Vorort Ffm.,
Laden 50, Café 100, Nebenr.
60 qm, 5 ZW; Ums. 250 000,-,
Mt. 1000,-, Preis 60 000,-.

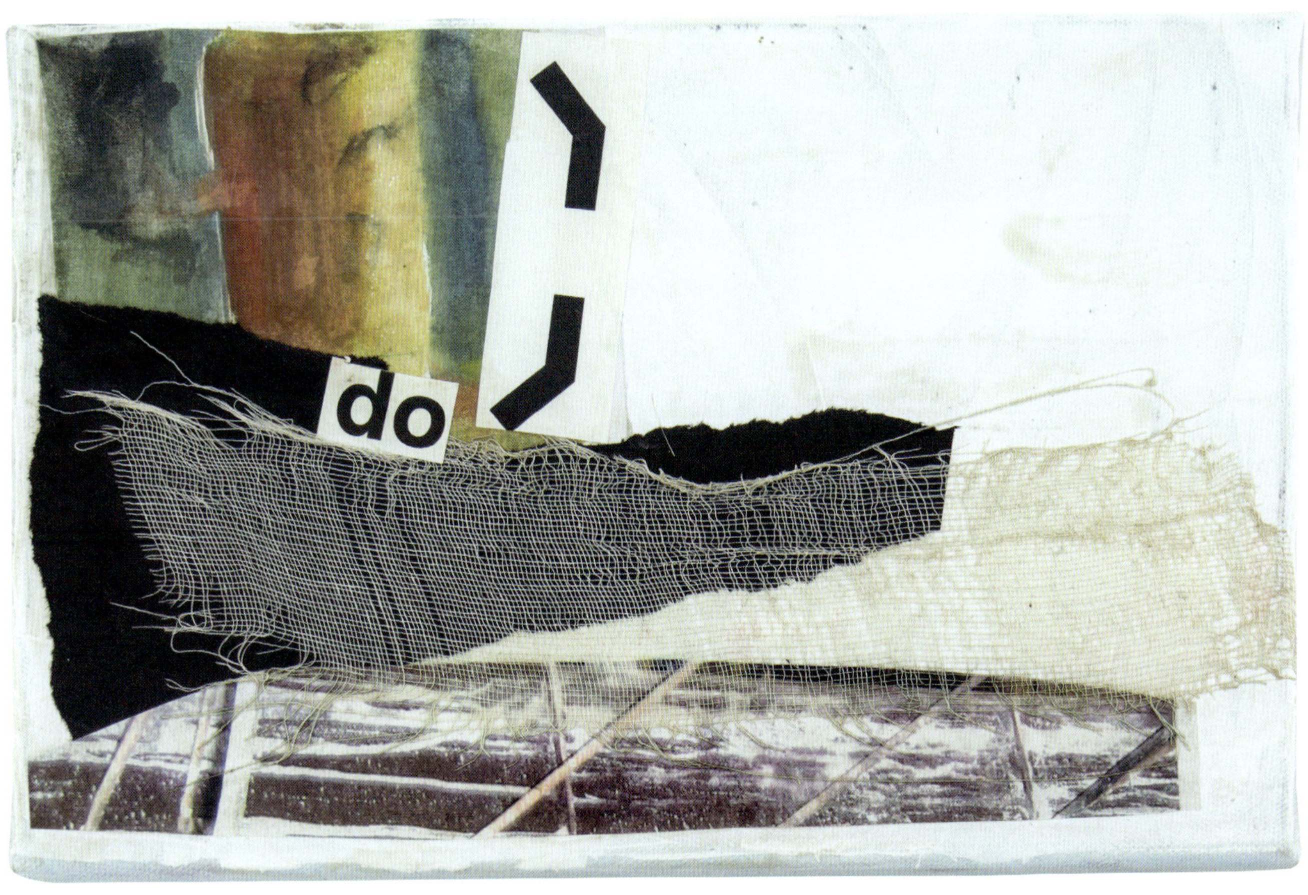
do

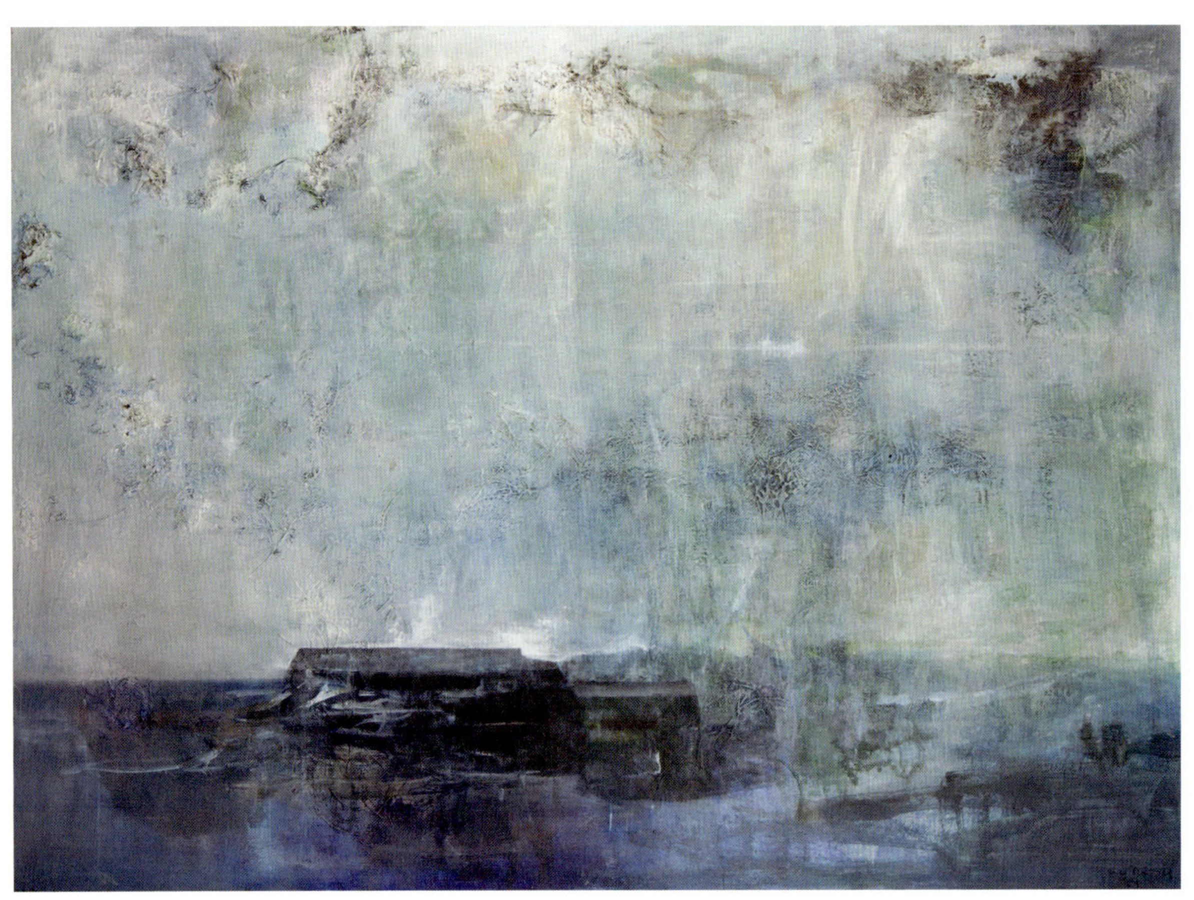

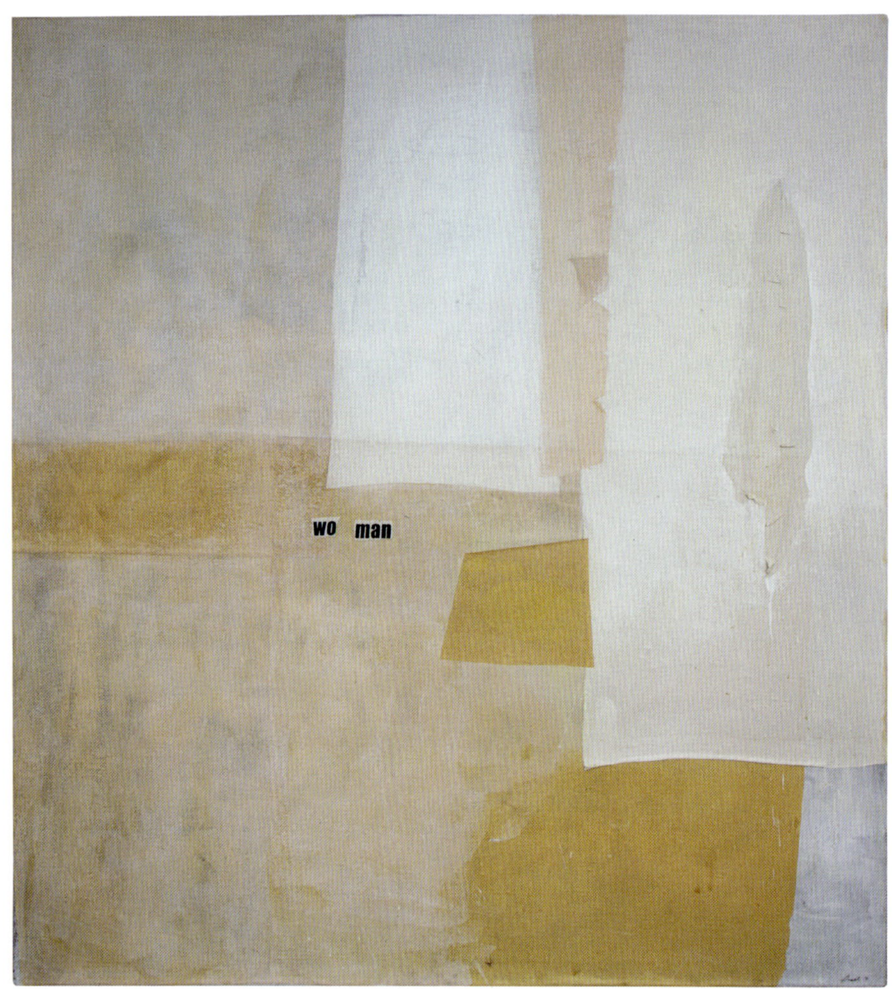
wo man

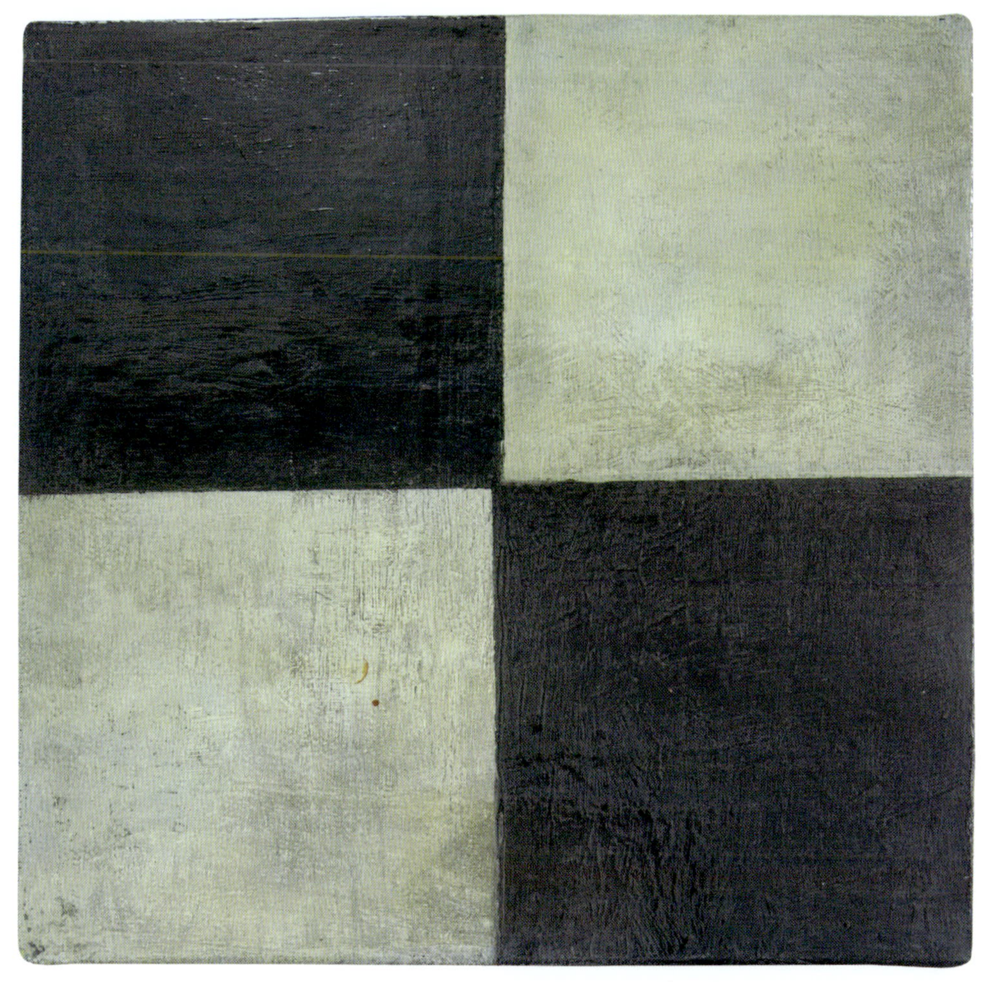

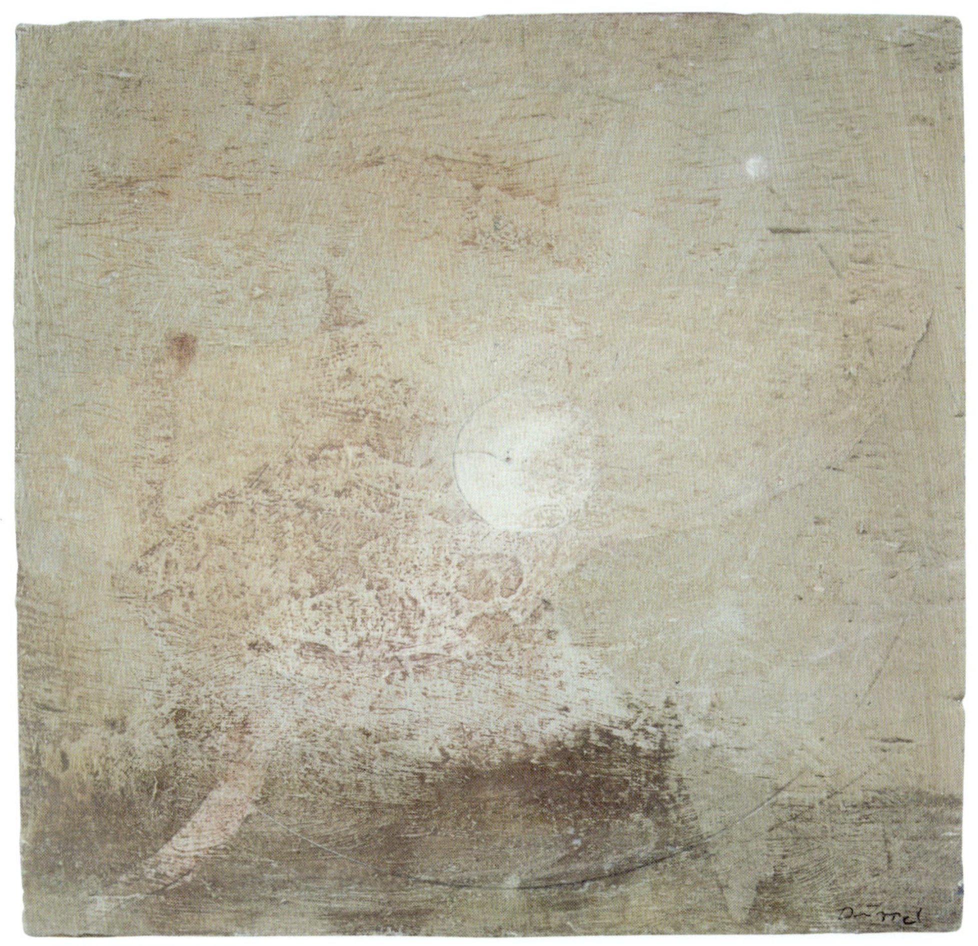

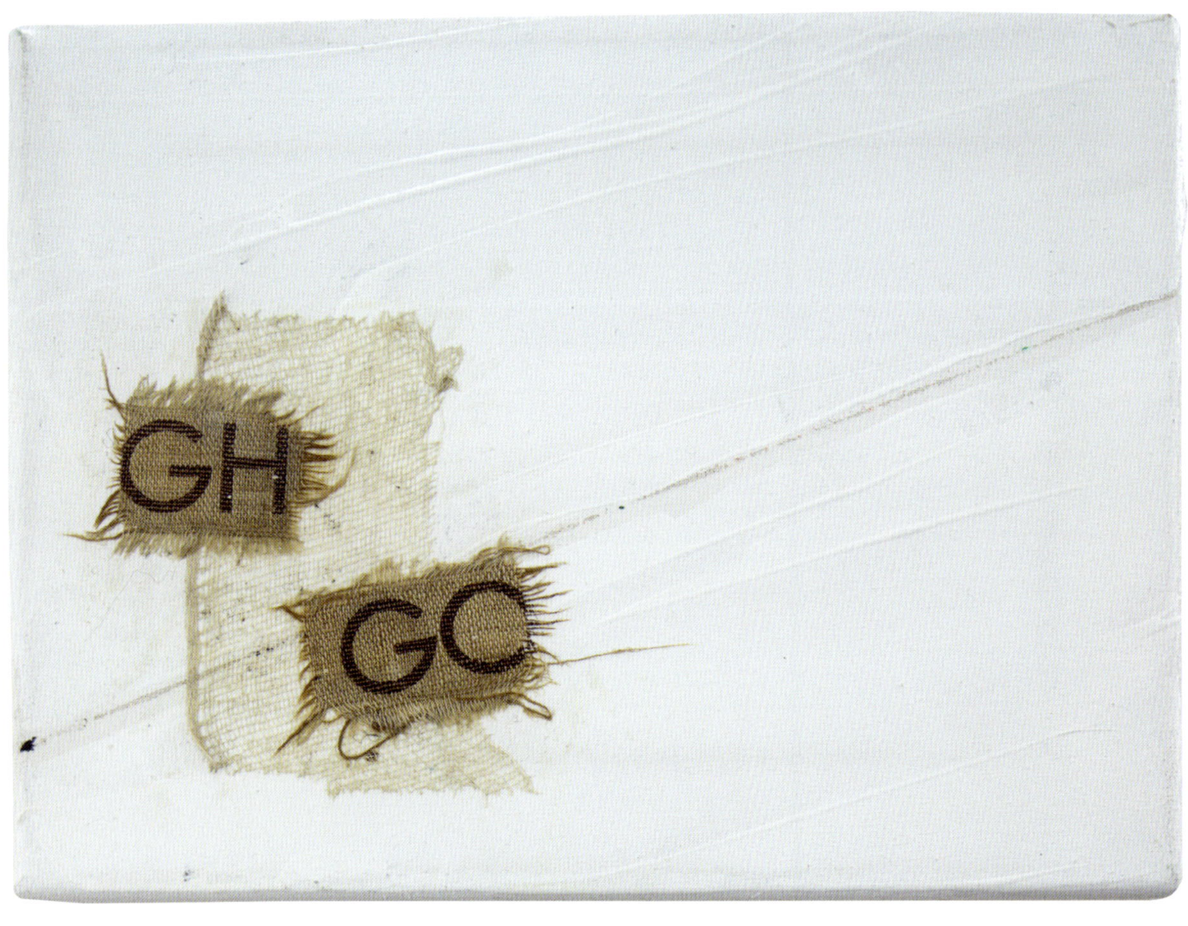
GH
GC

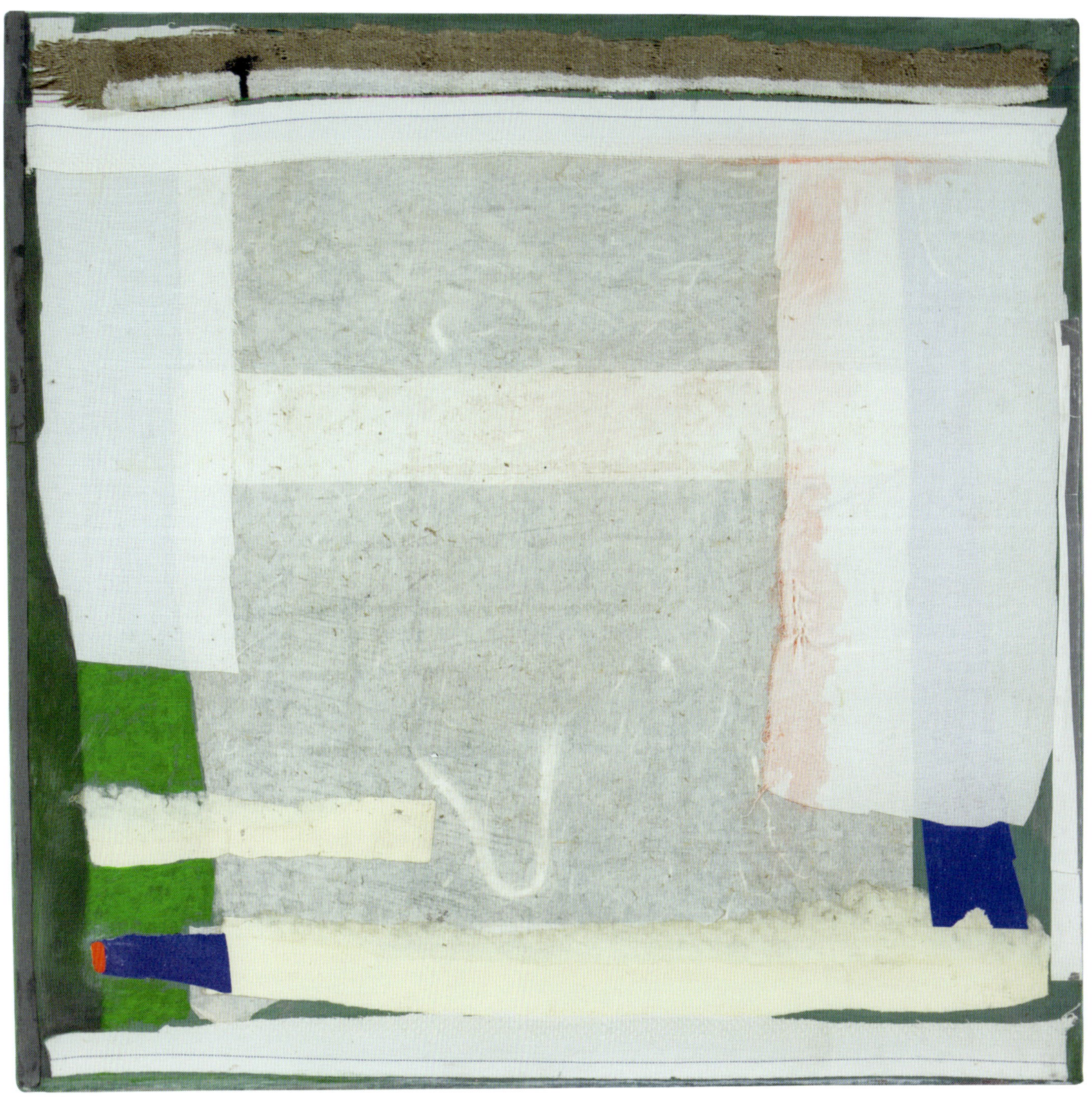

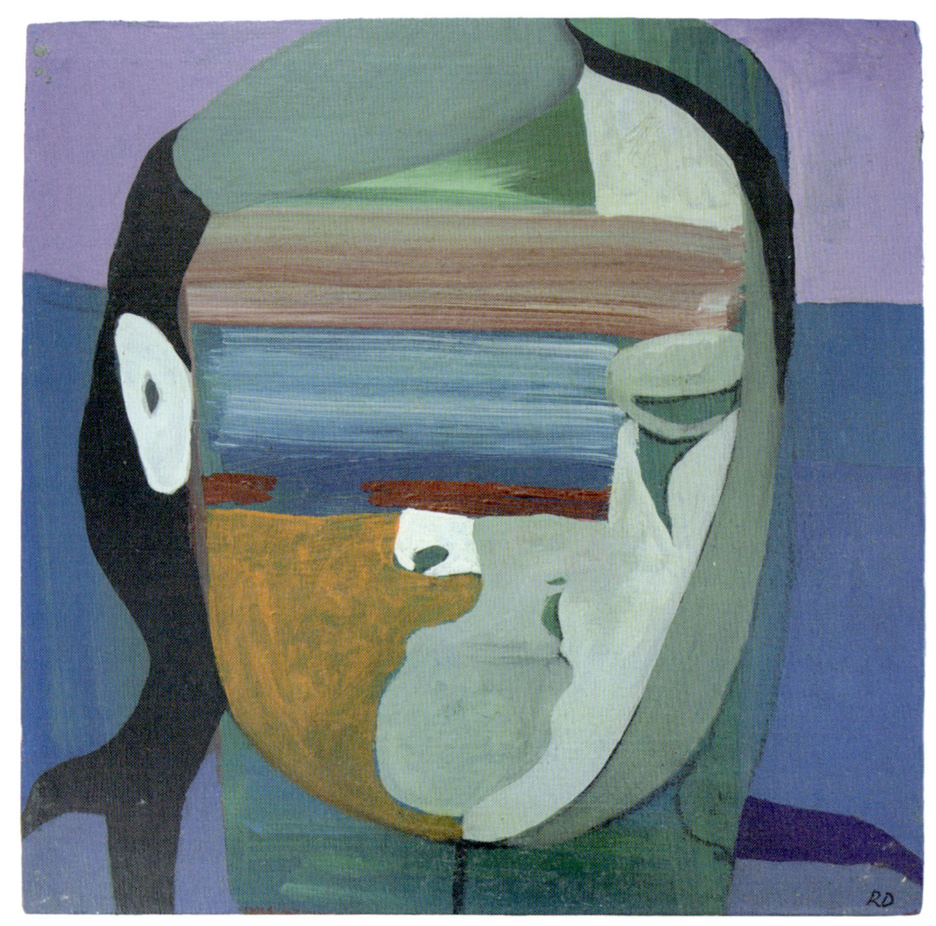
RD

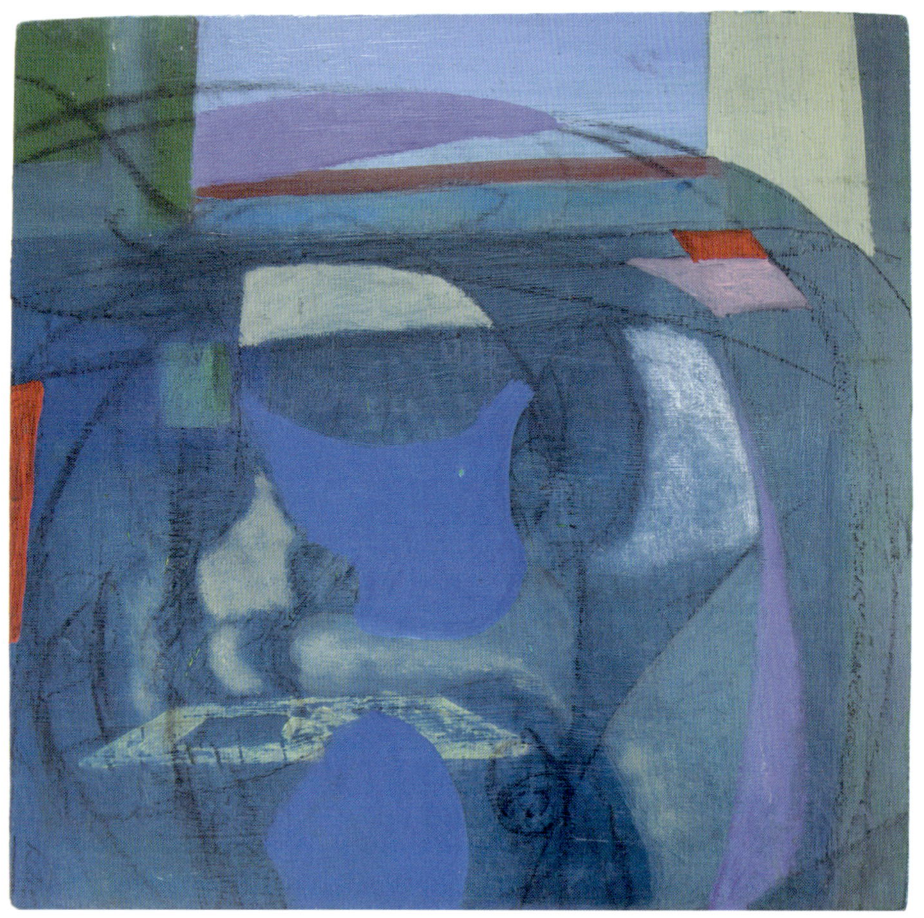

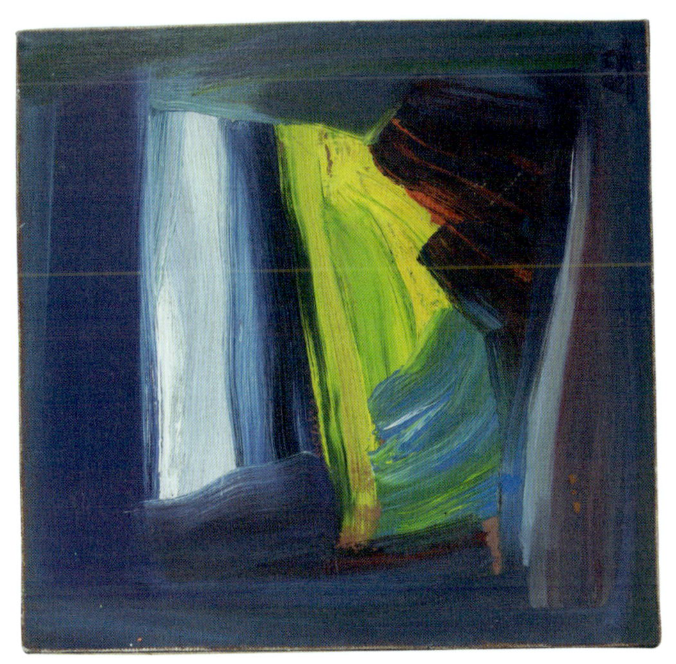

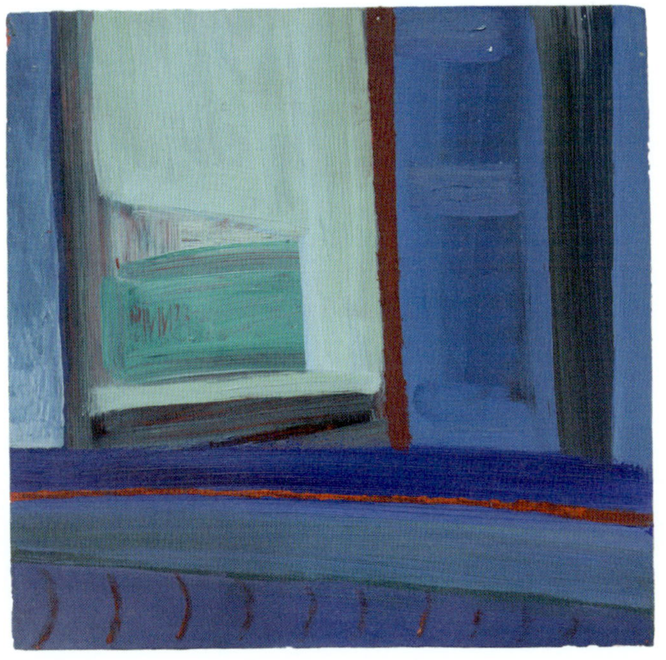

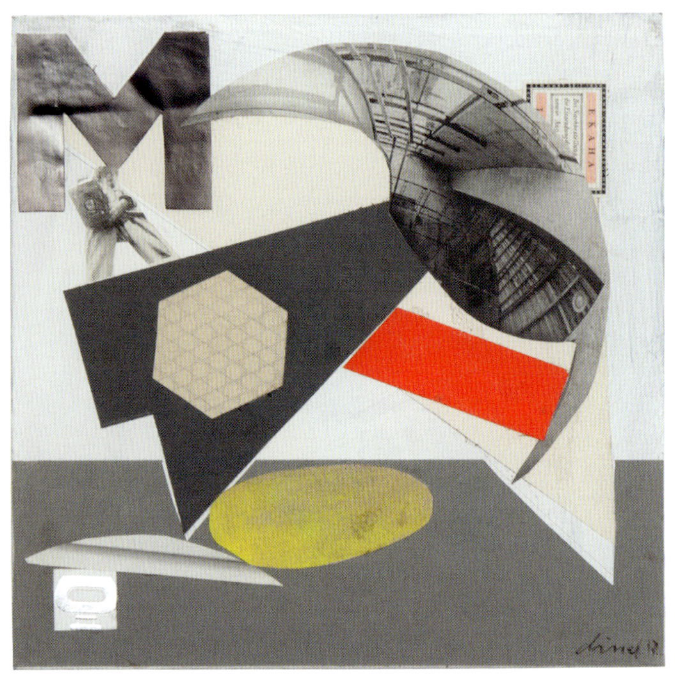

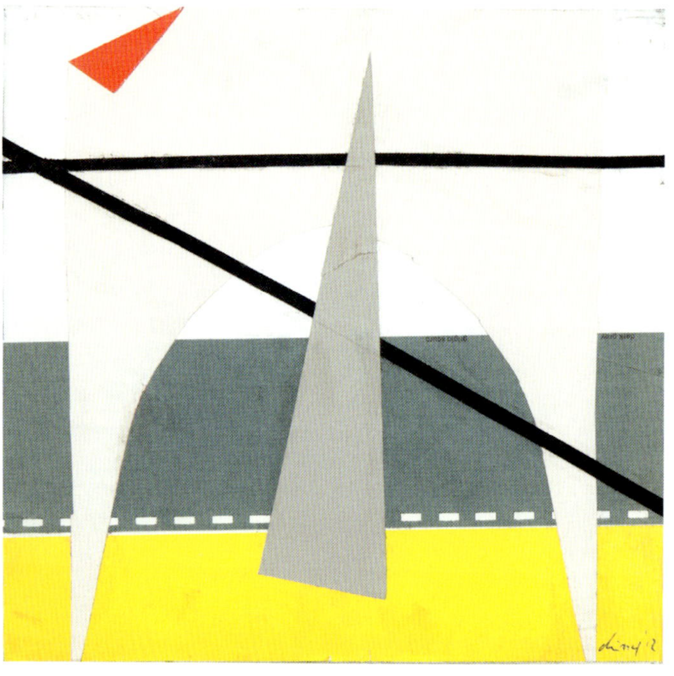

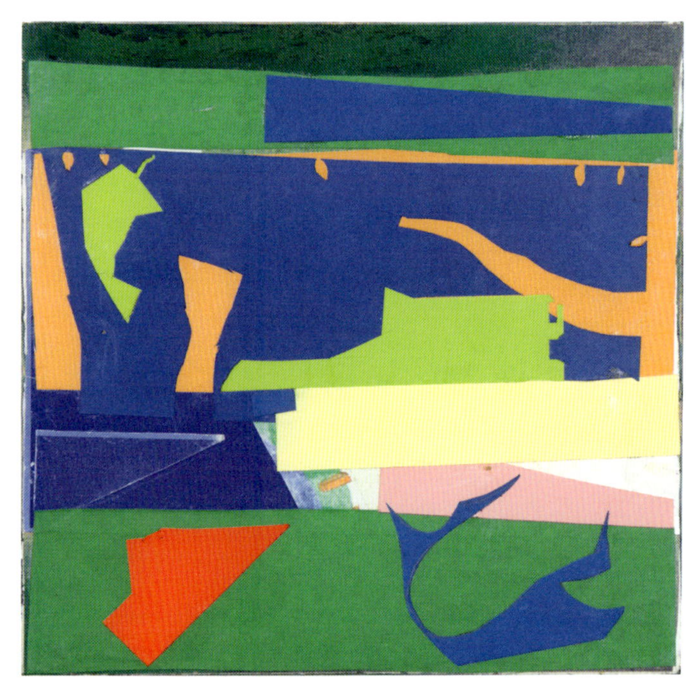

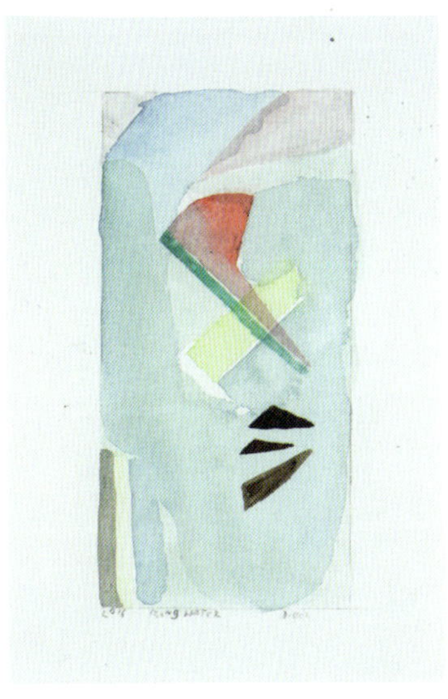

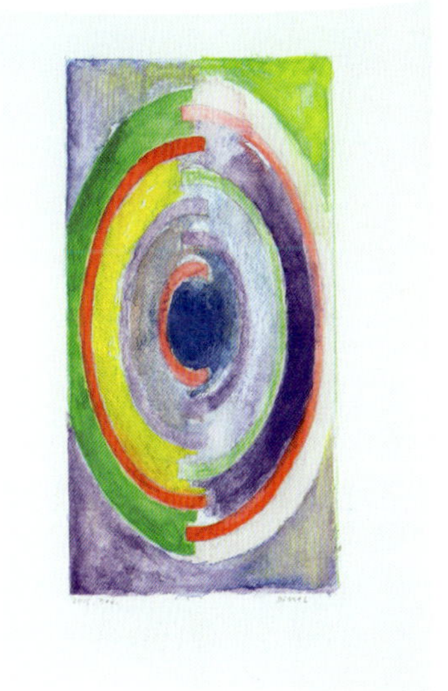

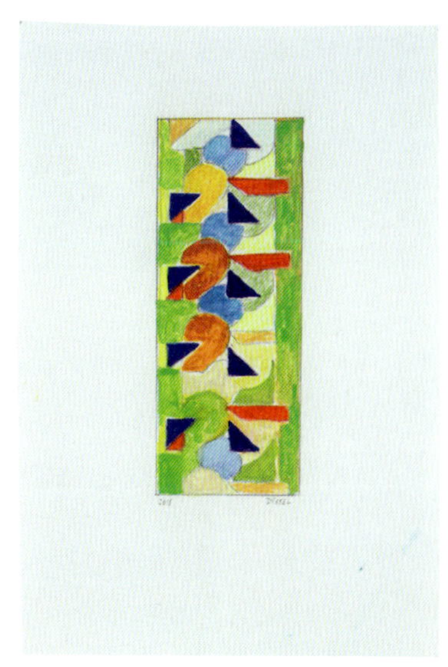

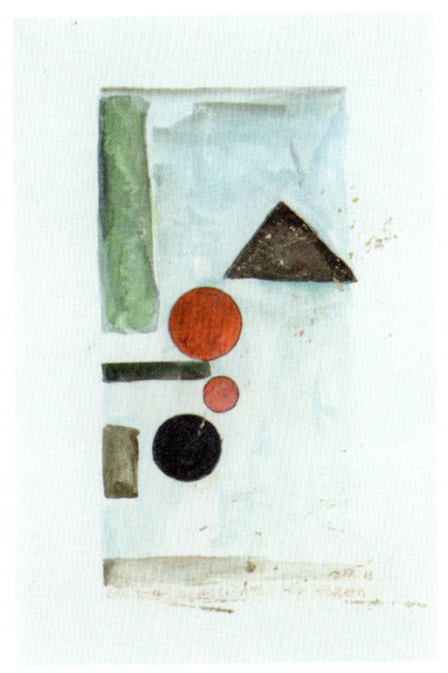

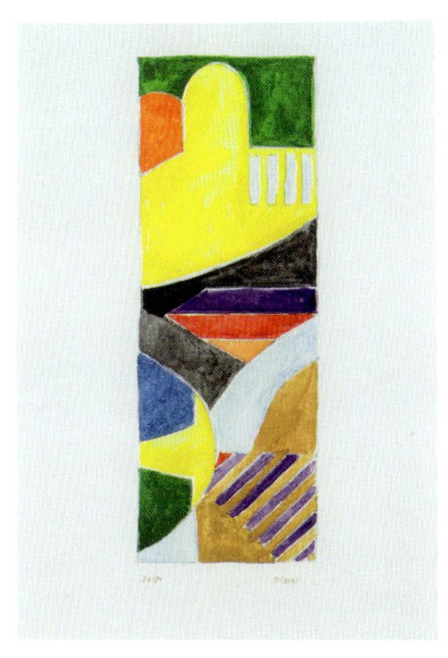

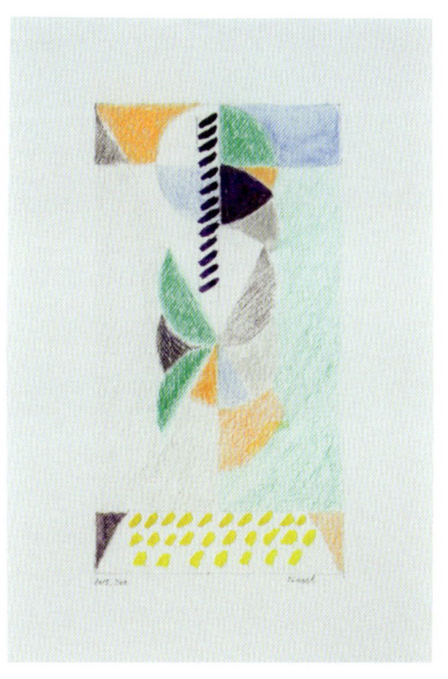

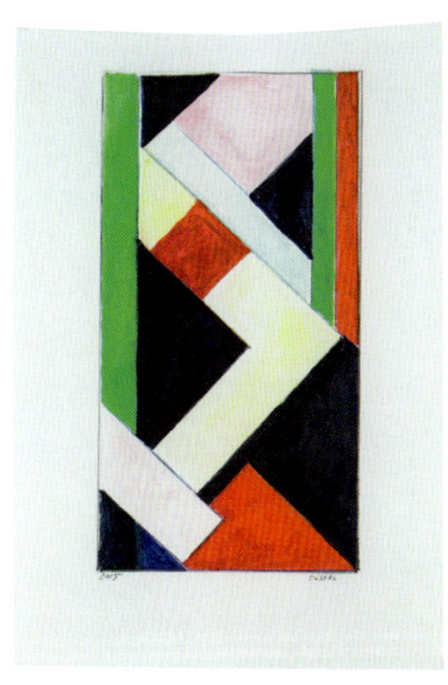

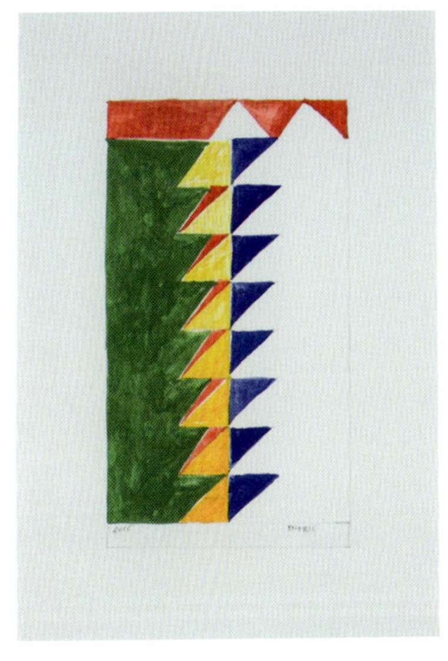

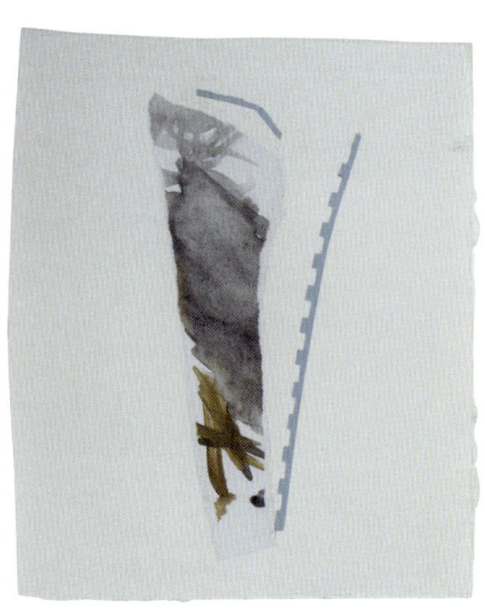
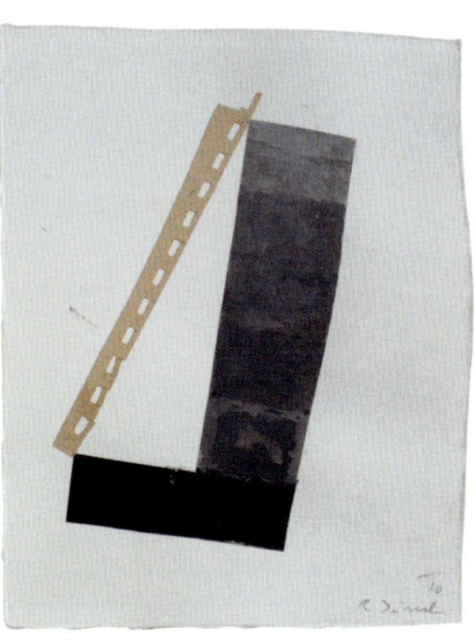
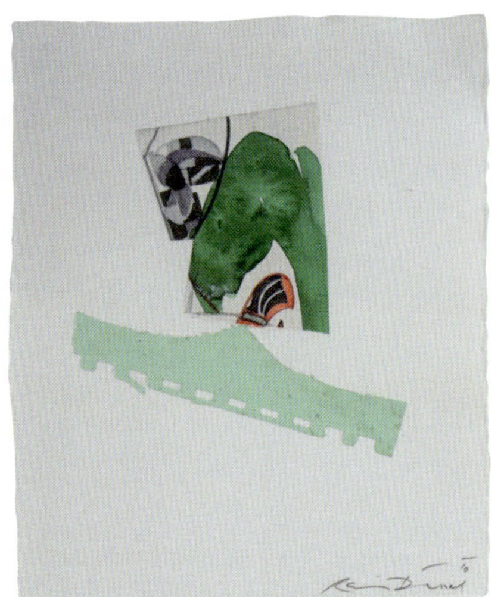

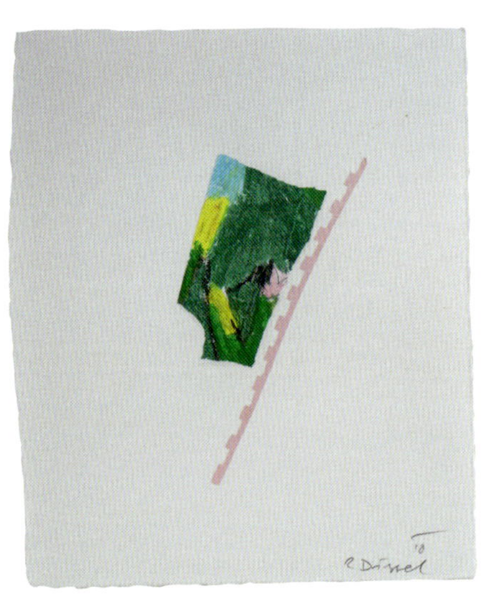
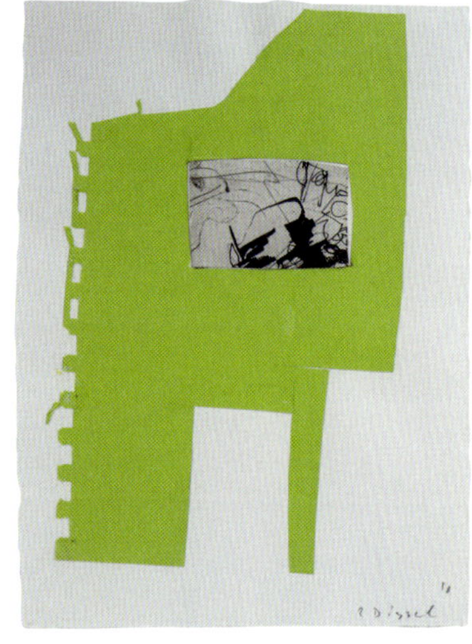
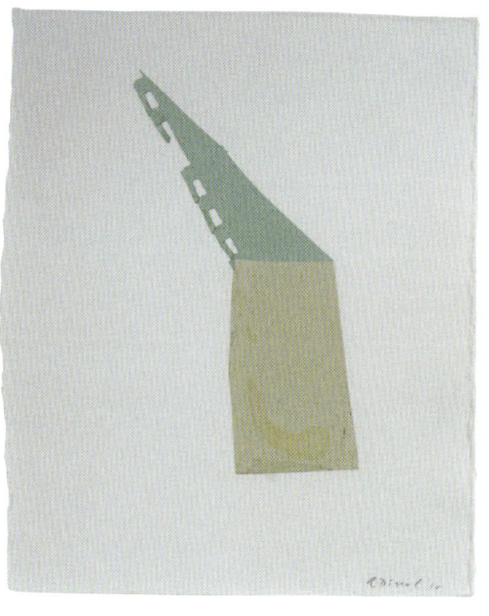
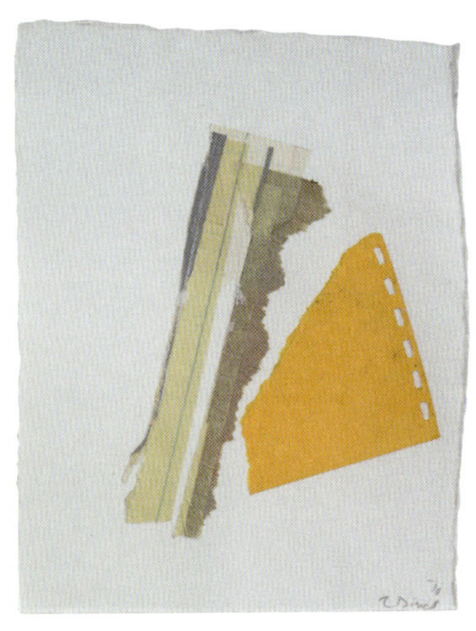
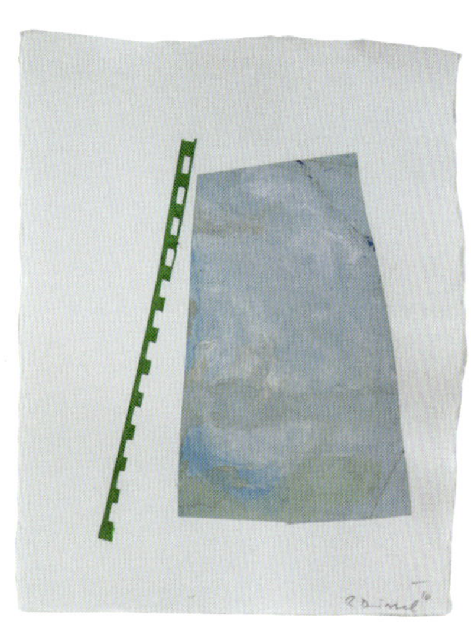
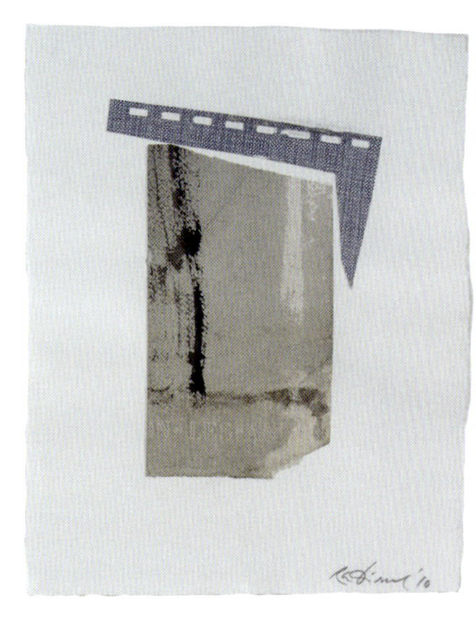

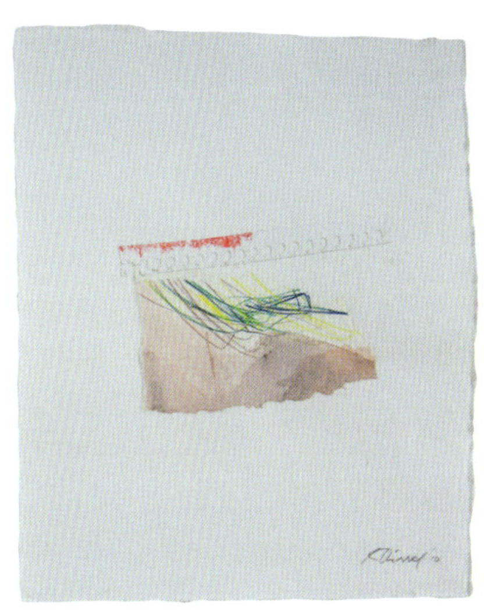
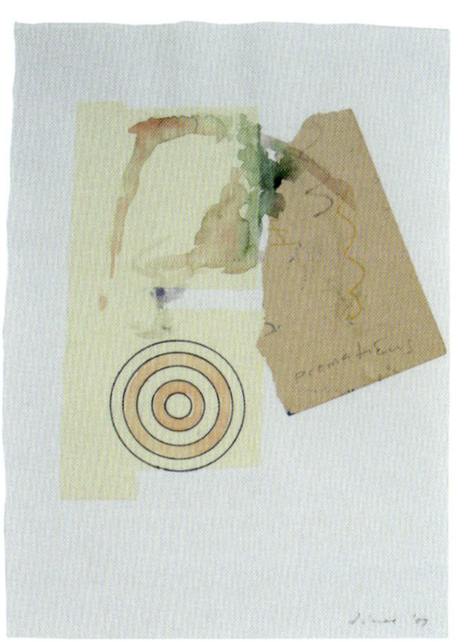
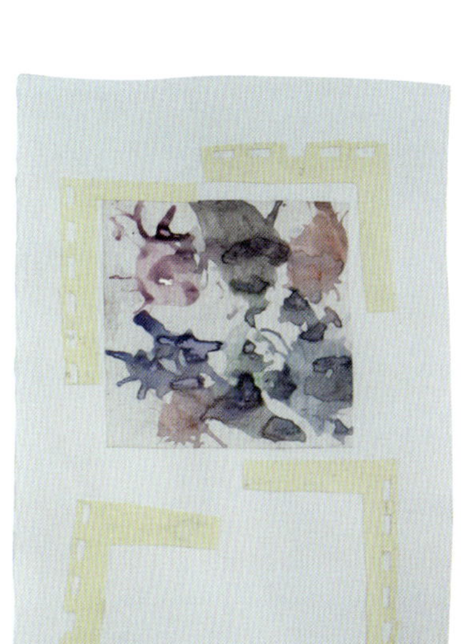
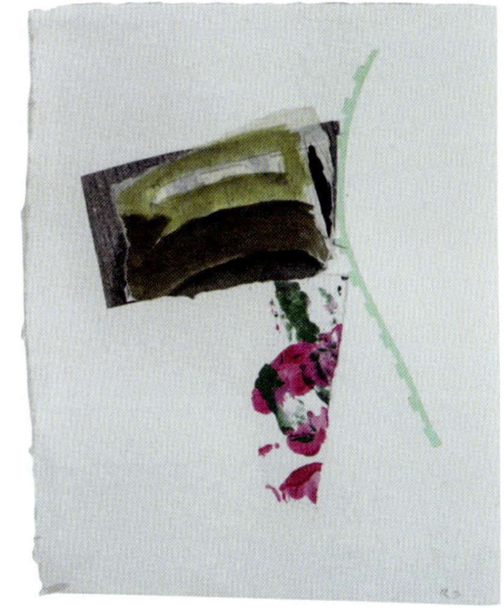
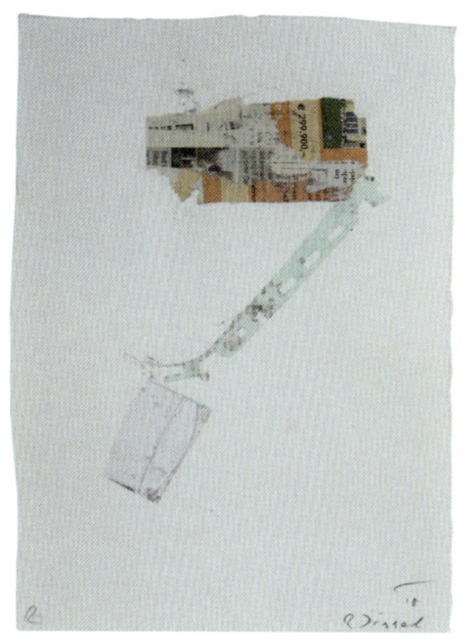
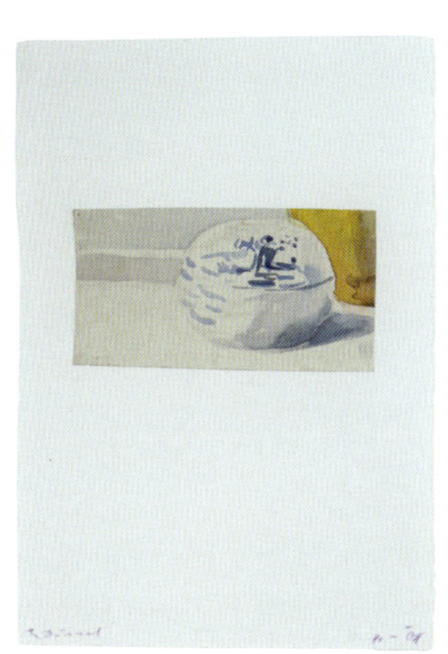

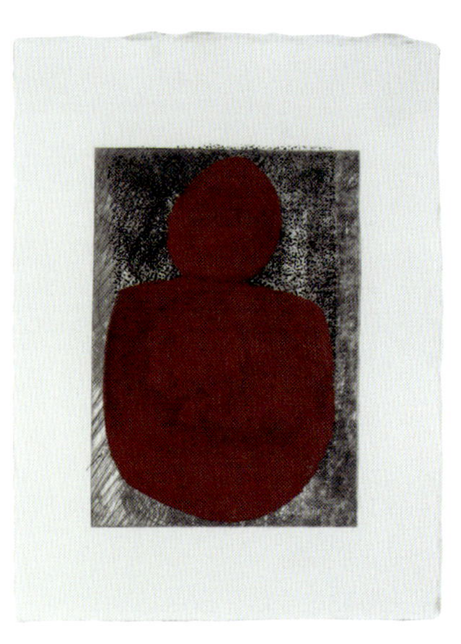

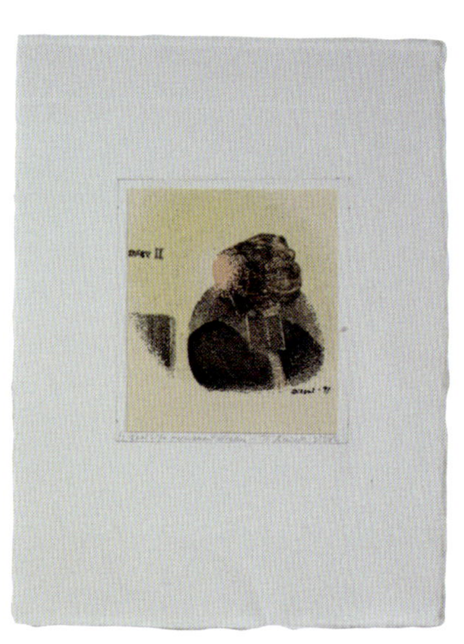

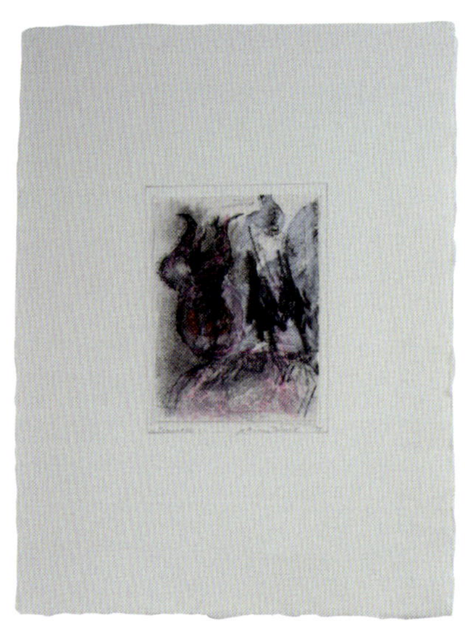

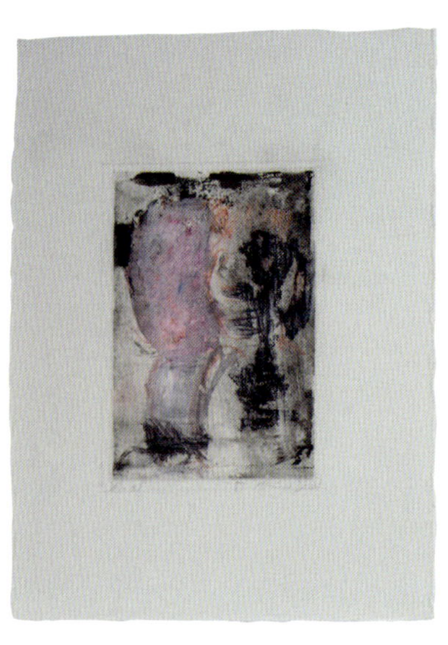

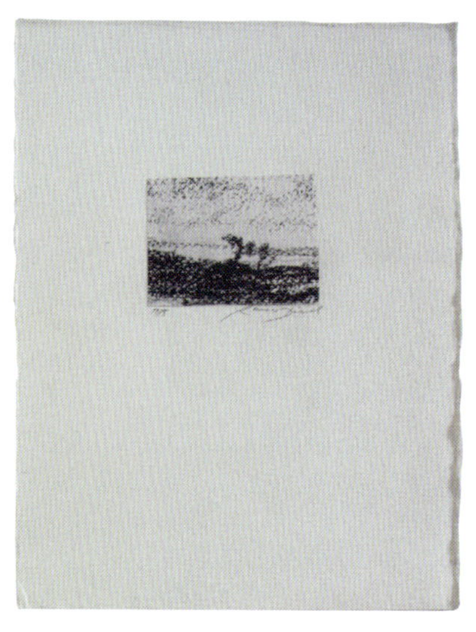

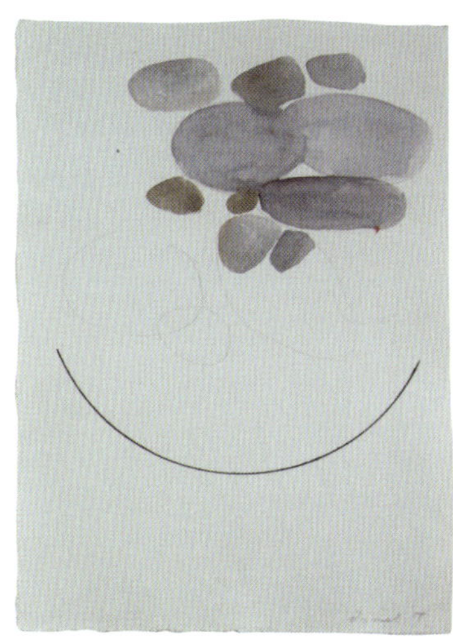

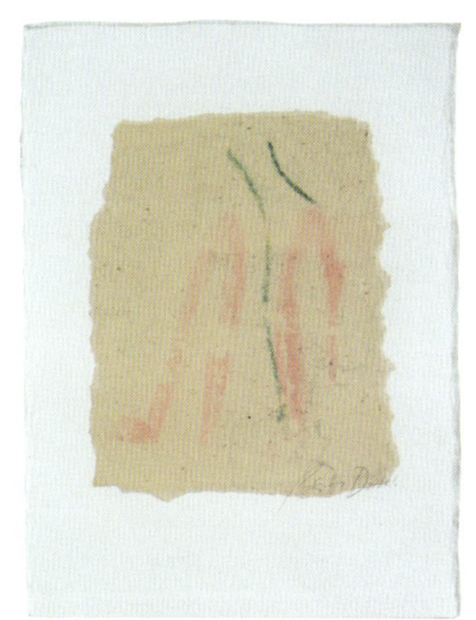

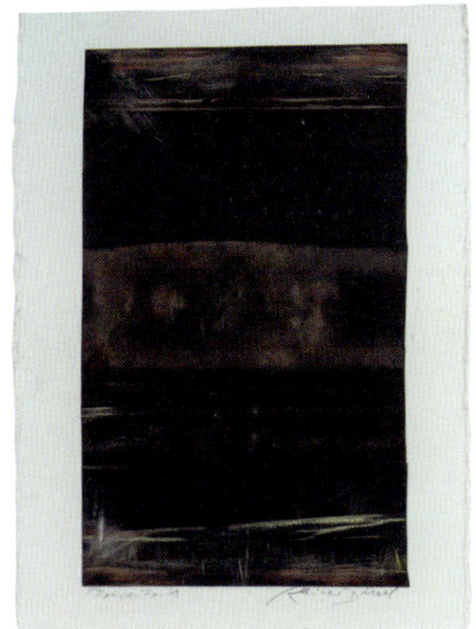

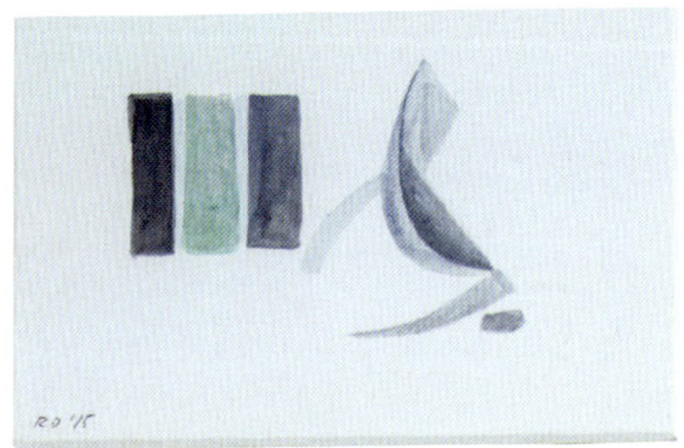
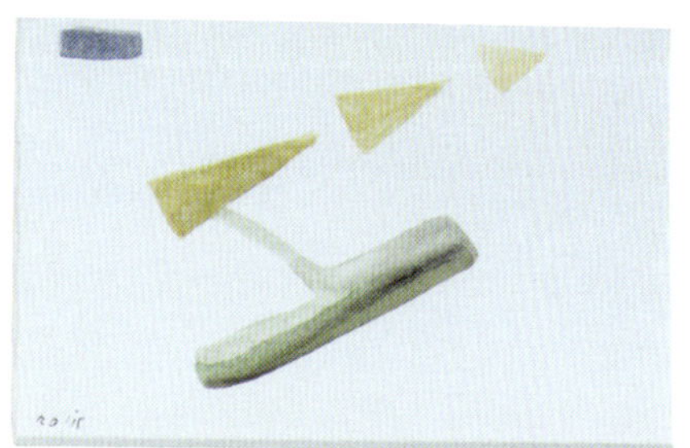

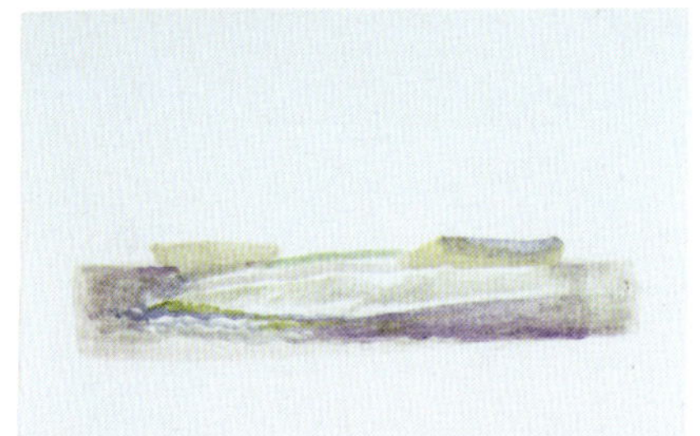
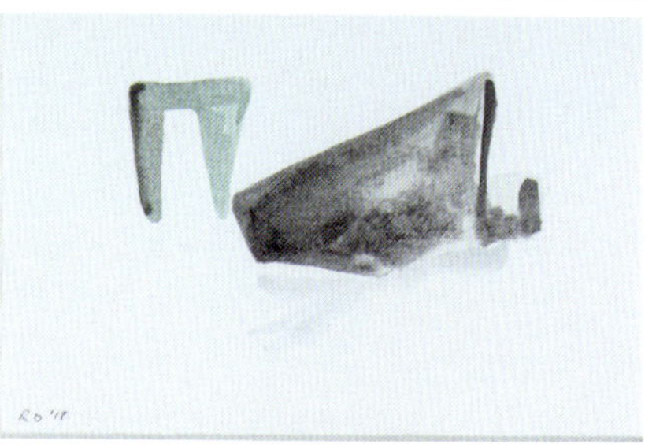
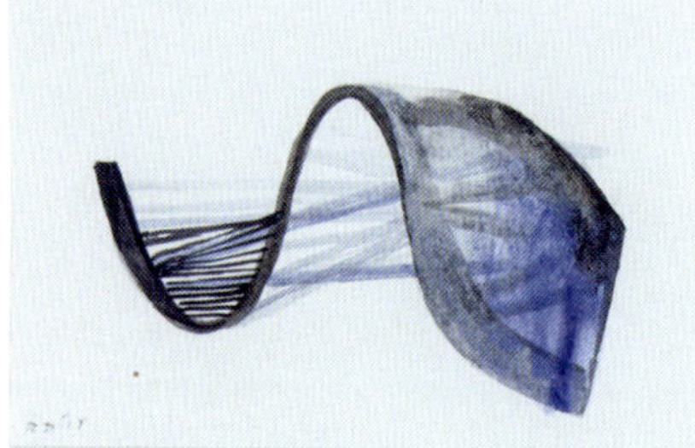
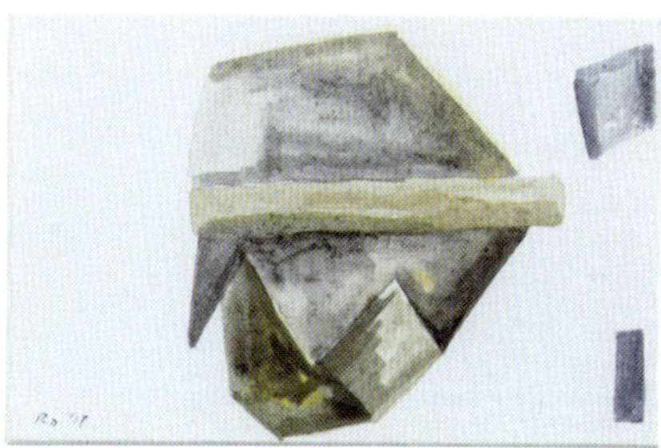
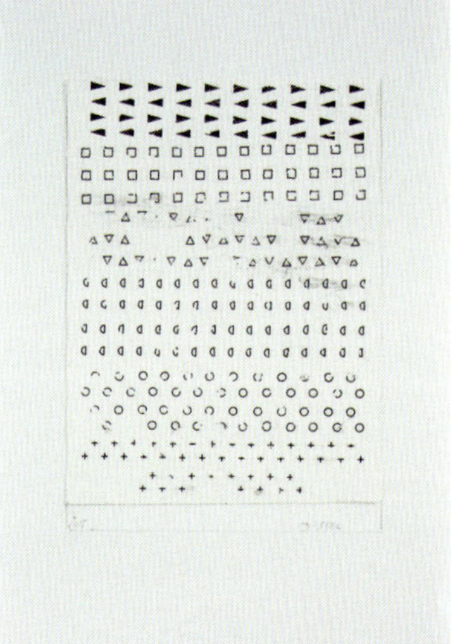
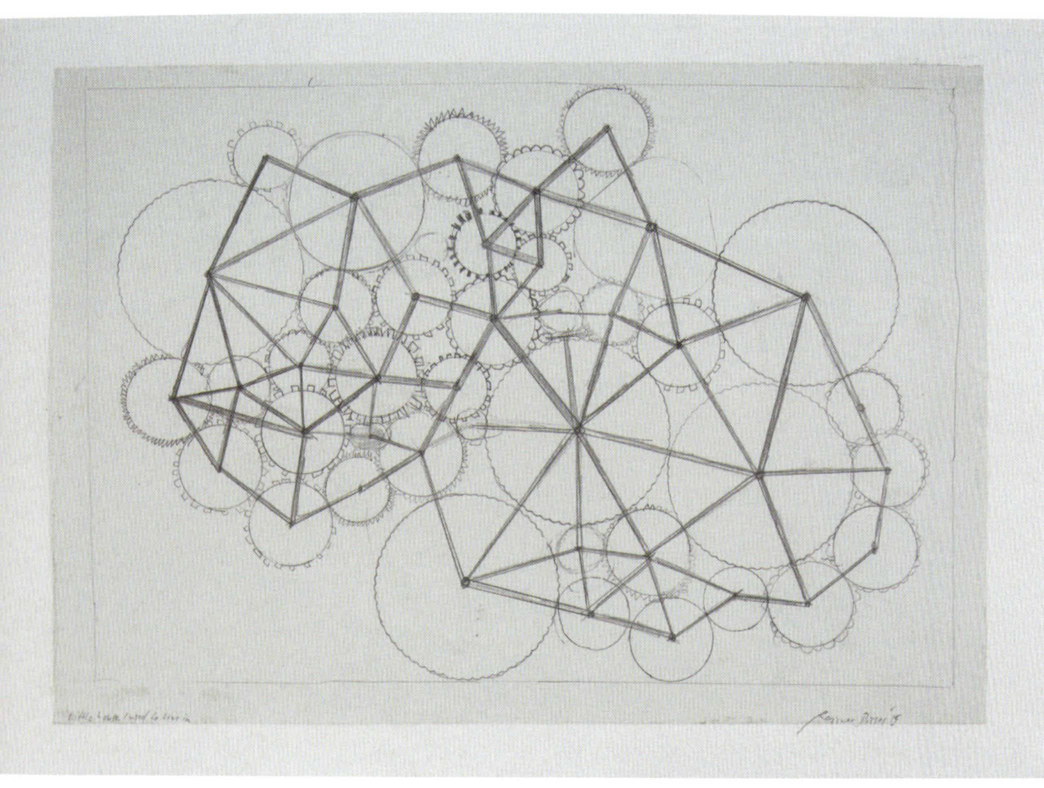

VOM URSPRUNG DES ALPHABETS

Hans Thill

Die Kunst ist die wilde Tochter der Freiheit

Friedrich Schiller

In meinem Schlafzimmer hängt ein Weinschlauch sehr alten Datums. In meinem Schlafzimmer hängt eine sprechende Konfrontation zweier Männer, einer mit, einer ohne Revolver. Es sind Bilder von Rainer Dissel. Eines nahmen wir auf den Umschlag meines ersten Buchs: Gelächter Sirenen (1985).
Seit Anbeginn ist Rainer Dissels Kunst auf der Suche nach dem Ursprung. Die Inspiration kämpft sich durch die Finsternis mancher Leinwand ins Licht. Es ist eine Art Ruderbewegung der Vernunft, die, wenn sie einmal in höhere Sphären gelangt, doch noch von ihrer schlammigen Herkunft weiß. Man kann das zwischen den Fingern spüren, an den Sohlen der Sandalen.
Wenn ich Bilder von Rainer Dissel betrachte, kommen mir immer wieder vergessene eigene Zeilen ein. Wir haben uns nicht abgesprochen. Wir haben vor langer Zeit in Familie grosse Teller mit gegrilltem Fleisch verzehrt, das bald schon erkaltet war. Damals rang ich mit dem semantischen Fluch der Sprache. Ich hätte alles gegeben, eine Sprache ohne Bedeutung zu schaffen. Die Schwierigkeiten Mitte der achtziger Jahre des letzten Jahrhunderts lagen darin, dass alles Aussage, Inhalt, Meinung werden wollte. Rainer Dissel und Annegret Emrich waren damals ein Paar der direkten Aktion. Rainer Dissel griff zu einem Fundstück und befestigte es ohne zu zögern an einer Leinwand. Wenn wir uns anderswo trafen, schilderte er mir seine Bilder anhand der verwendeten Materialien und fragte: wie findest du das? Ich habe eine Collage vor Augen, ein Stillleben mit Zigarettenpapier, das sich und andere Zettel zu einer Komposition fügt: GIZA PYRAMIDS, Collage, Tusche, Papier auf Leinwand, 30 x 30cm, 2010. Dass die ewigen Pyramiden zu Asche verglühen, wenn man ein wenig Tabak in sie hineinwickelt, war für mich schon immer ein Wunder. Wieviel Imagination in einem Produktnamen stecken kann! Man muss das Papier nur dünn genug schneiden.

Vom Ursprung des Alphabets in pebble tools
und gizeh papers ist auszugehen, aber auch ein
Stierkopf und der Himmel Hé stehen dabei.

Schon lange ist es um die Lettern eng geworden,
sie rücken zusammen, jedes ein Glied, bis sie,
ein Gitterwerk aus der Bauernzeit, dem Laien
die Sicht versperren.

Ich habe das alles in mir, es steht auf Lücke wie
die Zähne in Parzellen, es webt sich griechisch
rechts-links und links-rechts, verwechselbar, es
endet somit recte auf Kufen

Das Wort erstarrt zur Schrift: es ist tote Sprache, auf ein Papier gebannt. Die Bilder der Marken und Zeichen sind bei Rainer Dissel vorzugsweise schwarz-weiß. Von einem öligen Schwarz, einer trockenen Viskosität, die uns als Pulver in die Augen steigt. MAKING OUR MARK, Gummistempeldruck auf Holz, 25 x 25cm, 2000. In der selben Serie stehen geometrische Figuren herum wie Leute auf einem Platz. O.T., Tusche, Eitempera, Papier auf Leinwand, 35 x 40cm, 2001. Der erste surrealistische Text, verfasst von dem Duo Philippe Soupault und André Breton, trug den Titel: Die magnetischen Felder. Eine Ordnung, die sich von selbst zusammenfindet. Ich dachte immer, in der Sprache stelle sich diese leichter ein als auf einer Leinwand. Aber auch das Auge ist eine Ordnung schaffende Instanz, ein Organ, dem man nichts verbieten kann. Immerhin erhält es Lektionen von uns bzw. von Rainer Dissel, diesmal im Farbigen einer Gouache: LESSON, Collage, Gouache, Bleistift, Karton auf Baumwollsegeltuch, 40 x 30cm, 2013. Die Farben: Dark grey.
Man liest auf den Bildern. Man liest ohnehin zu viel. Man wäscht seine Hände in Unschuld. Einst gab es eine Lady, die ihre Hände in Blut wusch. MAC BETH, Collage, Papier, Stoff, Pappe auf Baumwollsegeltuch, 30 x 24cm, 2014; also eines von Dissels Bildern der ungemütlicheren Art. Mit Einklebungen von Texten, die er irgendwo auf einem Dachboden fand. Man könnte sie auch im Kopf finden, Textreste, oder in einem staubigen Winkel auf der Festplatte eines Schoßgeräts.
Das Blut ist vielleicht aus dem sehr alten Weinschlauch (Rotwein), der bei mir im Schlafzimmer hängt? Man sucht sich seine Fundstücke zusammen. Es ist wie Assoziationen haben. Wer Assoziationen hat, möge zum Arzt gehen. Lady Mac Beth möge zum Arzt gehen.
»Als Richard Strauss mit zweiundzwanzig Jahren auf seine erste Italienreise ging, besuchte er als Bildungsbürger des 19. Jahrhunderts natürlich vor allem Rom

und Neapel, und es wirkt fast wie eine Pflichtübung, dass er die Eindrücke dieser Reise in eine sinfonische Fantasie verwandelt hat.« So heißt es auf einer Plattenhülle der Firma RONDO über die sinfonische Fantasie Mac Beth. Ein runder Text, wie geschliffen für das Männchen mit dem Licht, das in Form des Schattens eines Tintenflecks rechts oben übers Bild geht: wer kennt ihn nicht? Deutsche Urgemütlichkeit, in der Nachkriegszeit propagiert von der Firma DARMOL, deren Namen, wer hätte es gedacht, für ein Abführmittel steht. Kaum vorzustellen, dass einer da im Hausrock mit Licht auf das Klo zustrebt: »Er nahm Darmol und fühlt sich wohl.«

Die Texteinklebungen auf Rainer Dissels Collagen werfen unsere Köpfe hin und her. Man müsste das Bild drehen, aber es hängt ja einigermaßen fest an der Wand. Etwa die Stellenanzeigen auf dem Bild APO, Collage, Bleistift, Acryl- und Ölfarbe auf Baumwollsegeltuch, 71,5 x 71,5cm, 2014, bei dessen Titel wir endlich in einer Sprache angekommen wären, die man Out-door-Griechisch nennen könnte. Hier ist das Räderwerk des Luftpostbriefs ein treibendes Element, eine old fashioned Dadakonstruktion, auf der die Geometrie Männchen macht, die Mütze ein blaues Kreissegment, überschwebt von einem Bogenstück.

Es ist eine alte Dadamanie, die Kunst vollzuschreiben mit Botschaften, wie es auch die Frommen des 16. Jahrhunderts taten, die in allen Himmeln Texte sehen wollten. Aber Dada weiß wie man aus den Buchstaben Geräusche machen kann, die Texte beginnen zu keuchen und zu brüllen.

Bei Rainer Dissel haben wir es vorwiegend mit der Lakonie der nützlichen Schriften zu tun. Auch in solchen Schriften kann man immer gleich Gott vermuten.

Kinder des Alphabets

Die Heiserkeit hat er
von den
Konsonanten geerbt, den Eltern
mit der steifen Oberlippe. Die lauten
Vokale konnten ihm nichtmal
die Liebe erklären. Er findet
jetzt eine Trommel in seinem

Bauch und ein Wasser am Wegrand, das am
Freitag in einen See mündet. An den
waldigen Stellen das krumme
Holz der offenen Zeichen,
geständige Os, Fock, der

Hustenkapitän. Die Kinder füllen Fische und
Sand in Flaschen, der Freitag stellt
die Frage: wer Gott ist und
wer Mensch. Die Antwort liegt
wie Blech auf seiner Zunge.

Der Blick zerkaut die Schrift wie der berühmte Hund bei Rabelais seinen Knochen. Ist er auf Mark gestoßen, hat er ein Aha-Erlebnis. Dieses liegt nur ein paar Schritte vom Apo-Erlebnis entfernt. Wir gehen auf DISTANZ, eine Collage (auf Baumwolle, Gaze, Nessel, Papier, Öl- und Acrylfarbe, 70 x 90cm, 2014), der das architektonische Element Sprache genug ist. Bei BACKWARD EXPERIMENT (Öl-Eitempera, Kohle, Kreide, Papier, auf Leinwand, 180 x 165cm,2011_2012) ist aus dem Papier eine wahre Stadt gewachsen. Die Türme Babylons: man muß sich Babylon als eine glückliche Stadt vorstellen (Gregor Laschen). Wäre nur die Sprache der Formen eine gesprochene! Wir sind so satt der Theorien.

Wie sich die Schrift von selber frißt, teils
in mir, teils in uns zusammen, wird bald
gefährlich, eine Kerze zuviel beim Akt an
sich, ein schlechter Wein, ein wie-Vergleich

Ist die Gefahr vorbei, wirds endlich still im
Wort (Egger), dafür klirren Gläser weiter
in einer Art Geschrei.

Geht es um Kunsttheorie, wird in abgeklärten Kreisen gern Barnett Newman zitiert, der behauptet, Kunsttheorie sei ebenso relevant für Künstler wie die Ornithologie für Vögel. Doch was heißt das für die Pyramiden von Gizeh? Wer sagt denn, Herr Beuys, dass man einem Hasen erst die Kunst erklären sollte, wenn er tot ist?

Wenn ein Affe eine Bananenschale findet, wird er darin lesen. Wir lehren niemandem die Kunst, wir lehren nicht einmal, Aufstrich-Abstrich, das Alphabet. Wir bauen mit Steinen, die auf dem Acker liegen. Es erstehen graue Gebäude aus vergilbtem Zeitungspapier, eine Art Buntsandstein von Wüstenrot. Wir bauen uns in die Vorgartenzeit, direkt an der lauten Straße gelegen. Damals hießen die Städte Aschenberg und Kahl. Damals, als die Gartenzwerge noch geholfen haben.

Zum Autor

Hans Thill ist ein deutscher Lyriker und Übersetzer. Seit 2010 ist Hans Thill zudem künstlerischer Leiter des Künstlerhaus Edenkoben. 2004 erhielt er den Peter-Huchel-Preis für deutschsprachige Lyrik. Zudem ist er Mitbegründer des Heidelberger Verlags *Das Wunderhorn* und Leiter der jährlichen Übersetzer-Werkstatt *Poesie der Nachbarn. Dichter übersetzen Dichter* sowie Herausgeber der gleichnamigen Reihe und Mitherausgeber der Reihe P. Hans Thill ist außerdem »Writers-for-Peace« -Beauftragter im Präsidium des deutschen PEN.

ON THE ORIGIN OF THE ALPHABET

Hans Thill

Art is the wild daughter of freedom

Friedrich Schiller

In my bedroom hangs a very old wine skin. In my bedroom hangs a verbal confrontation between two men, one with, one without a revolver. Both are images by Rainer Dissel. One we used for the cover of my first book: Gelächter Sirenen (1985). Since the beginning, Rainer Dissel's art has been searching for the origins. Inspiration fights its way through the darkness of the one or other canvas into the light. It is a kind of rowing movement by Reason which, once it gains higher spheres, still knows of its muddy origins. You can sense it between your fingers, on the soles of your sandals.
When I consider Rainer Dissel's images some long forgotten lines come to mind. We didn't consult on it. Long ago we sat down in a family setting and ate grilled meat that soon went cold. At that time, I was wrestling with the semantic curse of language. I had given my all to create a language without meaning. The difficulties in the mid-1980s stemmed from the fact that everything sought to be statement, content, opinion. Rainer Dissel and Annegret Emrich were at the time a couple in direct action. Rainer Dissel took a found object and without thinking twice fixed it on a canvas. When we met elsewhere he described his images to me in terms of the materials used and asked: What do you think of this?
I have a collage in mind, a still life with cigarette paper that along with other pieces of paper forms a composition: GIZA PYRAMIDS, collage, ink, paper on canvas, 30 x 30cm, 2010. That the eternal pyramids burn to ash when you twist a little tobacco in them was something I always found miraculous. Amazing how much imagination can go into a product name! You only need to cut the paper thin enough.

The origin of the alphabet in pebble tools
and gizeh papers is something we can assume, but also
a bull's head and the Heaven Hé were in for the ride.

It has long since become tight for letters,
they huddle up closer, each a link, until,

a grid from farming days, they block
the layman's view.

I have it all within me, the gaps lined up
like teeth in their parcels, woven together Greek
right to left and left to right, mistakable, it
ends thus recte on slides

The word freezes as script: It is a dead language, banished to a page. The images of the marks and signs are, in Rainer Dissel's case, preferentially black and white. Of an oily black, a dry viscosity that gets in our eyes as powder. MAKING OUR MARK, rubber stamp print on wood, 25 x 25cm, 2000. In the same series, geometrical figures linger like people on a plaza. Untitled, ink, tempera, paper on canvas, 35 x 40cm, 2001. The first Surrealist text, authored by the duo of Philippe Soupault and André Breton, was entitled: THE MAGNETIC FIELDS. An order that converges of its own volition. I always thought that this occurs more easily in language than on a canvas. But the eyes is also an agent assisting order, an organ which you cannot forbid anything. At any rate, it is given lessons by us or by Rainer Dissel, this time in the colors of a gouache: LESSON, collage, gouache, pencil, card on cotton canvas, 40 x 30cm, 2013. The colors: Dark grey.
You can read the pictures. After all, we read too much anyway. You wash your hands of it. Once there was a lady who washed her hands in blood. MAC BETH, collage, paper, textile, card on cotton canvas, 30 x 24cm, 2014; meaning one of Dissel's paintings of the more unpleasant kind. With texts glued onto it that he found somewhere in an attic. You could also find them in your head somewhere, fragments of texts, or in a dusty corner of the hard drive on a lap device.
Perhaps the blood is from the very old wine skin (red wine) that hangs on my wall? You hunt out your own found objects. It is like having associations. Anyone having associations should see a doctor. Lady Mac Beth, please consult your physician.
When, aged 22, Richard Strauss headed off on his first trip to Italy, as an educated 19th-century gentleman he visited above all Rome and Naples, of course, and it has the feel of a compulsory exercise about it that he transformed the impressions the trip made of him into a symphonic fantasy." Or so we can read on the cover of an album made by RONDO on the symphonic phantasy Mac Beth. A perfected text

as if polished for the little man with the light who moves in the guise of the shadow of an ink blot across the picture on the upper right: Surely we all know him? Classical German coziness, propagated in post-War times by the company DARMOL, whose name, imagine that, is for a laxative. Hard to imagine that the guy is heading in his housecoat for the toilet: "He took Darmol and felt was on a roll."

The texts glued into Rainer Dissel's collages send our minds caroming. You feel a need to turn the picture, but it is mounted fairly firmly on the wall. For example the job ads in the picture APO, collage, pencil, acrylic and oil paints on cotton canvas, 71.5 x 71.5cm, 2014, the title of which means we have finally arrived in a language we could call outdoor Greek. Here the cogs of the airmail letter are the driving element, an old-fashioned Dada construction, where the geometry jumps about, the cap a blue circular segment, an arc floating over it.

It is an old Dada-mania to fill art up with messages the way the devout did in the 16th century, who thought they saw texts in all heavens. But Dada knows how to get sounds from the letters, the texts start to pant and roar.

With Rainer Dissel we primarily have to do with the laconic nature of useful writings. You can always suspect God in such writings.

Children of the Alphabet

He inherited the coarseness
From the
Consonants, the parents
with the stiff upper lips. The loud
vowels were never able to
declare their love for him. He now finds
a drum within his

stomach and water at the roadside that
culminates in a lake. At the woody
points the bent
Wood of open signs,
confessional Os, Fock, the

Captain of Cough. The children fill fish and
sand into bottles, Friday asks
the question: Who is God and
who is Man. The answer lies
heavily on his tongue.

The eye devours the script like Rabelais' famous dog chews his bone. When he hits the marrow, he has his Aha moment. This is not a far cry from an Apo experience.
We head for the DISTANZ, a collage (on cotton, gauze, nettle, paper, oil and acrylic, 70 x 90cm, 2014), which is satisfied with the architectural element of language.
With BACKWARD EXPERIMENT (oil tempera, charcoal, chalk, paper on canvas, 180 x 165cm,2011_2012) a veritable city has emerged on the paper. The towers of Babylon: You need to imagine Babylon as a happy city (Gregor Laschen). Were the language of shapes but verbal! We are so fed up with all the theory.

The way script devours itself, partly
in me, partly in us together, soon becomes
dangerous, one candle too many during the act
itself a bad wine, an as-if comparison

Once the danger's past, things finally fall silent
in the word (Egger), but the glasses continue to clink
in a kind of scream.

If the subject is art theory, then level-headed circles like to quote Barnett Newman who once claimed art theory is about as relevant for artists as an ornithologist is for birds. But what does that mean for the pyramids of Gizeh? Who will tell Herr Beuys that one should first explain art to a rabbit, considering he is dead?
If a monkey finds a banana skin then he will read it. We do not teach anybody art, we do not even teach, upstroke / downstroke, the alphabet. We build with stones that lie on fields. The result are grey buildings made of fading newspapers a kind of colorful sandstone courtesy of Wüstenrot. We are building our way into the front-garden age, directly adjacent to the loud road. Back then the cities were still called Ashville and Barrentown. Back then, when the garden gnomes still helped out.

About the author

Hans Thill is a German poet and translator. Since 2010 Hans Thill has been Artistic Director of Künstlerhaus Edenkoben. In 2004 he won the Peter Huchel Prize for German poetry. He is also co-founder of Heidelberg publishing company *Das Wunderhorn* and head of the annual translator workshop *Poesie der Nachbarn. Dichter übersetzen Dichter* as well as editor of the series of the same name and co-editor of Reihe P. Hans Thill is officer for “Writers-for-Peace” on the Presiding Council of the German PEN.

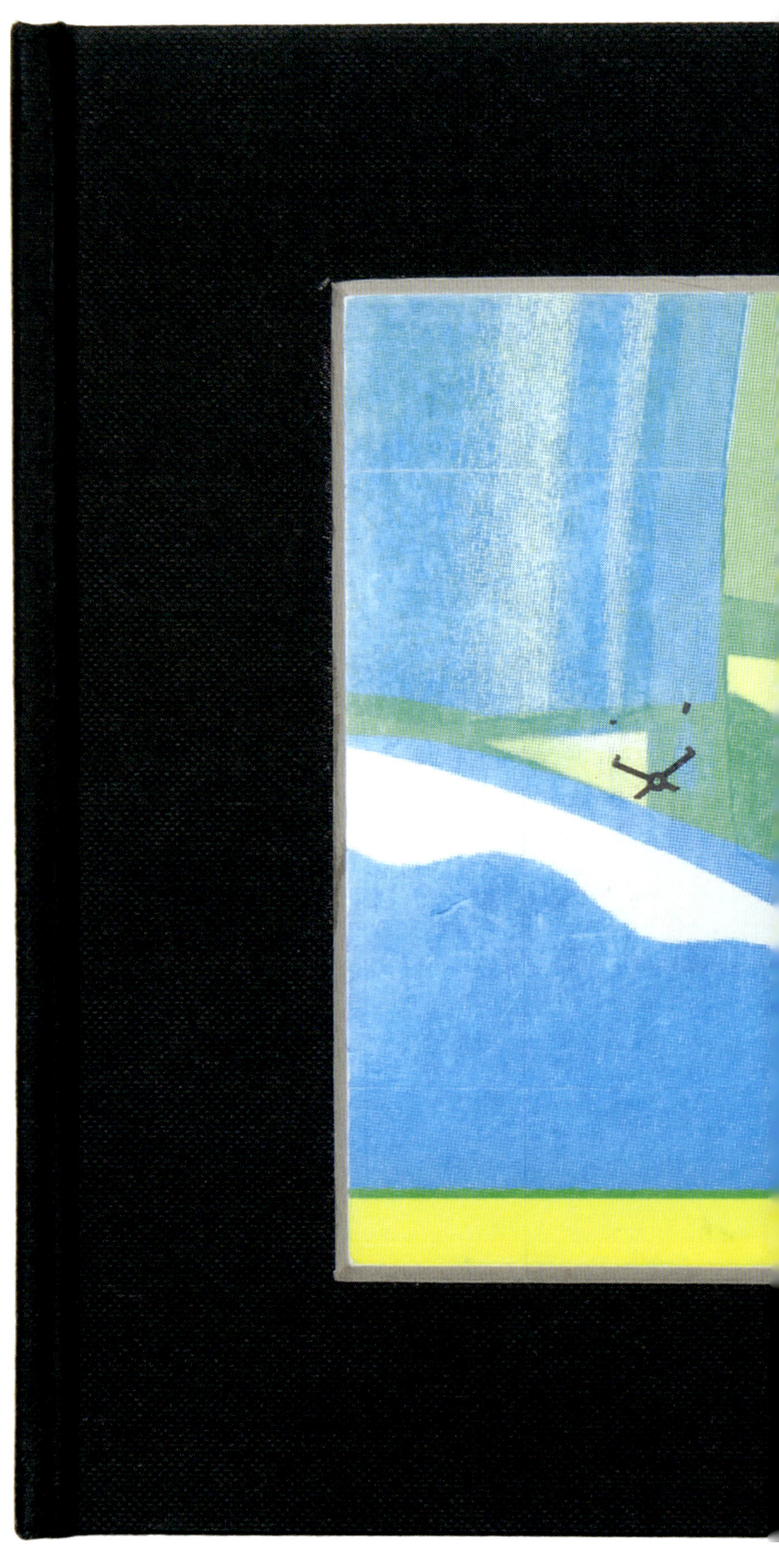

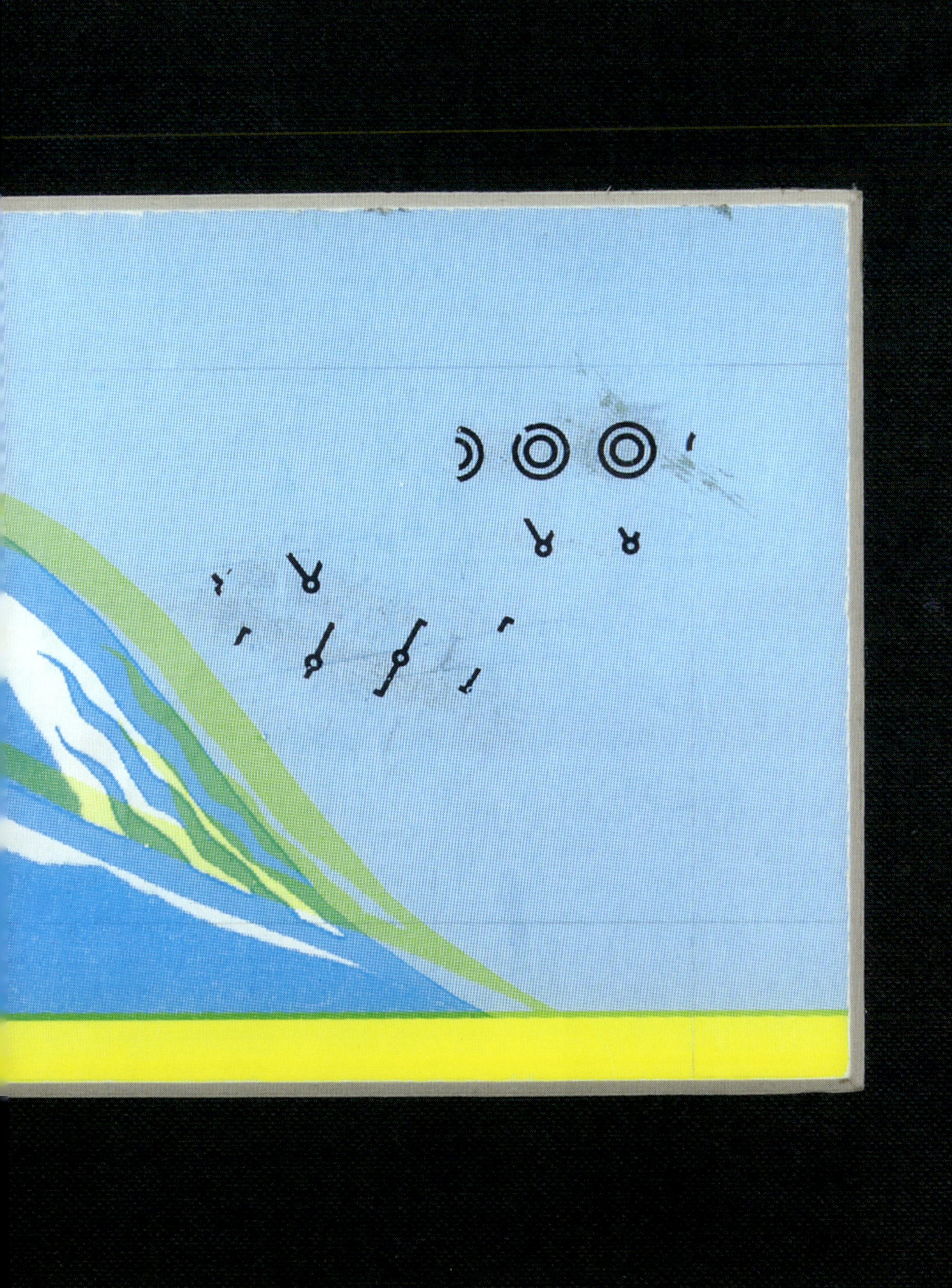

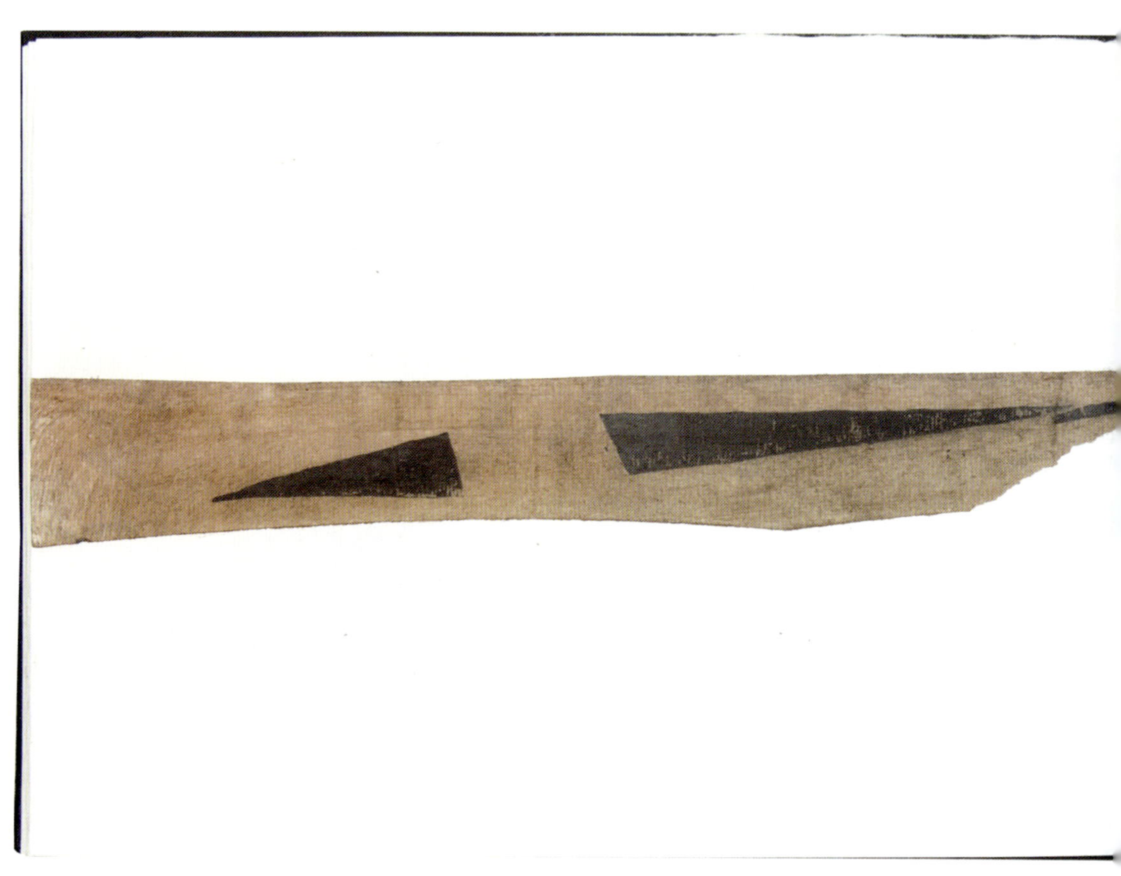

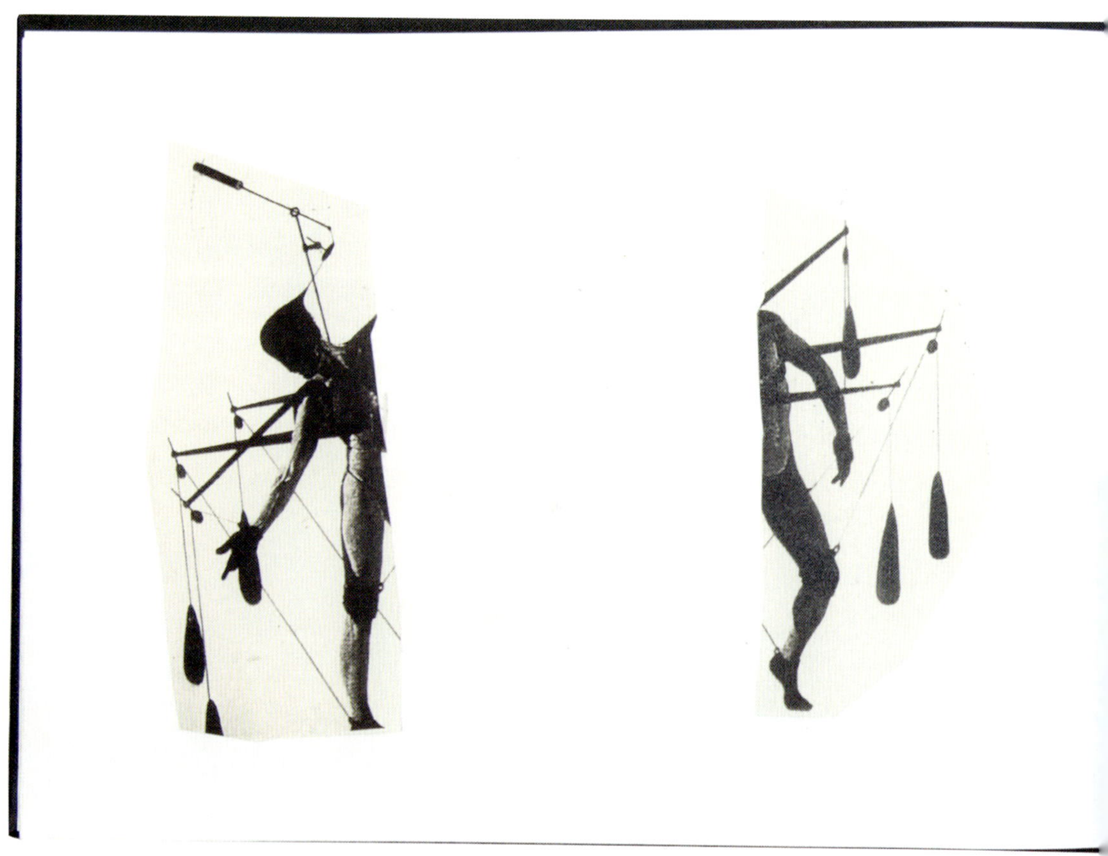

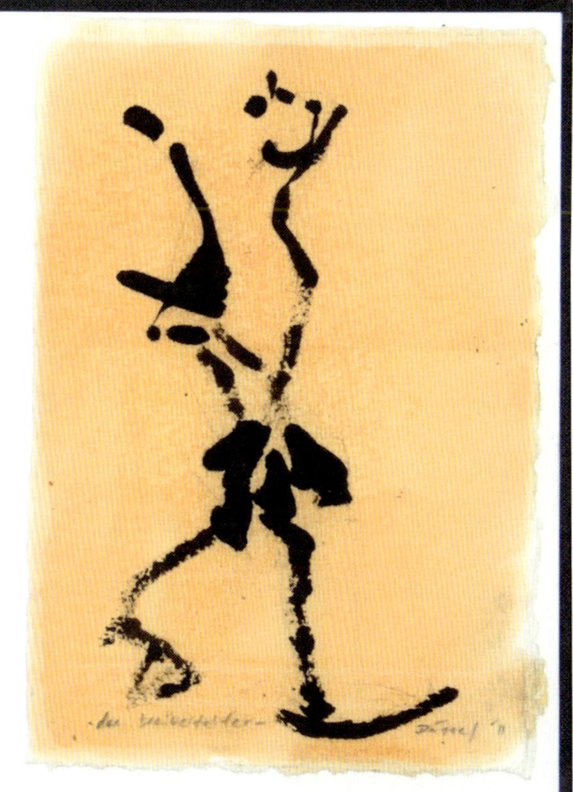

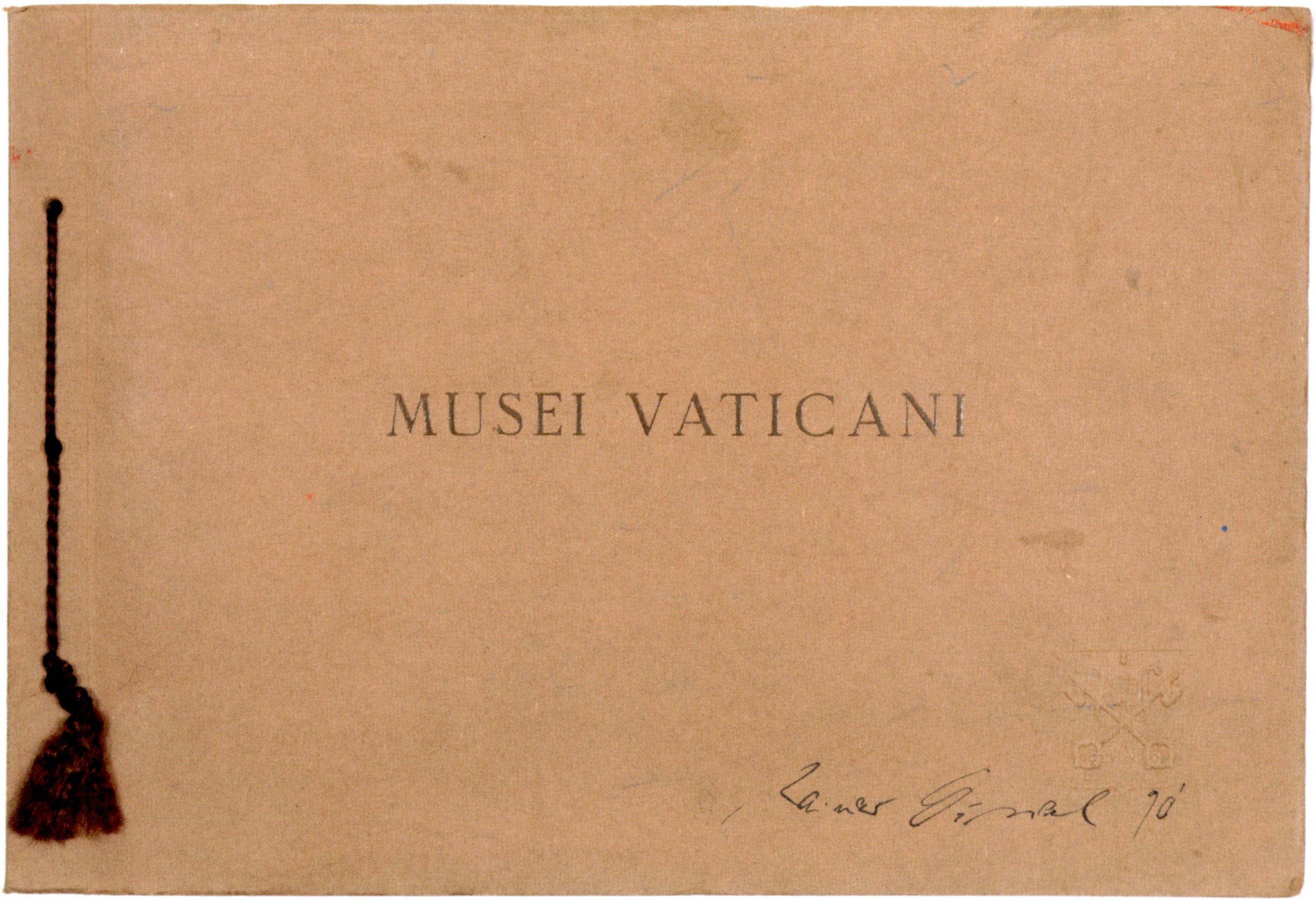

MUSEI VATICANI

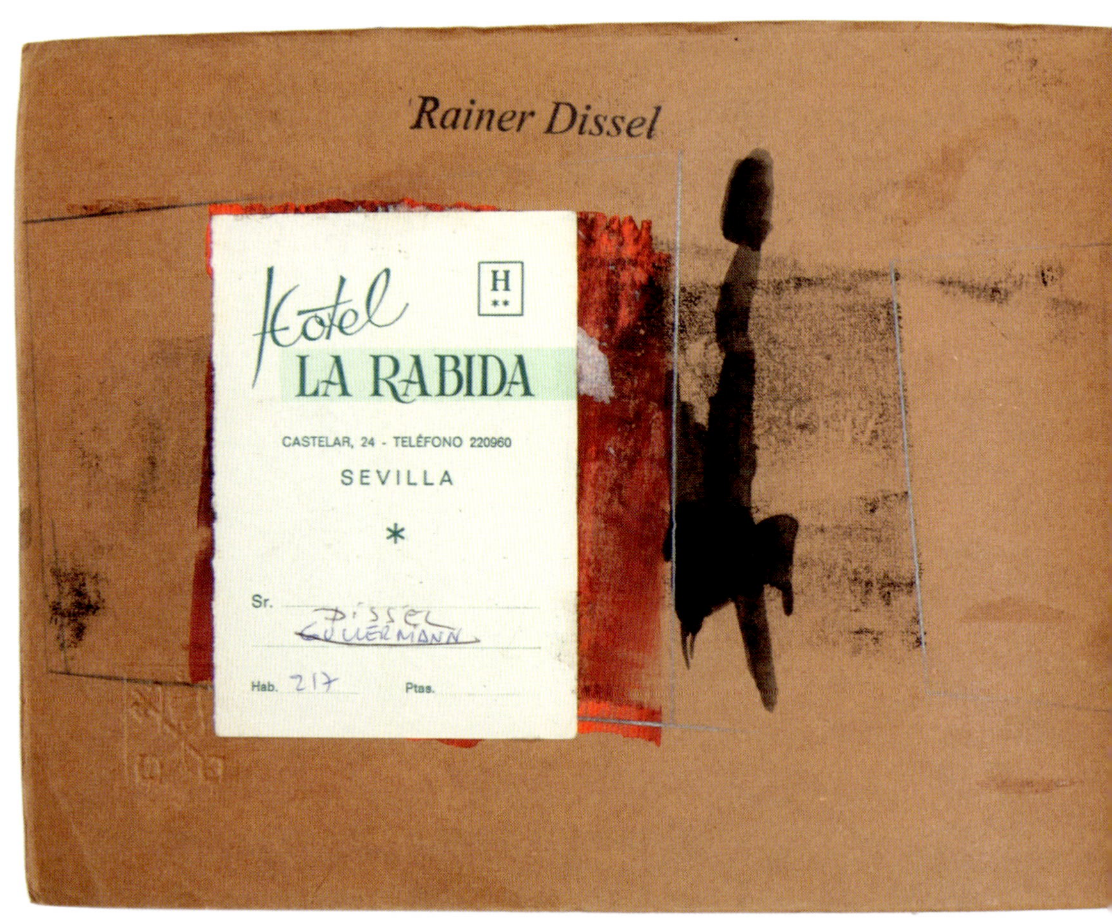

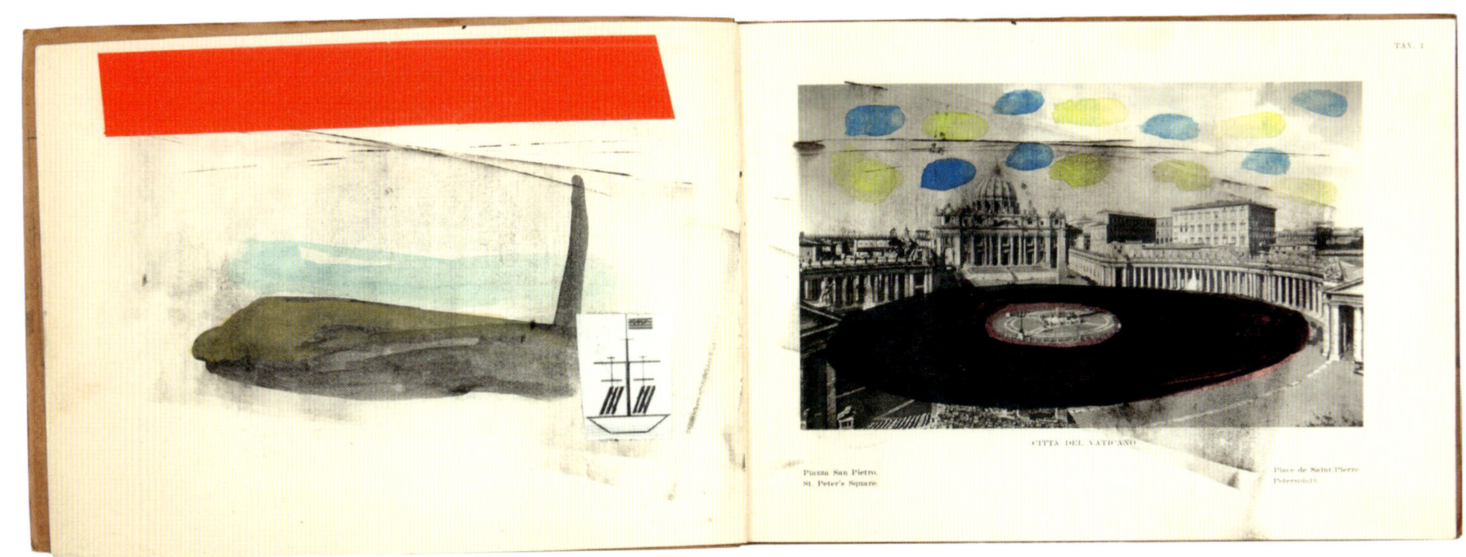
TAV. I
CITTA DEL VATICANO
Piazza San Pietro.
St. Peter's Square.
Place de Saint Pierre
Petersplatz

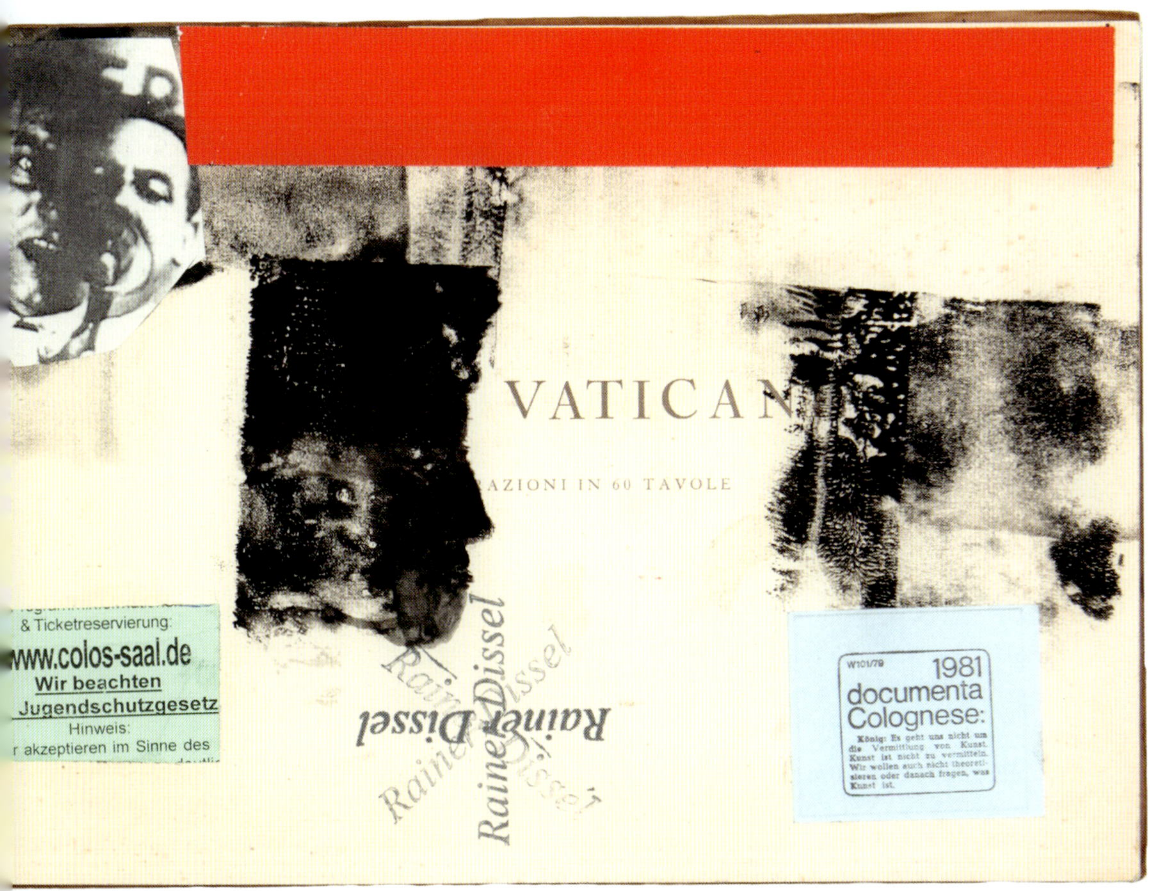
VATICAN
AZIONI IN 60 TAVOLE
& Ticketreservierung:
www.colos-saal.de
Wir beachten
Jugendschutzgesetz
Hinweis:
r akzeptieren im Sinne des
Rainer Dissel
Rainer Dissel
Rainer Dissel
W101/79
1981
documenta
Colognese:
König: Es geht uns nicht um die Vermittlung von Kunst. Kunst ist nicht zu vermitteln. Wir wollen auch nicht theoretisieren oder danach fragen, was Kunst ist.

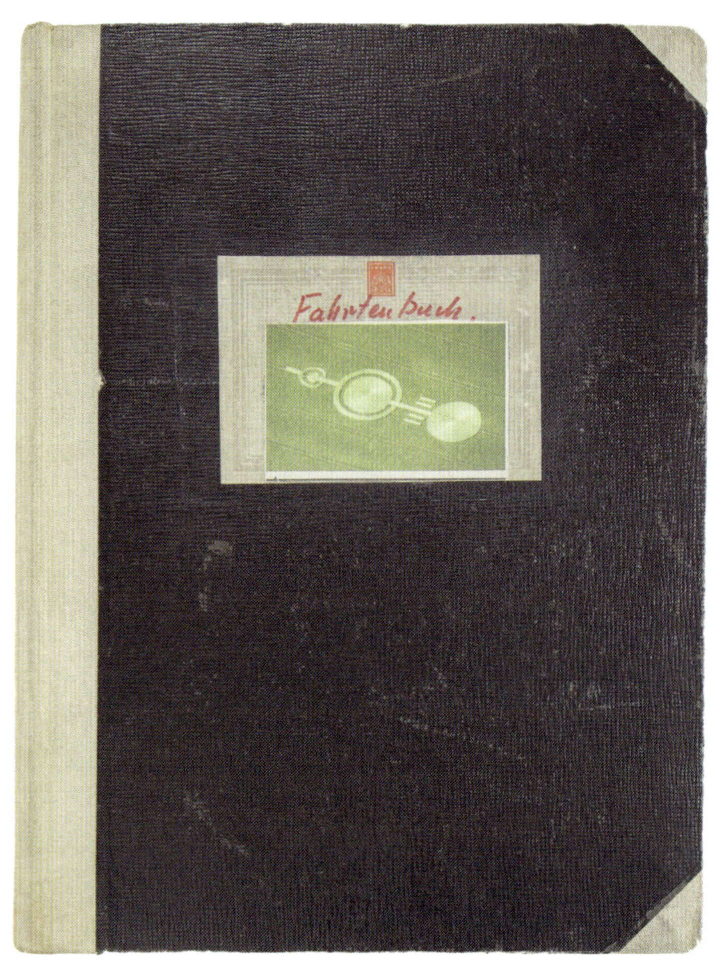
Fahrtenbuch.

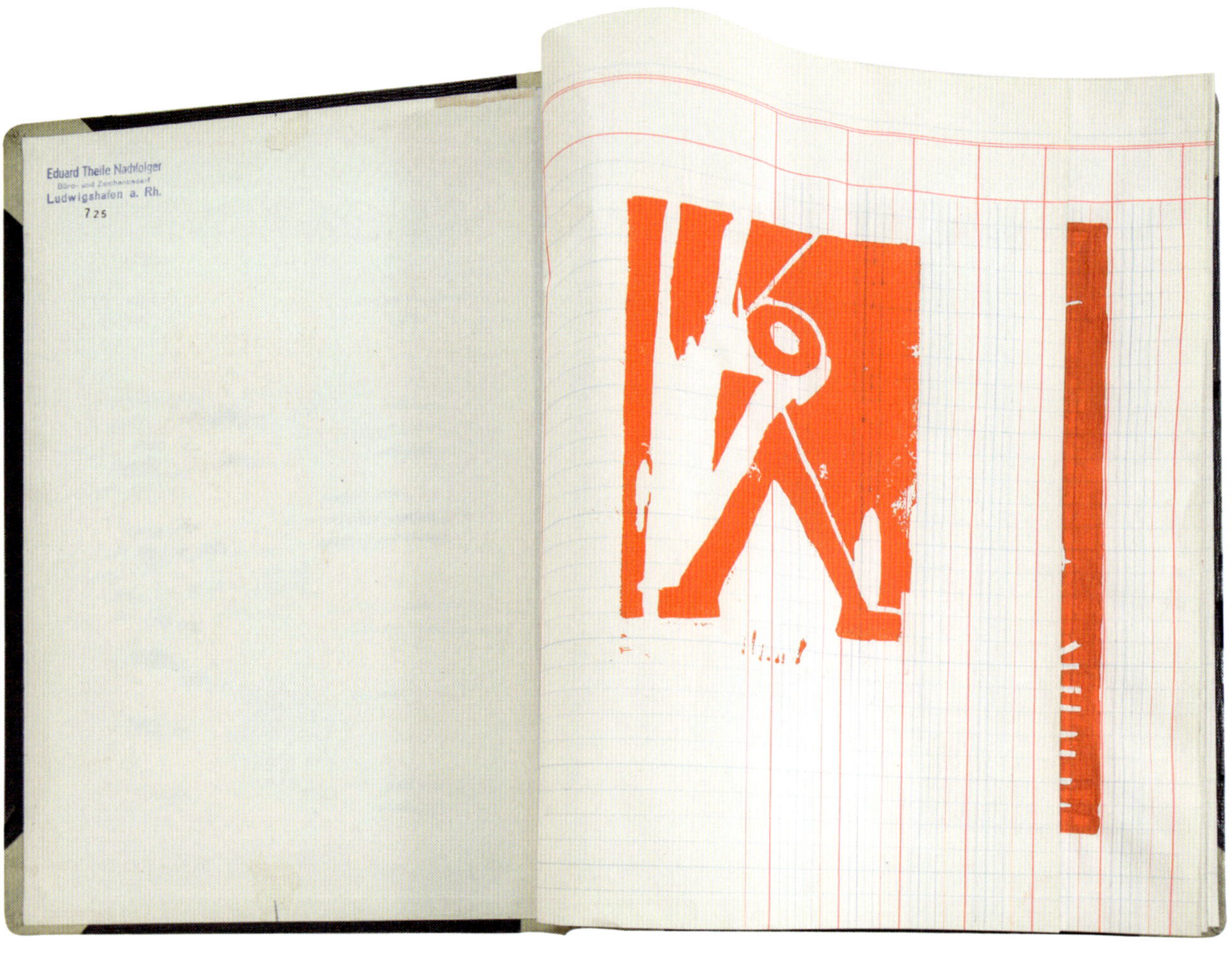

Eduard Theile Nachfolger
Büro- und Zeichenbedarf
Ludwigshafen a. Rh.
7.25

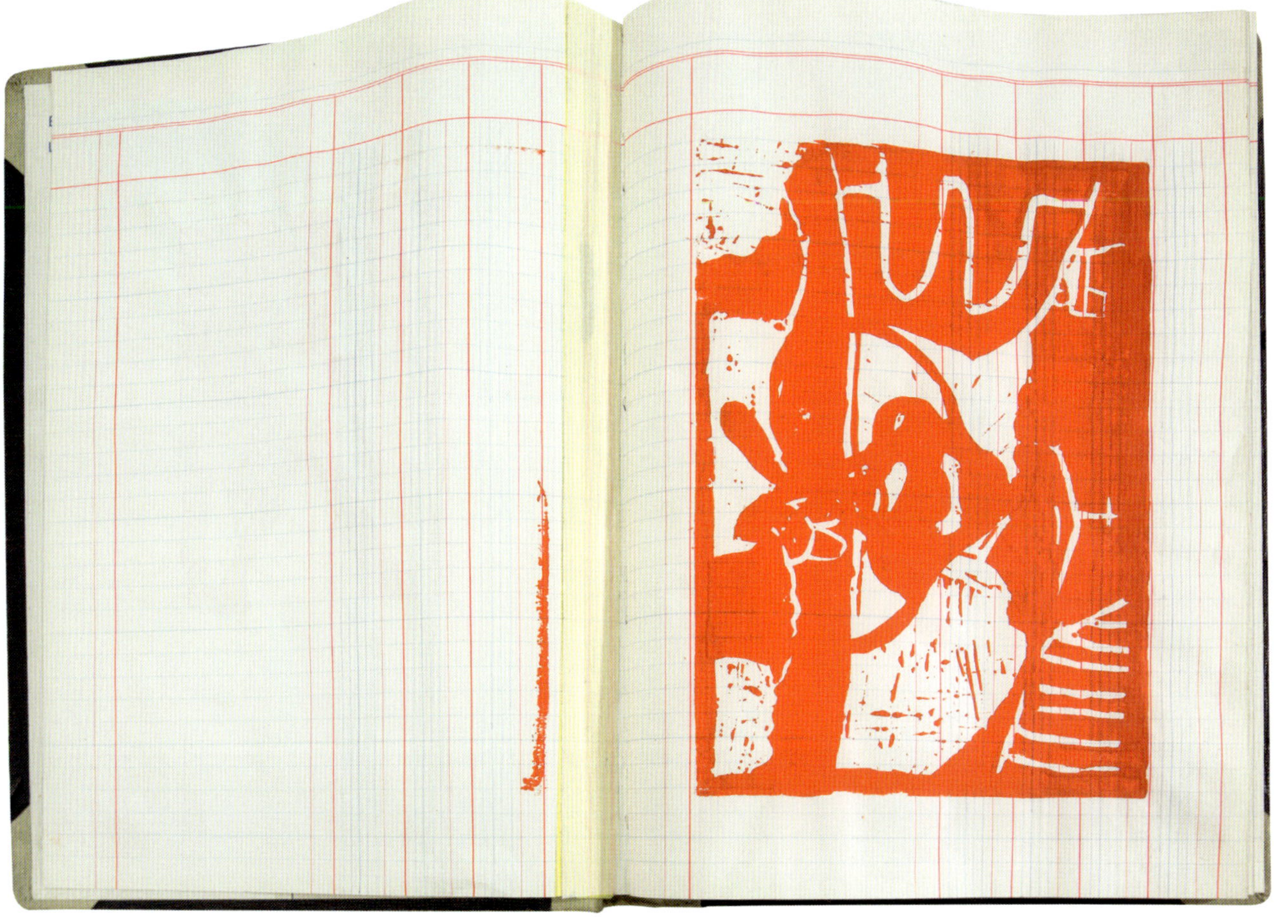

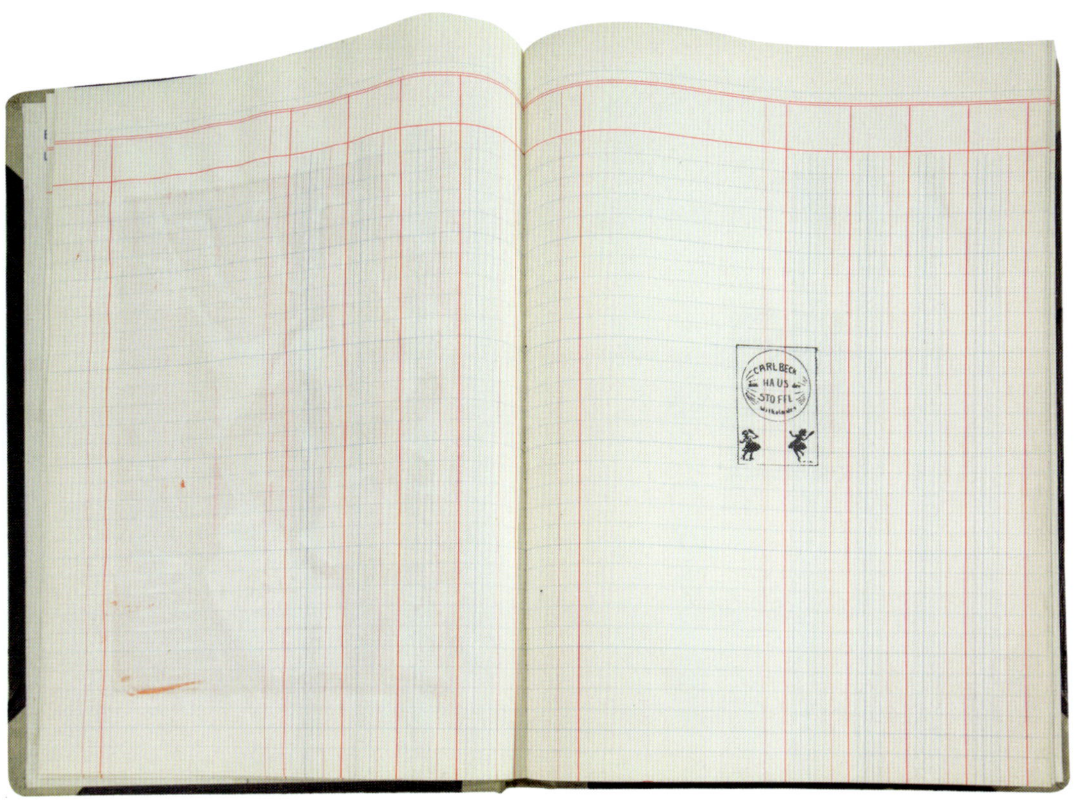
CARL BECK
HAUS
STOFFL

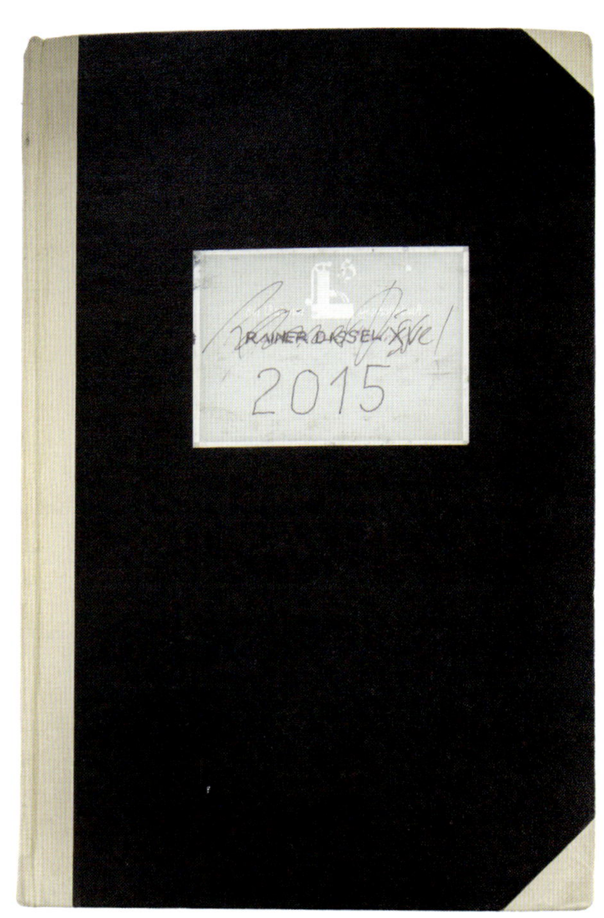
RAINER DIESEL
2015

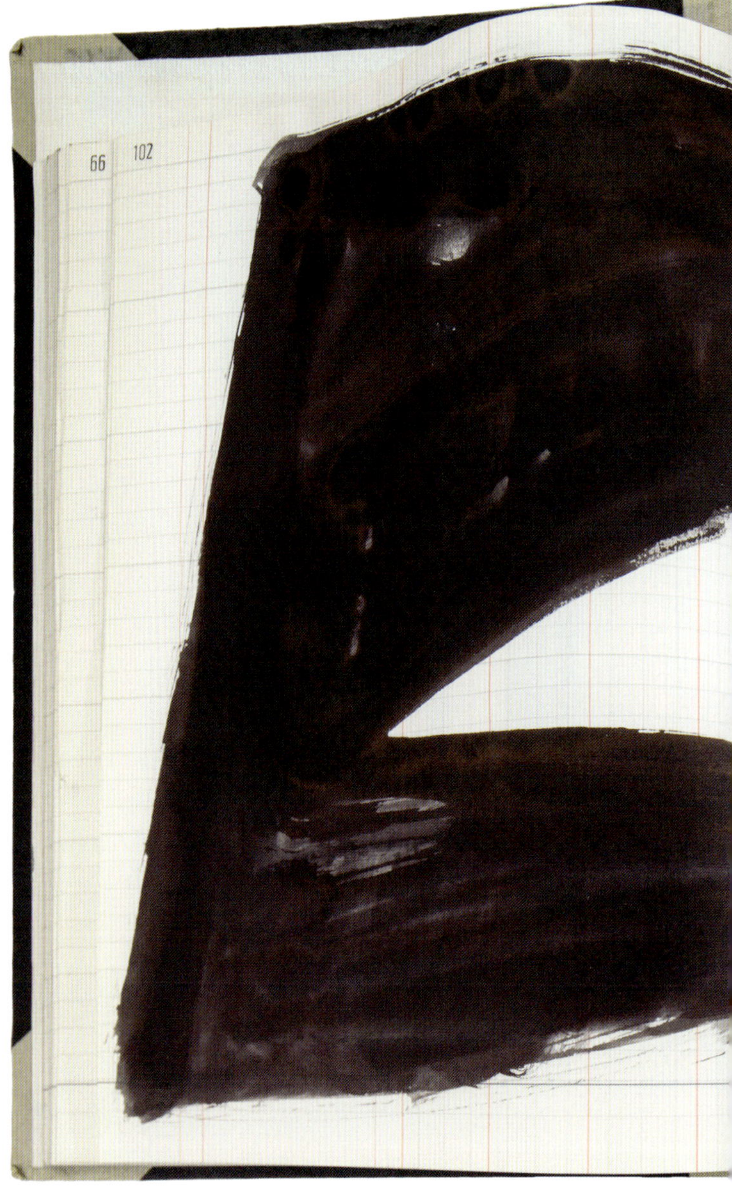
66
102

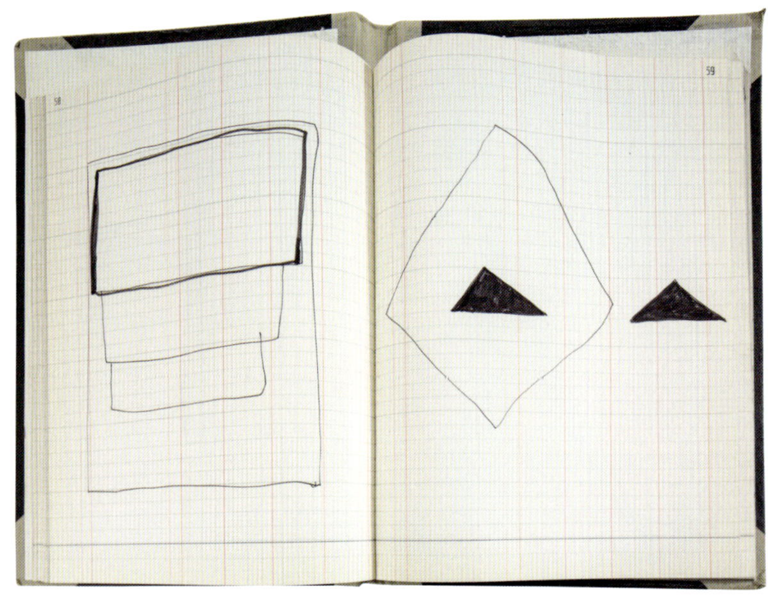

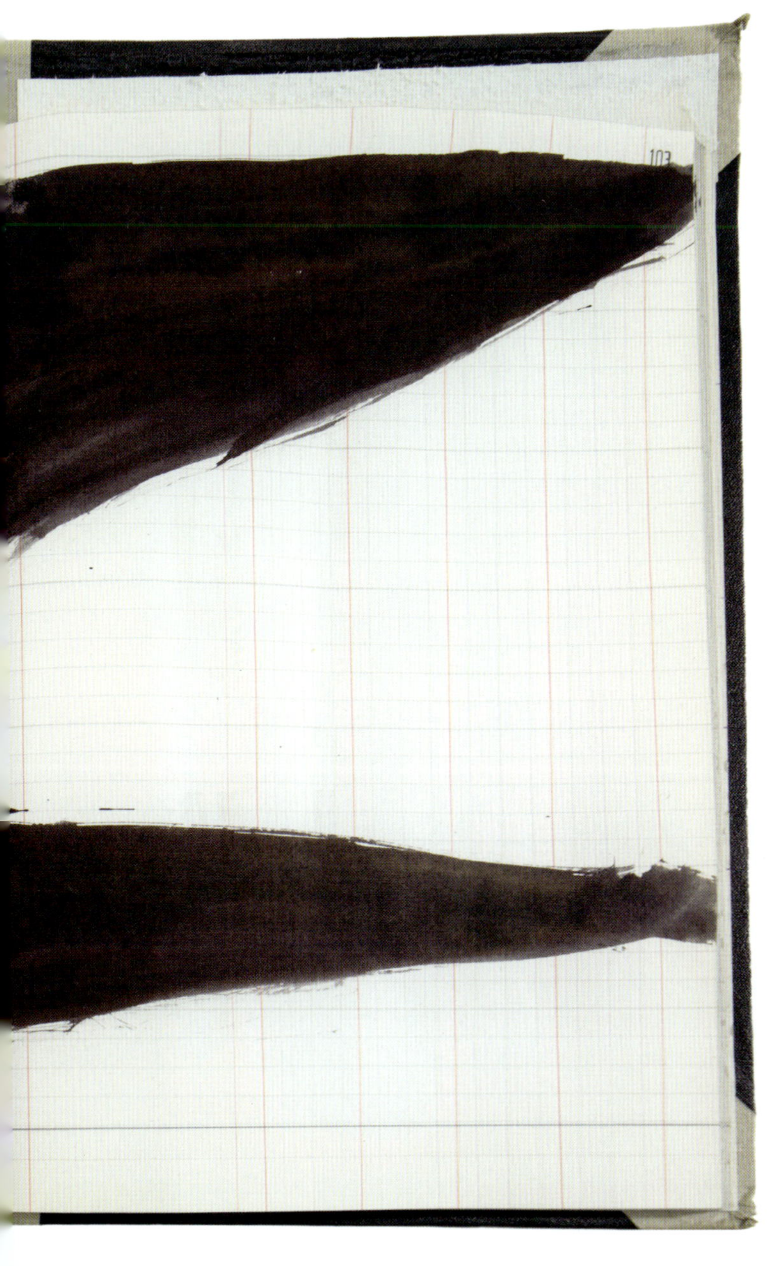

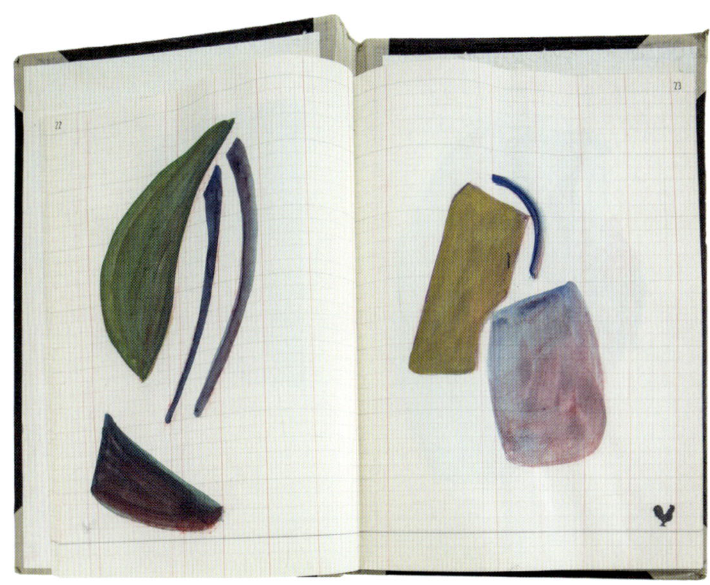

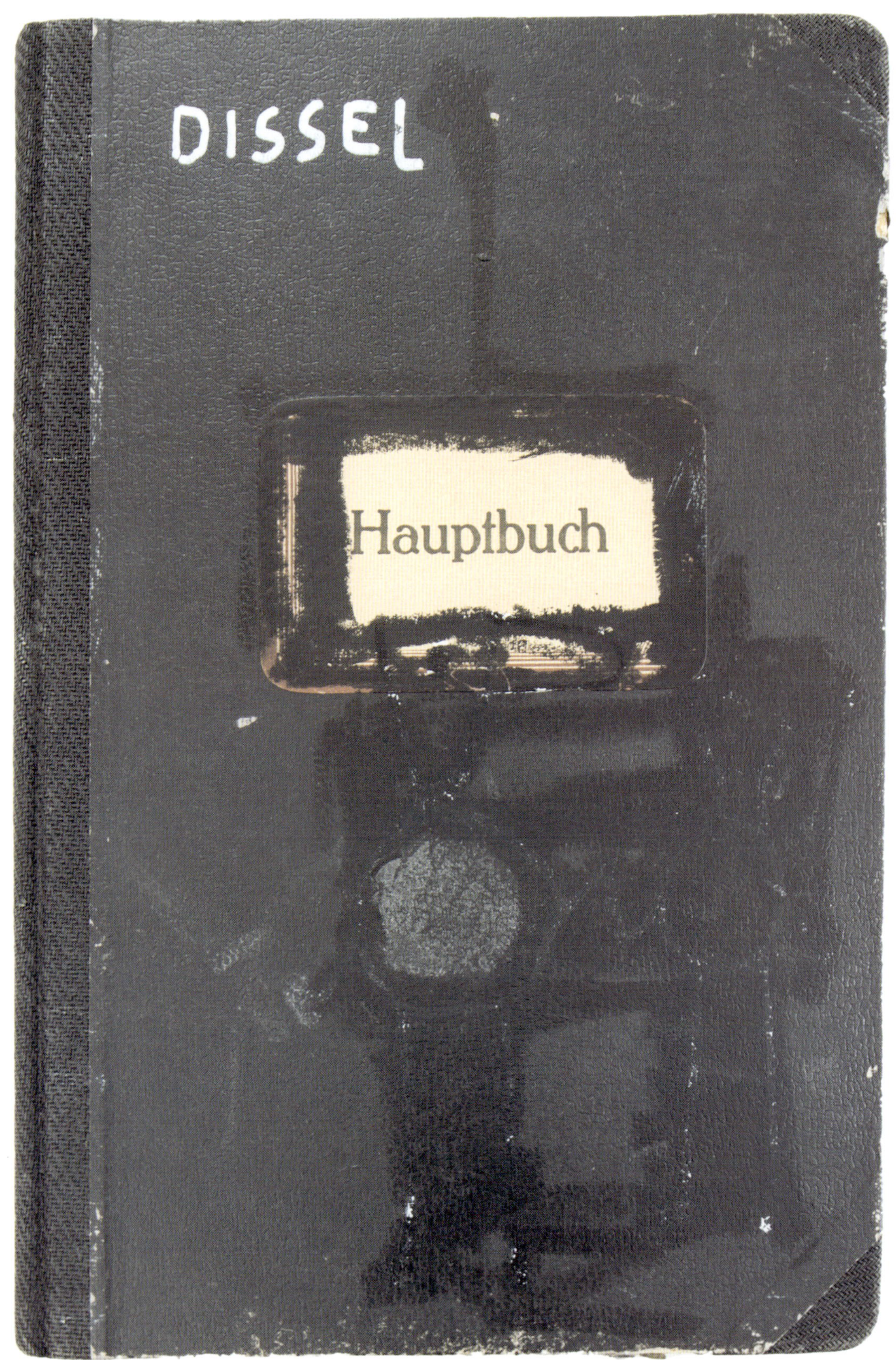
DISSEL
Hauptbuch

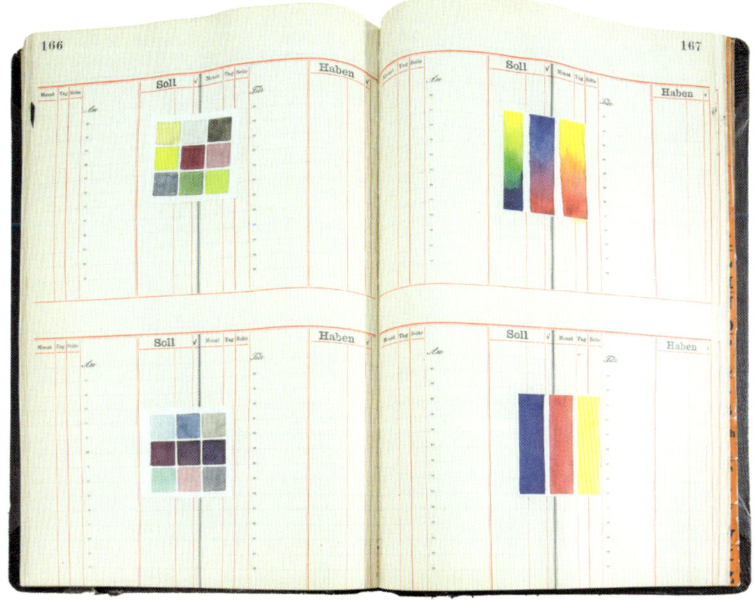
166
167
Soll
Haben

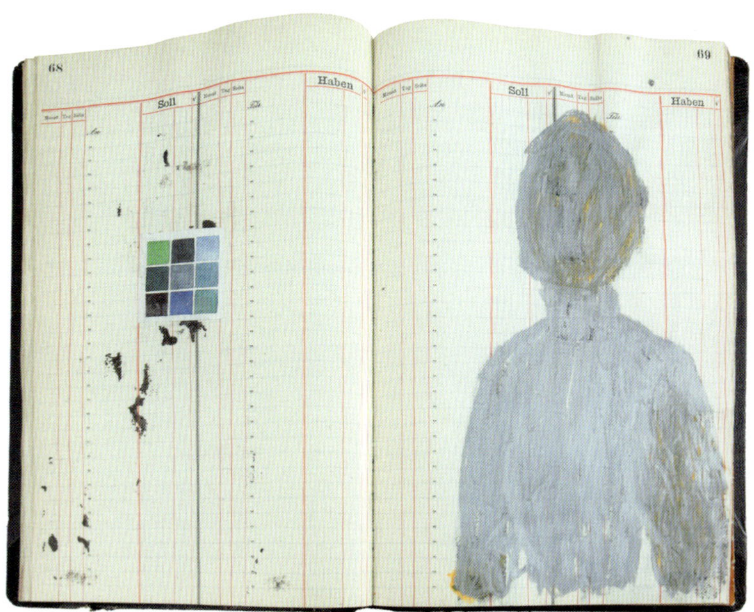
68
69
Soll
Haben

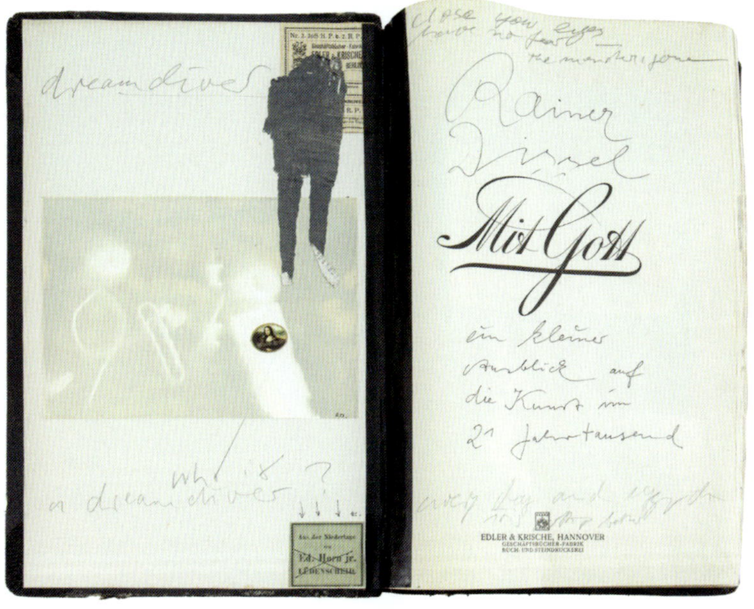
dream diver
Mit Gott
ein kleiner Ausblick auf die Kunst im 21 Jahrtausend
EDLER & KRISCHE, HANNOVER

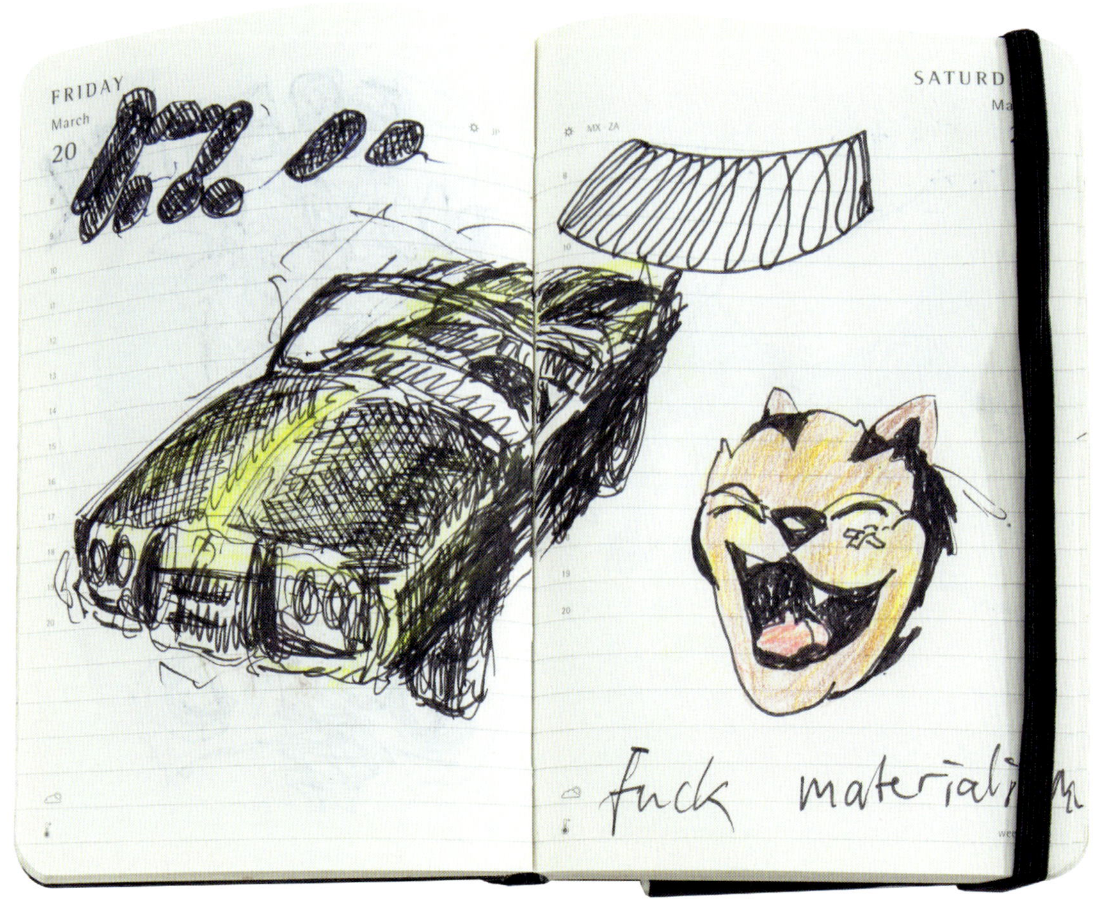
FRIDAY
March
20
SATURD
fuck materialism

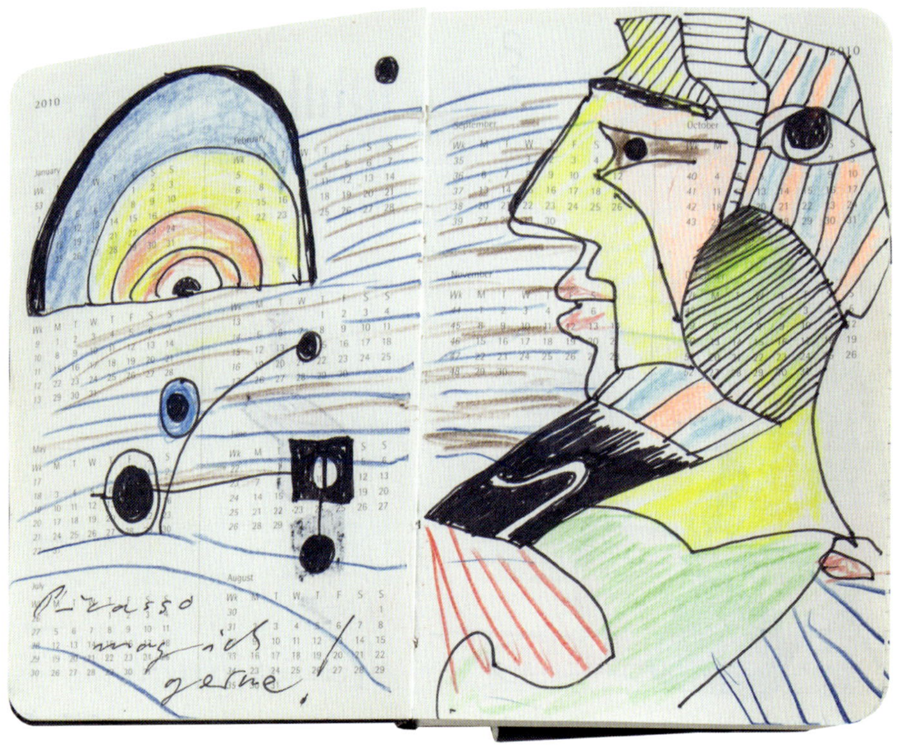
2010
Picasso
mag ich
gerne.

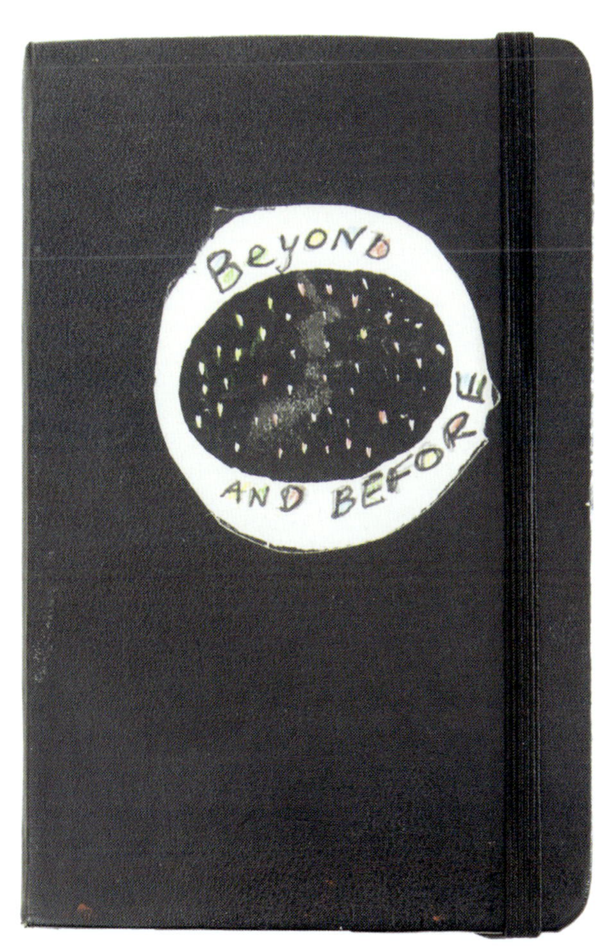
Beyond
AND BEFORE

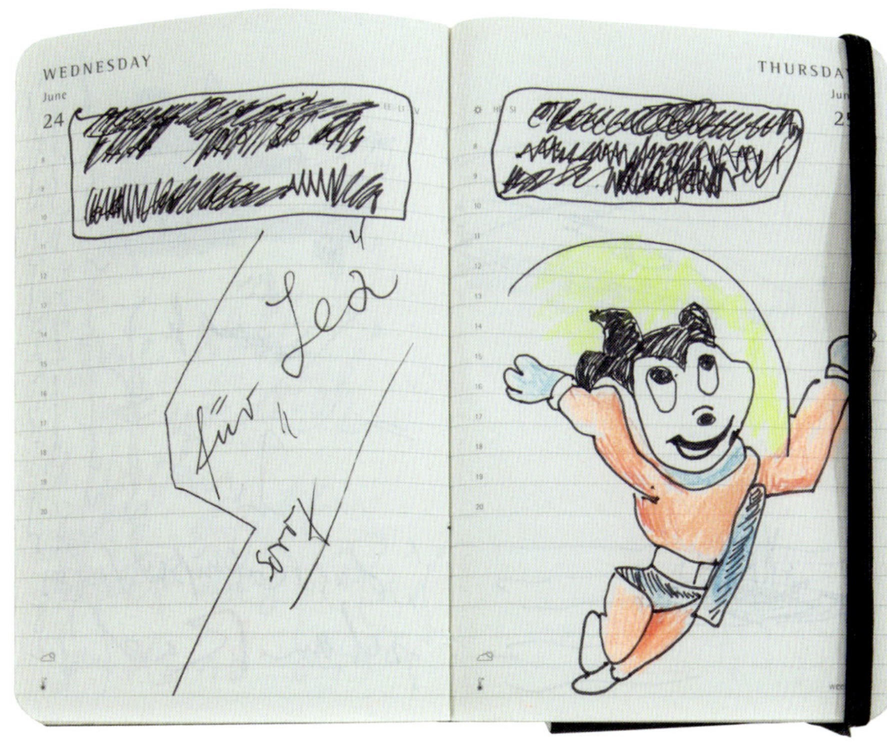
WEDNESDAY
June
24
THURSDAY
25
für Lea
sorry

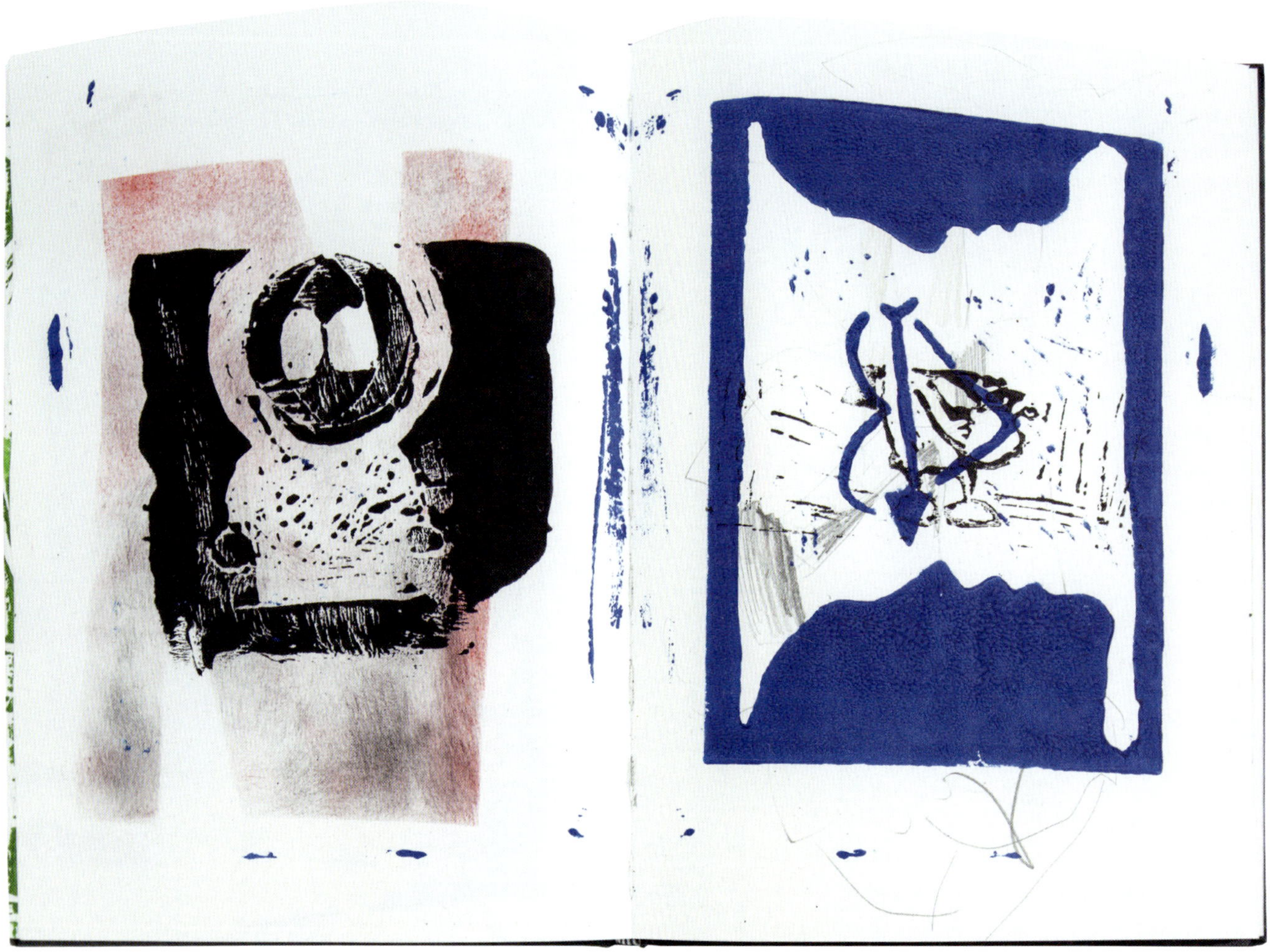

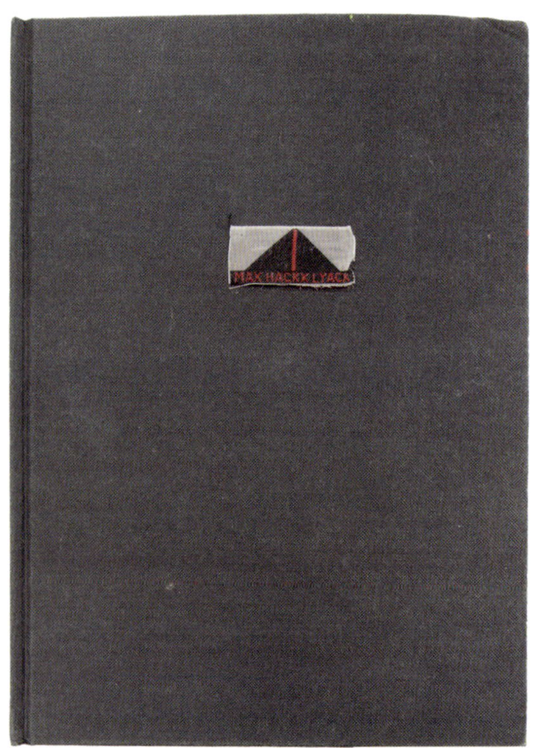

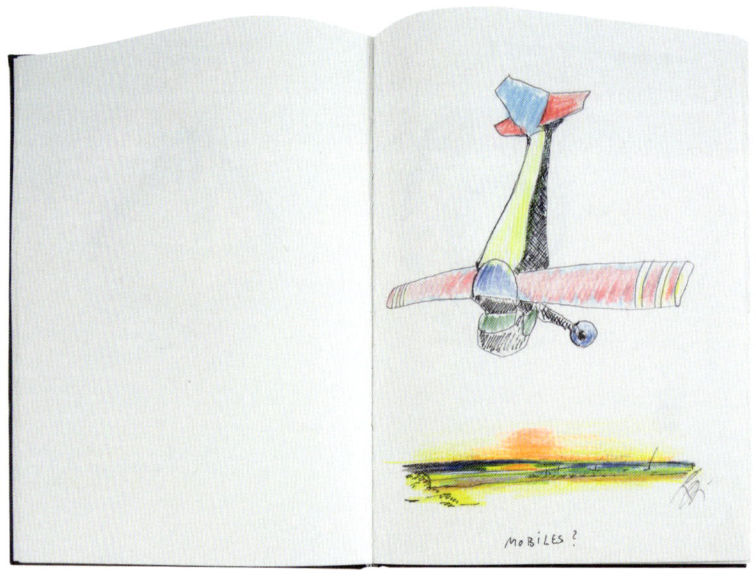
MOBILES ?

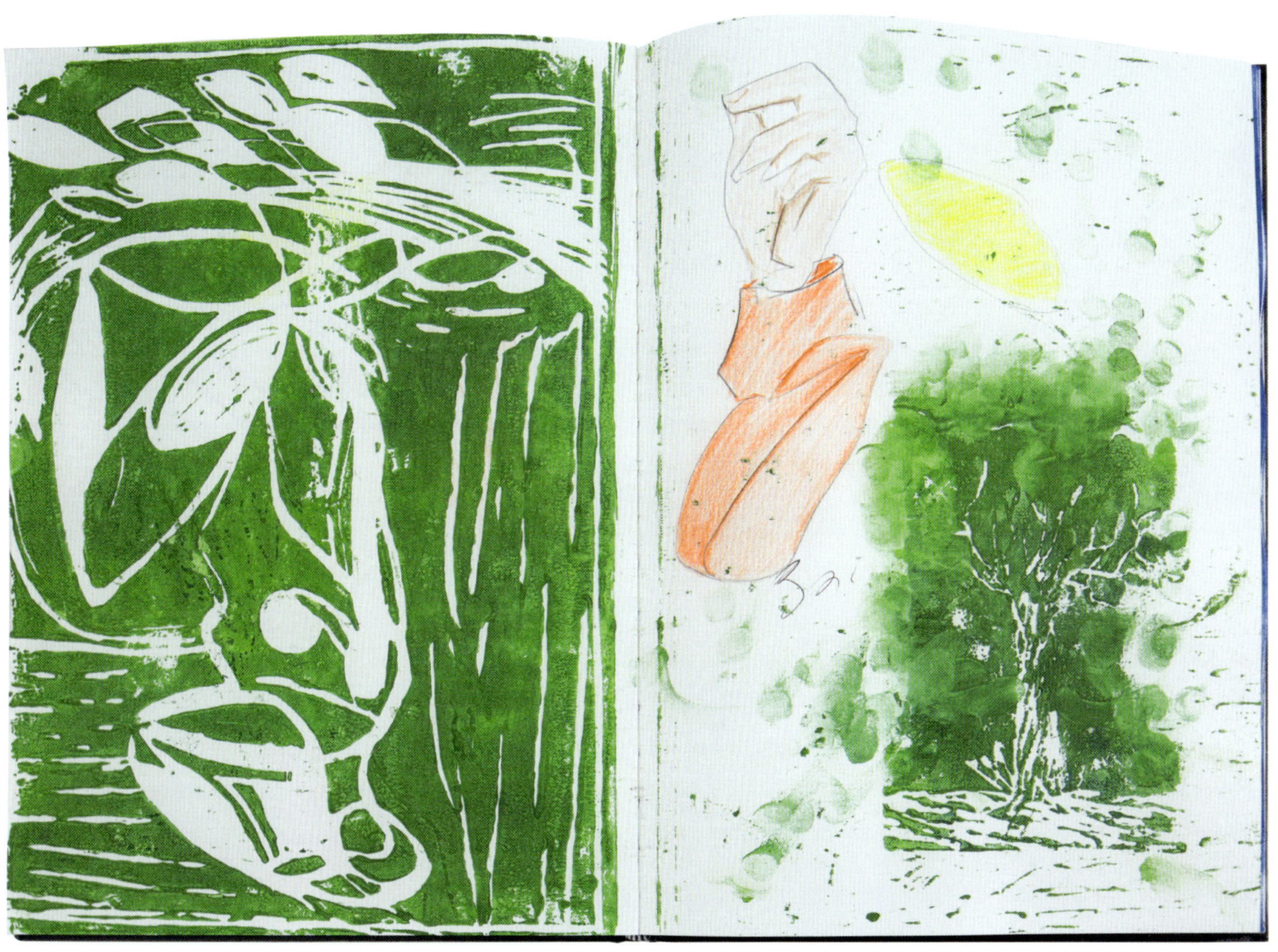

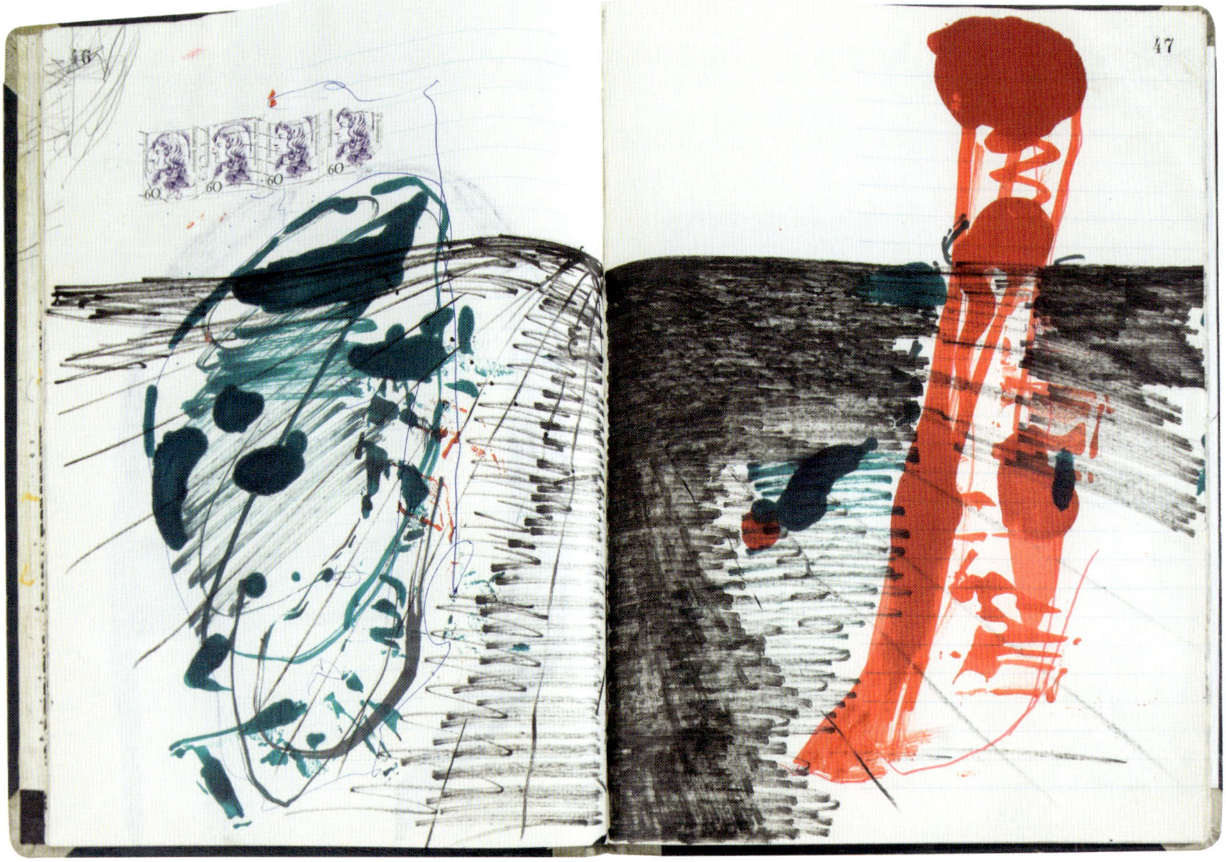

46

47

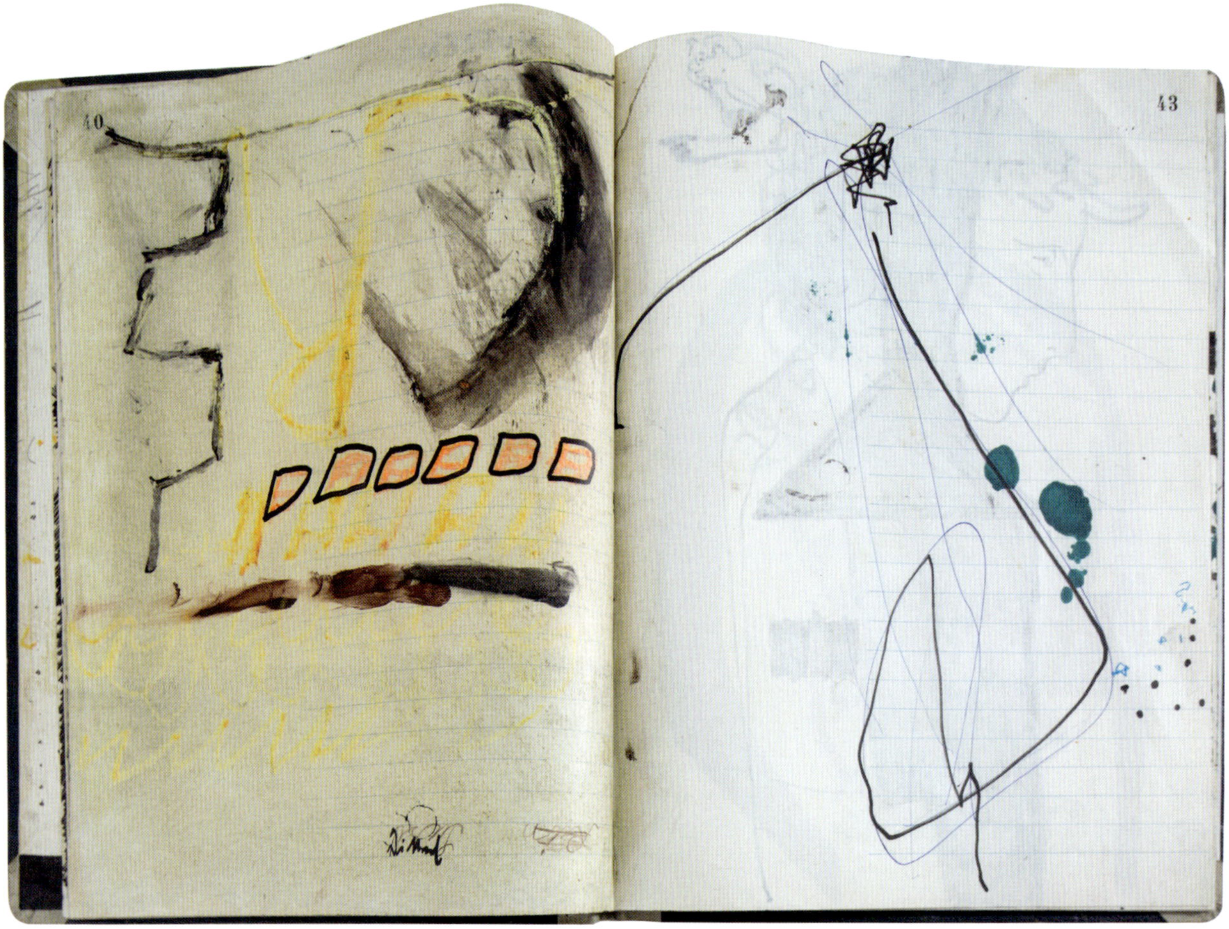

40

43

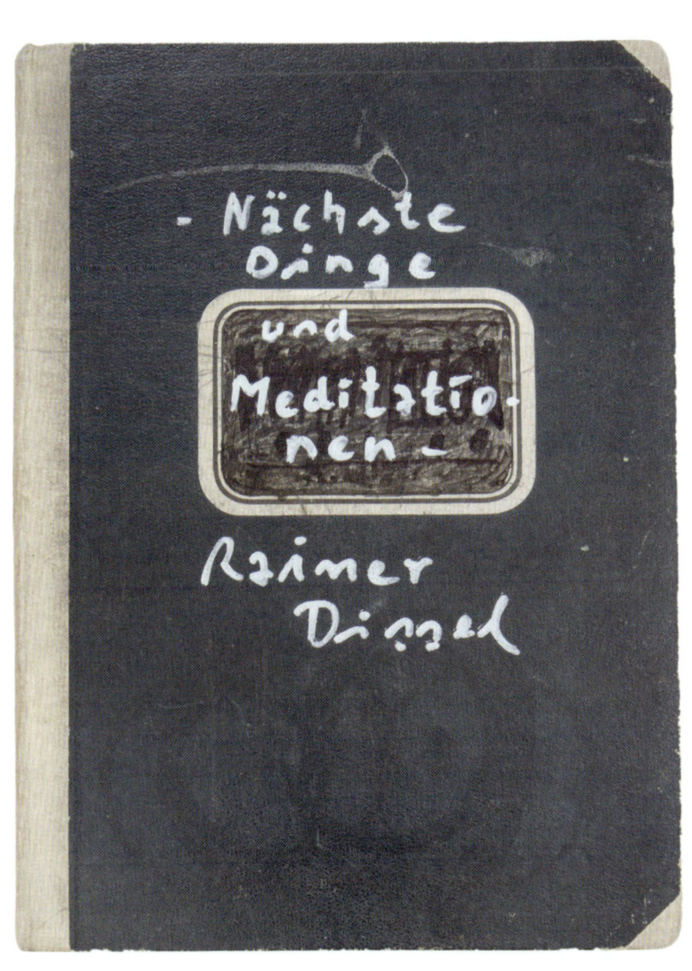
- Nächste
Dinge
und
Meditatio-
nen -
Rainer
Dissel

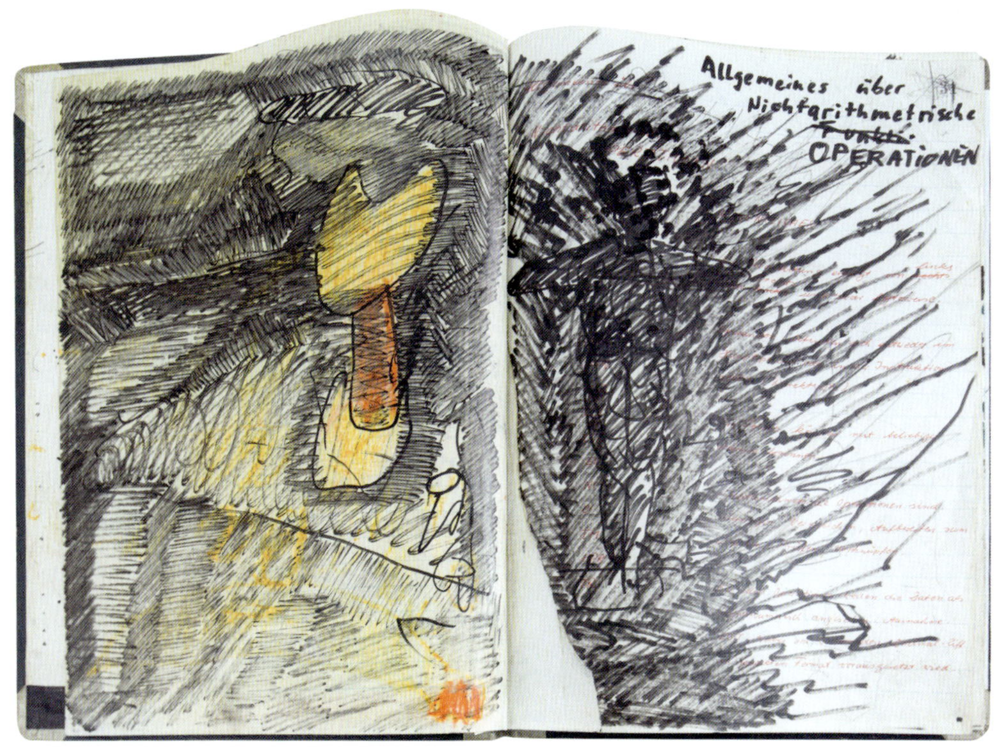
Allgemeines über
Nichtarithmetrische
OPERATIONEN

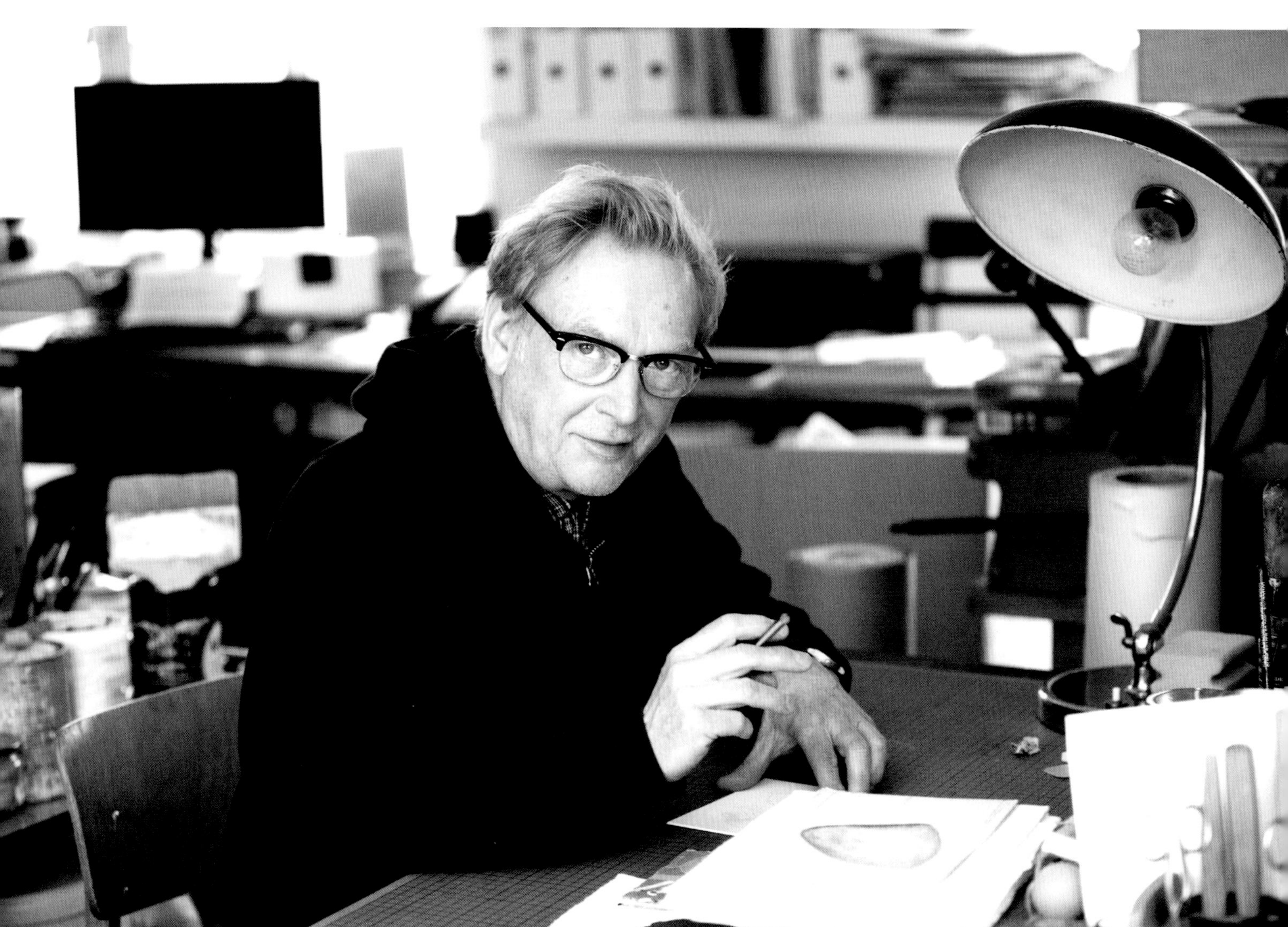

RAINER DISSEL

1975-1976 Grundstudium an der Hochschule für Gestaltung (HfG) Offenbach /
basic studies at the University of Art and Design (HfG) Offenbach

1976/77-1980 Studium an der Staatlichen Hochschule für Bildende Künste – Städelschule, Frankfurt/Main bei Thomas Bayrle und Johann Geyger /
studies at the Academy of Fine Arts, Frankfurt/Main under Thomas Bayrle and Johann Geyger

1981 Abschluss in freier Malerei und Grafik an der Staatlichen Hochschule für Bildende Künste – Städelschule, Frankfurt/Main (Meisterschüler) /
graduation in free painting and graphics at the Academy of Fine Arts, Frankfurt/Main (masterclass student)

Rainer Dissel lebt und arbeitet als freiberuflicher Künstler im Raum Frankfurt/Main und ist zudem in der Lehre tätig. Bis 2013 war er verheiratet mit der Künstlern Annegret Emrich, er hat eine Tochter. /
Rainer Dissel lives near Frankfurt/Main where he works and lives as an artist and art teacher. He was married to the artist Annegret Emrich until 2013. He has one daughter.

Preise · Stipendien / grants

1985 Berlin, Galeriestipendium
1985 Nominierung Schmidt-Rottluff Stipendium
1985 RischArt-Preis, München
1987 Nominierung Lehmbruck-Stipendium
1986-1991 Auslandsaufenthalt, Galeriestipendium Boston (USA)
1987-1990 Darmstädter Sezession (auf Einladung / at invitation)

Messebeteiligungen / fairs

Erste Frankfurter Kunstmesse
Art Zürich

Art Miami
Chicago Art Fair
Art Cologne
Art Nürnberg
ICAF, Los Angeles
Artexpo New York

Permanente Sammlungen / permanent collections

Museum Schweinfurt
Fraunhoferinstitut Darmstadt
Museum of Contemporary Art, Miami
Museum Berger, Amorbach
Stadt Freudenberg
Stadt Freiburg (Brsg.)
Reiffeisen Volksbank Aschaffenburg
Sammlung Henkel, Düsseldorf
ehem. Sammlung Rolf Dittmar, Wiesbaden
Hochheimer Kunstsammlung, Villa Burgeff

Ausgewählte Ausstellungen / exhibitions

Städelmuseum, Frankfurt/Main; Galerie Thieme, Darmstadt (1981)
Haus der Kunst, München; Galerie Phönix, Würzburg; Marielies-Hess-Stiftung HR, Frankfurt/Main (1982)
Nationalgalerie, Berlin; Galerie Thieme, Darmstadt (1983)
Kunsthalle Düsseldorf; Haus der Kunst, München; Galerie Leithold, Würzburg und Galerie Thieme, Darmstadt (1984)
Darmstädter Sezession Jahresausstellung, Darmstadt; Hartje Gallery, Boston (1985)
HEAG Halle, Darmstadt; Kunsthaus Wiesbaden; Galerie Hähnel, Frankfurt/M. und Hartje Gallery Boston (1986)
Lehmbruckmuseum, Duisburg; Darmstädter Sezession, Darmstadt; Galerie Kraushaar Düsseldorf (1987)

Museum of Contemporary Art Krakau (MOCAK); Darmstädter Sezession, Darmstadt (1988/89)
Fraunhofer Institut, Darmstadt; Hartje Gallery Boston/Frankfurt und Galerie Thieme, Darmstadt (1990)
Museum/Städtische Sammlungen Schweinfurt, Schweinfurt; Museum Berger, Amorbach und Galerie Menzel, Berlin (1991)
Art Nürnberg 7, Forum für aktuelle Kunst (1992)
Galerie Menzel, Berlin (1995)
IG Metall, Mannheim (1996)
Städtische Galerie Freudenberg (1997)
Museum Schweinfurt, Städtische Galerie (1998)
Preis der Sparkasse Esslingen-Nürtingen; IGMetall, Frankfurt/Main (1999)
Galerie Hufgard, Aschaffenburg (2000)
Airport Conference Center, Frankfurt/Main (2001)
Gesamtausgestaltung Kundenzentrum RV-Bank eG, Aschaffenburg (2003)
Museum KunstWerk, Walldürn (2005)
Galerie Cornelissen, Wiesbaden (2006)
Hochheimer Kunstsammlung Villa Burgeff (2007)
Kunstverein Kirchzarten - Freiburg (2008/9)
Remisengalerie Schloss Phillipsruhe, Hanau (2010/11 und 2012)
Kunst in Konstanz, Konstanz (2014)
Preventon, Frankfurt/Main (2015)
Torrance Art Museum, Torrance California (USA) (2016)

Medienbeiträge / media

Reportage zu Rainer Dissel in: Aspekte, ZDF- Mainz, 5. Januar 1990.

Ausstellungskataloge / exhibition catalogues

- Doppelganger, Torrance Art Museum, 2016
- Macht, PreventOn, Frankfurt/Main, 2015, S. 6 und 18-19.
- 4. Kunstpreis der Industriegewerkschaft Metalle, Miteinander Leben und Arbeiten,

Metallgalerie Frankfurt, 1.11.1999-1.12.1999, S. 18.
- Morbus Alzheimer – Bilder einer vergessenen Ausstellung, Heidelberg, 1997 (Hrsg. zus. mit A. Emrich).
- Zukunft der Arbeit – Arbeit der Zukunft, Hrsg. IG Metall Mannheim, 1995, o. S.
- Katalog Art Nürnberg 7, Forum für aktuelle Kunst - Copy Connection - Tendenz - Grenzenlos - Kommunikation, Nürnberg, 09.-12. April 1992, S. 90-91.
- Rainer Dissel. Bilder einer Ausstellung – Städtische Sammlung Schweinfurt, Schweinfurter Museumsschriften, Heft 34/1991.27.
- Ausstellung der Darmstädter Sezession - Schwarzweiß in der Fläche - Farbe im Raum, 1991, S. 36-37.
- Rainer Dissel, Katalog zur Ausstellung 01-02 1986, Hartje Gallery, Frankfurt a. M.
- Thesaurus - Bilder und Zeichnungen : Rainer Dissel et al., Galerie Parterre, Darmstadt, 1985, S.1-8.
- RischArt Preis, Bilder im Vorbeigehen mit Texten von Dr. Helmut Friedel und Gerhard Müller Rischart, München 1985, o. S.
- Marielies-Hess-Stiftung, Hessischer Rundfunk, Frankfurt am Main, 1982.
- Neue Malerei aus Deutschland, München, 1982.

Zeitschriftenbeiträge · Besprechungen / journal articles

Critica-Zeitschrift für Philosophie und Kunsttheorie, Ausg. II/2013, S. 36-37.
Brink – Zwischen Kunst und Wissenschaft, Ausg. 2/2012, S. 42-43.
Artforum USA: Cambridge Rainer Dissel, Besprechung v. Nancy Stapen, Ausg. Nov 1986, S.133.
Zahreiche Ausstellungsbesprechungen in nationalen und internationalen Tageszeitungen (u.a. Boston Globe, Frankfurter Rundschau, Frankfurter Allgemeine, Badische Zeitung, Wiesbadener Kurier, Main-Echo)

Lexikonartikel print / encyclopedia articles

Bildende Kunst im Spessart. Ein Lexikon, Hanau, 2009.

WERKVERZEICHNIS / CATALOGUE OF WORKS

P.018 Distanz, Collage auf Baumwolle, Gaze, Nessel, Papier, Öl- und Acrylfarbe, 70 x 90 cm, 2014 / Distanz, collage on canvas, gauze, calico, paper, oil and acrylic paint, 27,5 x 35 inch., 2014

P.019 Hindernissparcours, Ölfarbe, Stoff, Papier auf Baumwollsegeltuch, 72 x 102cm, 2014 / Obstacle cours, oil paint, cloth, paper on cotton canvas, 28,3 x 40,1 inch., 2014

P.020 Ballungsanalyse, Collage, Bleistift auf Baumwollsegeltuch, 130 x 130 cm, 2014 / Cluster Analysis, collage and pencil on cotton canvas, 51,2 x 51,2 inch., 2014

P.023 Cours, Collage auf Leinwand, 41,5 x 51,5 cm, 2014 / Cours, collage on canvas, 16,3 x 20,3 inch., 2014

P.024 Handbuch, Collage und Eitempera auf Holz, 34 x 32,5 cm, 2014 / Hand Book, collage and egg tempera on wood, 13,4 x 12.6 inch., 2014

P.025 San Diego, Collage auf Baumwollsegeltuch, 71 x 71 cm, 2014 / San Diego, collage on cotton canvas, 28 x 28 inch., 2014

P.026 L'art decorative d'aujourdhui, Collage auf Leinwand, 52 x 52 cm, 2012/13 / L'art decorative d'aujourdhui, collage on canvas, 20,5 x 20,5 inch., 2012/13

P.028 Giza Pyramids, Collage, Tusche, Papier auf Leinwand, 30 x 30 cm, 2010 / Giza Pyramids, collage, ink, paper on canvas, 11,8 x 11,8 inch., 2010

P.031 MacBeth, Collage, Papier, Stoff, Pappe auf Baumwollsegeltuch, 30 x 24 cm, 2014 / MacBeth, collage, paper, cloth, cardboard on cotton canvas, 11,8 x 9,4 inch., 2014

P.032 Fort La Latte, Collage, Papier, Grundierung, Farbe auf Leinwand, 30 x 40 cm, 2013 / Fort La Latte, collage, paper, prime coat, color on canvas, 11,8 x 15,7 inch., 2014

P.034 o.T., Tusche, Eitempera, Papier auf Leinwand, 35 x 40 cm, 2001 / untitled, ink, egg tempera, paper on canvas, 13,8 x 15.7 inch., 2001

P.035 Vincent, Stoff, Gipsbandage, Acryl auf Leinwand, 28 x 25 cm, 2014 / Vincent, cloth, plaster bandage, acryl on canvas, 11 x 9,8 inch., 2014

P.037 Making our mark, Gummistempeldruck auf Holz, 25 x 25 cm, 2000 / Making our mark, rubber stamp print on wood, 9,8 x 9,8 inch., 2000

P.038 Erinnerung, Collage, Ölfarbe auf Baumwolle, 40 x 50 cm, 2014 / reminiscence, collage, oil paint on canvas, 15.7 x 19,7 inch., 2014

P.040 Goldener Schnitt, Tusche, Papier auf Leinwand, 40 x 30 cm, 2013 / golden cut, ink, paper on canvas, 15,7 x 11,8 inch., 2014

P.041 Erster Schnee, Decollage, Stoff, Papier, Plakat auf Baumwollsegeltuch, 21 x 29 cm, 2013 / First snow, decollage, paper, poster on cotton canvas, 8,3 x 11,4 inch., 2013

P.042 APO, Collage, Bleistift, Acryl- und Ölfarbe auf Baumwollsegeltuch, 71,5 x 71,5 cm, 2014 / APO, collage, pencil, acrylic and oil paint on cotton canvas, 28,1 x 28.1 inch., 2013

P.043 Dürer, Collage und Bleistift auf Baumwollsegeltuch, 40 x 30cm, 2013 / Dürer, collage and pencil on cotton canvas, 15,7 x 11,8 inch., 2013

P.045 Radieuse, Collage auf Baumwolle, 41,5 x 41,5 cm, 2014 / Radieuse, collage on canvas, 16,3 x 16,3 inch., 2014

P.046 Wahrgenommen, Stoff, Gaze, Ölfarbe auf Baumwollsegeltuch, 81,5 x 81,5 cm, 2012/14 / Perceived, cloth, gauze, oil paint on cotton canvas, 32,1 x 32,1 inch., 2012/14

P.048 Distanz 2, Collage, Aquarellfarbe auf Baumwollsegeltuch, 81,5 x 101,5 cm, 2014 / Distanz 2, collage, watercolor on cotton canvas, 32,1 x 40 inch., 2014

P.051 Black Flag – Let's Putzen (für Ernst Jandl), Collage auf Baumwolle, Grundierung, Acrylfarbe, 40 x 50 cm, 2014 / Black Flag – Let's Putzen (for Ernst Jandl), collage on cotton, prime coat, acrylic paint, 15,7 x 19,7 inch., 2014

P.052 Distanz 3, Collage, Stoff , Öl, Grundierung auf Leinwand, 180 x 160 cm, 2014 / Distanz 3, collage, cloth, oil, prime coat on canvas, 70,9 x 63 inch., 2014

P.053 Form, Acryl, Öl, Gaze auf Baumwolle, 170 x 150 cm, 2014 / Form, acryl, oil, gauze on canvas, 66,9 x 59 inch., 2014

P.054 Piece of S., Collage, Öl, Grundierung auf Baumwollsegeltuch, 130 x 130 cm, 2014 / Pieces of S., collage, oil, prime coat on canvas, 51,2 x 51,2 inch., 2014

P.055 o.T., Collage, Acryl, farbiger Karton, Papier auf Holz, 35 x 35 cm, 2013 / untitled, collage, acryl, colored cartboard, paper on wood, 13,8 x 13,8 inch., 2013

P.056 Nummer 10, Öl-Eitempera und Papier auf Nessel, 200 x 130 cm, 1991 / number 10, oil-egg tempera, paper on nettle, 78,7 x 51,2 inch., 1991

P.057 Run, Collage, Papier, Stoff auf Leinwand, 20 x 20 cm, 2013 / Run, collage, paper, cloth on canvas, 7,9 x 7,9 inch., 2013

P.058 Cabinet, Collage, Papier auf Baumwollsegeltuch, 20 x 20 cm, 2013 / Cabinet, collage, paper on cotton canvas, 7.9 x 7,9 inch., 2013

P.059 Mechaniker, Collage, Öl-Eitempera auf Baumwollsegeltuch, 40 x 40 cm, 2013 / mechanic, collage, oil-egg tempera on cotton canvas, 15,7 x 15,7 inch., 2013

P.060 Salah Al-Din, Collage, Öl-Eitempera, Tusche auf Leinwand, 40 x 30 cm, 2014 / Salah Al-Din, collage, oil-tempera, ink on 15,7 x 11,8 inch., 2014

P.061 Allegro, Collage, Papier auf Baumwollsegeltuch, 40 x 30 cm, 2013 / Allegro, collage, paper on cotton canvas, 15,7 x 11,8 inch., 2014

P.062 MacBeth2, Collage auf Baumwollsegeltuch, 51,5 x 41,5 cm, 2013 / MacBeth2, collage on cotton canvas, 20,3 x 16,3 inch., 2013

P.063 Etude sur le movement d' Art decorative, Collage, Tusche, Öl auf Baumwollsegeltuch, 130 x 130 cm, 2014 / Etude sur le movement d' Art decorative, collage, ink, oil on cotton canvas, 51,2 x 51,2 inch., 2014

P.064 Paint yourself, Collage, Öl-Eitempera, Holz auf Leinwand, 30 x 30 cm, 2013 / Paint yourself, collage, oil-egg tempera, wood on canvas, 11,8 x 11,8 inch., 2013

P.065 o.T., Öl, Holz auf Holz, 27,8 x 30 cm, 2000 / untitled, oil, wood on wood, 10,9 x 11,8 inch., 2000

P.066 Lesson, Collage, Gouache, Bleistift, Karton auf Baumwollsegeltuch, 40 x 30 cm, 2013 / Lesson, collage, gouache, pencil, cartboard on cotton canvas, 15,7 x 11,8 inch., 2013

P.067 Sunrise, Collage, Aquarellfarbe, Papier auf Holz, 25 x 19,5 cm, 2013 / Sunrise, collage, watercolor, paper on wood, 9,8 x 7,7 inch., 2013

P.069 Backward Experiment, Öl-Eitempera, Kohle, Kreide, Papier auf Leinwand, 180 x 165 cm, 2011/12 / Backward Experiment, oil-egg tempera, charcoal, paper on canvas, 70,9 x 65 inch., 2011/12

P.071 Argonauten, Öl-Eitempera, Kohle, Papier auf Leinwand, 230 x 270 cm, 2012 / Argonauts, oil-egg tempera, charcoal, paper on canvas, 90,5 x 106,3 inch., 2012

P.072 Circus Maximus, Öl-Eitempera, Kreide, Papier auf Leinwand, 180 x 200 cm, 2011/12 / Circus Maximus, oil-egg tempera, charcoal, paper on canvas, 70,9 x 78,7 inch., 2011/12

P.073 Scientia, Öl-Eitempera, Tusche, Kreide, Papier auf Leinwand, 230 x 200 cm, 2010 / Scientia, oil-egg tempera, ink, chalk, paper on canvas, 90,5 x 78,7 inch., 2010

P.074 Design, Papier, Öl-Eitempera auf Leinwand, 180 x 160 cm, 2012 / Design, paper, oil-egg tempera on canvas, 70,9 x 63 inch., 2012

P.075 Design 2, Papier, Öl-Eitempera auf Leinwand, 210 x 285 cm, 1996/2012 / Design 2, paper, oil-egg tempera on canvas, 82,7 x 112,2 inch., 1996/2012

P.076 Cataract 7 (Stromschnelle), Stoff, Kohle, Bleistift auf Leinwand, 30 x 30 cm, 2015 / Cataract 7 (rapid), cloth, charcoal, pencil on canvas, 11,8 x 11,8 inch., 2015

P.077 Ströhmung, Öl-Farbreste, Kleber auf Leinwand, 30 x 35 cm, 2014 / Current, leftover oil paint, glue on canvas, 11,8 x 13,8 inch., 2014

P.078 Jugendstil, Eitempera, Papier auf Baumwollsegeltuch, 30 x 40 cm, 2015 / Art nouveau, oil tempera, paper on cotton canvas, 11,8 x 15,7 inch., 2015

P.079 Zusammenspiel, Eitempera, Papier auf Baumwollsegeltuch, 30 x 40 cm, 2014 / interaction, oil tempera, paper on canvas, 11,8 x 15,7 inch., 2014

P.080 Dreieck, Ölfarbe, Grundierung, Gaze, Stoff auf Leinwand, 100 x 120 cm, 2016 / triangle, oil paint, prime coat, gauze, cloth on canvas, 39,4 x 47,2 inch., 2016;
Drill, Ölfarbe, Eitempera, Grundierung, Silberstift, Papier auf Leinwand, 100 x 140 cm, 2016 / drill, oil paint, prime coat, silverpoint, paper on canvas, 39,4 x 55,1 inch., 2016

P.081 o.T. (Woge), Eitempera, Grundierung, Leinwand auf Leinwand, 30 x 30 cm, 2015 / untitled (wave), oil tempera, prime coat, canvas on canvas, 11,8 x 11,8 inch., 2015
o.T.(sechs Teile), Aquarellfarbe, Tusche, Eitempera, Stoff auf Leinwand, 30 x 30 cm, 2015 / untitled (six pieces), watercolor, ink, oil tempera, cloth on canvas, 11,8 x 11,8 inch., 2015

P.082 Vier und Sechzehn, Öl-Eitempera, Stoff auf Leinwand, 165 x 165 cm, 2015 / four and sixteen, oil tempera, cloth on canvas, 65 x 65 inch., 2015

P.083 Form (Widerstand), Eitempera, Grundierung auf Leinwand, 100 x 120 cm, 2016 / Form (resistance), egg tempera, prime coat on canvas, 39,4 x 47,2 inch., 2016

P.084 Struggle for curve (Diptychon), Öl-Eitempera, Bleistift, Kohle, Blattgold, Stoff, Bindfaden, Papier auf Baumwollsegeltuch, 160 x 240 cm, 2015 / struggle for curve (diptychon), oil tempera, pencil, charcoal, gold, cloth, thread, paper on cotton canvas, 63 x 94,5 inch., 2015

P.086 Lachen, Stoff, Papier, Wasserfabe auf Leinwand, 30 x 40 cm, 2014 / Laughter, cloth, paper, watercolor on canvas, 11,8 x 15,7 inch., 2014

P.087 do, Eitempera, Gaze , Stoff, Papier auf Leinwand, 30 x 40 cm, 2014 / do, egg tempera, gauze, cloth, paper on canvas, 11,8 x 15,7 inch., 2014

P.088 Matter and More, Öl-Eitempera, Reisig, Teer auf Leinwand, 180 x 230 cm, 2003 / Matter and More, oil tempera, brush wood, tar on canvas, 70,9 x 90,5 inch., 2003
Wo man, Eitempera, Stoff, Papier auf Baumwollsegeltuch, 170 x 150 cm, 2014 / Wo man, oil tempera, cloth, paper on cotton canvas, 66,9 x 59 inch., 2014

P.089 Vier Quadrate, Öl-Eitempera auf Leinwand auf Holz, 25 x 25 cm, 2012 / four squares, oil-egg tempera on canvas and wood, 9,8 x 9,8 inch., 2012
Planeten , Öl-Eitempera auf Leinwand auf Holz, 25 x 25 cm, 2015 / planets, oil tempera on canvas on wood, 9,8 x 9,8 inch., 2015

P.090 GH GO, Grundierung, Druckfarbe, Bleistift, Leinwand, Gaze auf Leinwand, 20 x 30 cm, 2015 / GH GO, prime coat, printing paint, pencil, canvas, gauze on canvas, 7,9 x 11,8 inch., 2015

P.091 O.T. (mit Faden), Eitempera, Stoff, Papier auf Leinwand, 50 x 50 cm, 2013 / untitled (with thread), egg tempera, cloth, paper on canvas, 19,7 x 19,7 inch., 2015

P.093 Stromschnellen 1-6, Öl-Eitempera auf Leinwand auf Holz, á 25 x 25 cm, 2002 / cataract 1-6, oil-egg tempera on canvas on wood, each 9,8 x 9,8 inch., 2002

P.094 Drei Grundrisse für Architekturen, Papier, Bleistift auf Leinwand auf Holz, 25 x 25 cm, 2013 / Three floor plans for architectures, paper, pencil on canvas on wood, 9,8 x 9,8, 2013

P.095 Arbeiten auf Papier O.T. (Farbstudien), Aquarell auf Papier, 26,4 x 17,4 cm, 2015 / works on paper untitled (color study), watercolor on paper, 10,4 x 6,8 inch., 2015

P.096 Arbeiten auf Papier O.T. (Kompositionsanalysen), Papier auf Graupappe, 29 x 21 cm, 2008 / works on paper untitled (compositional analysis), paper on chipboard, 11,4 x 8,3 inch., 2008

P.097 Arbeiten auf Papier O.T. (Auswahl), Wasserfarbe,Tusche, Bleistift, Papier auf Graupappe, 29 x 21 cm, 2008 / works on paper untitled (selection), watercolor, ink, pencil on chipboard, 11,4 x 8,3 inch., 2008

P.098 Arbeiten auf Papier O.T. (Auswahl), Wasserfarbe, Tusche Eitempera, Kohle, Kreide, Schleifpapier auf Graupappe, 29 x 21cm, 2004-05-06-07 / works on paper untitled (selection), watercolor, ink, oil tempera, charcoal, sandpaper on chipboard, 11,4 x 8,3 inch., 2004-05-06-07

P.100 Sechs Postkarten, Aquarell auf Arches auf Graupappe aufgezogen / six postcards, watercolor on arches on chipboard
O.T., Bleistift auf Bütten, 29 x 21 cm, 2015 / untitled, pencil on hand made paper, 11,4 x 8,3 inch., 2015
Letrasett, Transfer auf Bütten, 29 x 21 cm, 2015 / Letrasett, transfer on hand made paper,11,4 x 8,3 inch., 2015
Little house I used to live in, Bleistift auf Papier auf Bütten, 24,5 x 35 cm, 2015 / Little house I used to live in, pencil on paper on hand made paper, 9,6 x 13, 8 inch., 2015

P.114 Künstlerbuch Painting Box (Umschlag), diverse Materialien, 21,5 x 30 cm, 47 Seiten, 2015 / artist book Painting Box (cover), diverse materials, 8,5 x 11,8 inch., 47 pp. 2015

P.116 Zwei Seiten aus „Painting Box" / two pages from Painting Box

P.118 Künstlerbuch Musei vaticani, Umschlag und zwei Innenansichten, 18 x 27 cm, 61 Seiten, diverse Materialien, 2006 / artist book Musei vaticani, cover and two pages, 7,1 x 10,6 inch., 61 pp., diverse materials, 2006

P.121 Künstlerbuch Fahrtenbuch, Umschlag und drei Innenansichten, Linoldrucke und Stempeldrucke, 30 x 22 cm, 98 Seiten, 2013 / artist book logbook, cover and three pages, lino-cut prints and stemp prints, 11,8 x 8,7 inch., 98 pp., 2013

P.122 Künstlerbuch Rainer Dissel 2015, Umschlag und drei Innenansichten, diverse Materialien, 33,5 x 22 cm, 180 Seiten, 2015 / artist book Rainer Dissel 2015, cover and three pages, diverse materials, 13,2 x 8,7 inch., 180 pp., 2015

P.124 Künstlerbuch Hauptbuch, Umschlag und drei Innenansichten, diverse Materialien, 33,5 x 22 cm, 200 Seiten, ca.1990-2008 / artist book Main book, cover and three pages, diverse materials, 13,2 x 8,7 inch., 200 pp., ca.1990-2008

P.126 Künstlerbuch Beyond and Before, Umschlag und drei Innenansichten, Kugelschreiber, Buntstift, 14 x 9 cm, 370 Seiten, 2014 / artist book Beyond and Before, cover and three pages, pen, crayon, 5,5 x 3,5 inch., 370 pp., 2014

P.129 Künstlerbuch MaxHackxLyacx, Umschlag und drei Innenansichten diverse Materialien, 30 x 21cm, 90 Seiten, 2014 / artist book MaxHackxLyacx, cover and three pages, diverse materials,11,8 x 8,3 inch., 90 pp., 2014

P.131 Künstlerbuch Nächste Dinge und Meditationen, Umschlag und drei Innenansichten, diverse Materialien, Papier teilweise geschnitten, 30 x 21 cm, 32 Seiten, 1984-2016 / artist book Next Things and Meditations, cover and three pages, diverse materials, paper partly cut, 11,8 x 8,3 inch., 32 pp., 1984-2016

DANK GILT ALLEN FÖRDERERN UND UNTERSTÜTZERN, OHNE DIE DIESES PROJEKT NICHT HÄTTE REALISIERT WERDEN KÖNNEN, INSBESONDERE AUCH DER SE-DENTALTECHNIK GMBH SOWIE CRITICA-ZPK UND DEM HMKW, DES WEITEREN AUCH DR. JULIA-CONSTANCE DISSEL, FERDINAND SCHWIEGER, STEFAN & ANGELIKA EUTENEUER UND CHRISTA & GERHARD KELLERSMANN.

IMPRESSUM / IMPRINT

GESTALTUNG / DESIGN
RICHARD PRUSS

TEXTE / TEXTS
DR. DANIÈLE PERRIER,
HANS THILL

ÜBERSETZUNG / TRANSLATION
DR. JEREMY GAINES / GAINES TRANSLATIONS

LEKTORAT / COPY EDITING
MARIA-ELISABETH RUDOLF
(LEKTORAT SCHUSTERJUNGE)

PRODUKTION / PRODUCTION MANAGEMENT
DISTANZ VERLAG, SONJA BAHR

GESAMTHERSTELLUNG / PRODUCTION
OPTIMAL MEDIA GMBH, RÖBEL/MÜRITZ

VERTRIEB / DISTRIBUTION
GESTALTEN BERLIN
WWW.GESTALTEN.COM
SALES@GESTALTEN.COM

ISBN 978-3-95476-152-4
PRINTED IN GERMANY

ERSCHIENEN IM / PUBLISHED BY
DISTANZ VERLAG
WWW.DISTANZ.DE